CURRENT STUDIES ON RITUALS

perspectives for the psychology of religion

HANS-GÜNTER HEIMBROCK &
H. BARBARA BOUDEWIJNSE (eds.)

D1732847

Amsterdam - Atlanta, GA 1990

CIP-GEGEVENS KONINKLIJKE BIBLIOTHEEK, DEN HAAG

Current

Current studies on rituals : perspectives for the
psychology of religion / H.-G. Heimbrock & H.B.
Boudewijnse (ed.). — Amsterdam - Atlanta, GA : Rodopi. — (International
series in the psychology of religion 2, ISSN 0925-4153)
Met lit. opg.
ISBN 90-5183-178-1
SISO 239.2 UDC 264-2
Trefw.: riten.
©Editions Rodopi B.V., Amsterdam - Atlanta, GA 1990
Printed in The Netherlands

CONTENTS

Introduction

1. Theories and Concepts Reconsidered

2. Empirical Studies: A Selection of Christian Rituals

3. From Christian to Psychological Interpretation

INTRODUCTION

This collection of articles concerning psychological aspects of ritual serves a threefold purpose. In first instance the various studies try to investigate an issue which has been rather overlooked in the psychology of religion. Secondly, focusing on specific issues, these articles represent the present state of affairs within our discipline as a whole. Thirdly these contributions present important challenges not only for the study of ritual but also for the psychology of religion as a discipline. In these introductory remarks we will outline our intentions as well as the context of the volume.

Looking back at a history of one hundred years of psychology of religion, studies of ritual behavior and ritual experience can not be identified as a central theme. Compaired to issues like conversion, religious orientation, religion and mental health or religious development, the problem of ritual for a long time played only a marginal role on the scene of academic discussion. This is clearly illustrated by the minimum of titles presented under the heading 'psychology of religion' in the bibliography edited by Grimes (1985). A comparison of the psychological branch of religious studies to other disciplines, like the history or sociology of religion, leads to striking discoveries however. Research of both religious and secular rituals figures as one of the most prominent issues of the social sciences. When the occurrence of international conferences is taken as an indication of the academic attention to a theme, in the case of 'ritual' a series of famous meetings can be reiterated. Shortly after the Second World War one of the venerable Eranos meetings in Switzerland was dedicated to ritual phenomena (see Fröber-Kapteyn, 1951). Two decades later, Sir Julian Huxley organized a remarkable conference in London, titled *A Discussion on Ritualization of Behaviour in Animals and Men* (Huxley, 1966). Another twenty years thereafter, a meeting concerning the ritual issue was organized in Chicago, titled *Symposium on Ritual in Human Adaptation* (see Moore, 1983). Allthough all these conferences were also attended by psychologists (e.g. Neumann, 1951; Erikson, 1966) and even though various of the other studies that were presented included statements on the nature and function of rituals with reference to individuals, only the conference of Chicago had a dominantly psychological signature.

As a result of all these socio-cultural investigations of ritual, we are quite well informed about the collective aspects of ritual behavior. Due to the studies of Durkheim (1912), Van Gennep (1909), Malinowski (1948), Goffman (1967) and others, we have learned much about the functional values of ritual for the solving of social conflicts and the transitions from one social status to another. Anthropologists like Turner (e.g. 1977a (1969)) and Douglas (1973) have provided insight into the symbolic meanings of ritual in small-scale 'traditional' (non-western) contexts as well as large-scale postindustreal societies, while Lévi-Strauss (1973) has focused on structural patterns of ritual.

The various articles bundled in this volume try to advance our knowledge of ritual phenomena in general and of ritual experience in particular by approaching them from a psychological angle with psychological concepts and methods. However, this is more than a collection of articles on ritual. Ritual is the topic through which virtually every author begins to envision a new or different way of doing psychology of religion. In fact, the focus on ritual itself marks a significant development of the psychology of religion. This volume is an attempt to further the revisioning of psychology of religion, of how psychologists of religion are to understand what their discipline is about. In centering on the topic of ritual, the authors find themselves raising fundamental questions about what psychology of religion is. As a consequence, more attention is given to conceptual issues and problems, raised by the topic of ritual, than to concrete psychological analyses of existing rituals. Many of the studies here presented are of an explorative nature. Save for the contributions in the second part of this volume, no in-depth studies of extant rituals are presented. Nor do the authors avail themselves of existing analyses as provided by, for instance, anthropologists or historians, in order to demonstrate how a psychologist might interpret the same ritual differently. Instead, several authors suggest an interdisciplinary approach. They point out ways in which psychologists of religion might learn and benefit from the achievements reached within other disciplines.

The first section of this volume presents five contributions. These contributions aim at broadening the conceptual tools applied in psychological studies of ritual in order to achieve a better understanding of the cognitive, emotional and social aspects of ritual experience. The authors make use of anthropological, psychoanalytic or some combination of theories. Although referring to different theoretical frames of interpretation, they nevertheless converge in a common hermeneutical interest. In contrast to the quantitative approaches presented in the second section, the authors adopt qualitative strategies. Boudewijnse gives a survey of the theoretical legacy of Victor Turner, whose anthropological studies of ritual have recently begun to attract the attention of psychologists of religion. An interdisciplinary approach to the study of ritual is advocated, while at the same time some of the pitfalls of such an undertaking are pointed out. Inquiring into the meaning of ritual symbolism, Geerts focuses attention on a combination of semiotics (Peirce) and anthropology (Turner). Heimbrock, concentrating on the transitional qualities of ritual behavior, investigates the possibilities of psychoanalytic object relation theory for the qualitative analysis of ritual. Faber's article on Christian liturgy gives an indication of the usefulness of psychological studies of ritual (in this case the psychoanalytic approach of Erikson) for pastoral theology. Concluding this first section Wikström indicates how ritual studies in the history of religion challenge psychological conceptions of ritual and their ability to catch the essence of religious ritual experience.

The second section of this volume contains three contributions, in which the authors present the concrete results of their research on traditional Christian rituals. As the title of this section already implies, they have made use of psychological instruments of a strictly empirical signature. Their studies, based as they are on quantitative data analysis, each provide the reader with thorougly elaborated and empirically based hypotheses. Paying attention to situational factors from the perspective of environmental psychology, van der Lans & Geerts study the impact of the liturgical setting on generating religious behavior. Janssen et al. analyze the prayer-practices of young people in contemporary Dutch society, practices which are found to be of an individualized nature. Visscher & Stern, in their turn, conducted a survey to investigate in what ways family rituals function to transmit Christian beliefs and values.

The cornerstone of a discipline's capability to conduct fruitful scientific investigations, lies in its capacity to be self-critical. While we opened the present volume with discussions in which concepts and theories are being reconsidered, we conclude the volume with four contributions that deal with the fact that the object of the psychology of religion can no longer be contained within the more conventional interpretations of it. Especially European traditions within our discipline have often put an unquestioned emphasis on the study of psychological dimensions of *Christian* religious experience and behavior. Even the focus on the 'psychology of unbelief' is an indirect indication of this trend. However, several studies in this volume call our attention to ritual experience and meaning attribution beyond these limiting boundaries. Especially the four concluding essays open up this whole issue, either by recognizing that participants in traditional Christian rituals attach new meanings to them rather than the traditional ones (van Uden & Pieper), or by noting that new rituals have come about to challenge or imitate the traditional Christian rituals. Ouwehand questions the adequacy and usefulness of current psychological theories of religious development for the interpretation of newly created women's rituals. The question whether traditional Christian rituals are being replaced by new rituals, is tackled by both Vandermeersch and Reich, although in different ways. Compairing psychotherapeutic and religious rituals, Vandermeersch adresses the issue of secularization, while Reich focuses on the moral dimension of modern phenomena such as the Live Aid rock marathon (which took place in 1985).

Of course studies of traditional Christian rituals continue to be carried out, like they should be, but they need to be complemented by studies of non-traditional rituals within what have been, until recently, Christian societies. Our field of research should renew contact with aspects of 'the variety of religious experience' within contemporary western society (cf. Kippenberg, 1986). Getting in touch with social and personal dimensions of ritual that transcend Christian religious experience or its negation, may challenge our discipline as a whole to look forward beyond theological preoccupations and even beyond the theoretical paradigm of secularization, in short: to move out of the shadows of a psychology of Christian religion.

Ever since its origin in the late 19th century, the psychology of religion has been a domain with an interdisciplinary character. From the days of William James and Sigmund Freud, a conflict of paradigms has developed, of medical, biological, phenomenological and even theological approaches. Due to this scientific tradition and due also to the variety of ritual symbolic action, it seems necessary to challenge psychologists of religion to look for new academic partners. The discovery of social and cultural sciences means in part a re-discovery of old academic ancestors. Also it could lead to a closer cooperation with these disciplines, which would be mutually rewarding. It is our conviction that modern religious studies as a whole could benefit from the psychology of religion, without which they would not be complete. One of the tasks for the psychology of religion should be to investigate the implicit or even hidden psychological assumptions of social and cultural theories of religion.

Certainly all these examinations provoke further questions. Neither the contributing authors nor the editors, however, have the illusion that a final stage of scientific perfection can be reached. Still, the present collection pretends to provide its readers with a general outline of the psychology of religion as it has developed in Europe until now. The variety of studies is an indication of the multitude of theoretical and methodological approaches and demonstrates the degree of exactness that can be achieved in empirical data analysis as well as the value of interpretive inquiries.

The present volume is the result of research as it has been conducted in various academic contexts, as well as the fruit of continuous international cooperation. Impulses to start this project date in first instance from the Fourth Symposium on the Psychology of Religion in Europe, which took place at the Catholic University of Nijmegen (The Netherlands) in september 1988. Another stimulating context, at least for the editors, was provided by the religious studies project 'Religious Symbols', located at the Theology Department of the University of Groningen (The Netherlands).

It is an established academic tradition of ritual importance to adress words of thanks to all partners whose cooperation has resulted in the present collection. We are grateful to the authors in Western Europe and Canada for contributing to our volume and for their tolerance concerning all our formalistic and fussy proposals. We also want to express our gratitude to H. Varkevisser for his technical assistance and to F. van der Zee for his patient cooperation and editorial advice. Last but not least we wish to thank E. van Gelein Vitringa for his substantial assistance in preparing the final manuscript.

Due to all these combined efforts, we are able to present this project to an even broader public in Europe and Northern America.

The editors.

THEORIES AND CONCEPTS RECONSIDERED

THE RITUAL STUDIES OF VICTOR TURNER
An anthropological approach and its psychological impact

H. Barbara Boudewijnse

1. Introduction

The study of symbols and symbolic meaning traditionally has occupied an important place within the general psychology of religion. As for the theoretical and empirical study of ritual symbolic action contemporary psychologists of religion have been concerned mainly with motivation and personality factors on the one hand and the effects of ritual experience on the personality on the other hand. The question of what happens within the ritual context itself has been underexposed, chiefly because of the applied methods of quantitative analysis. In order to study the meaning of symbols in the context of ritual action a different approach is much needed, as psychologists of religion have come to realise more an more.

Anthropologists in particular have a longstanding experience with qualitative methods of analysis, which they have conducted mainly on the basis of the so-called participant-observation method. It is not my intention here to concern myself with the general relationship of psychology and anthropology as academic disciplines or methods. For the purpose of this article it suffices to say that I consider the two disciplines, their methods and their fields of inquiry to be complementary. As Bock (1980) put it: cultural facts are partly to be explained in psychological terms just as psychological facts are partly to be explained in cultural or social terms. So, in order to conduct a balanced inquiry of symbolic action within the context of religious ritual, it is necessary to take full account of both the psychological and social-cultural dimensions which are involved. This calls for a differentiated approach, in which anthropological and psychological attainments are combined. Unfortunately, notwithstanding their common historical roots, on the whole anthropology and psychology followed separate roads, taking little notice of each other's accomplishments.

In recent years psychologists of religion have shown a growing interest in the work of Victor Turner, whose seminal studies of ritual symbolic action have been of major influence on the anthropological study of religion. It is not surprising that his theories should appeal to psychologists because of their far-reaching psychological implications. So far, however, psychologists of religion have incorporated Turner's ideas eclectically and often uncritically. In this article I will present a short survey of his work and clarify the partly implicit psychological premises which lie at the roots of his theories. Furthermore, an indication will be given of the clues this theoretical and methodological framework offers for the psychological study of religious ritual and of some pitfalls that should be avoided. Of course it is impossible to present a complete overview of Turner's writings, which cover about thirty years of scientific labour. His theoretical legacy is most impressive. In order to emphasize the shortcomings of the eclectic use to which it has been put, I have to present a general outline and omit details.

2. The ritual studies of Victor Turner

In the course of his extensive fieldwork among the Ndembu (a Bantu-speaking tribe in north-west Zambia) Turner developed a differentiated methodology for the qualitative analysis of religious symbolic action. Focusing on ritual performances, he wanted to devise a conceptual scheme that would do justice to the actual experiences of the ritual participants on the one hand but would still have explanatory value for the general occurence of religious rituals on the other hand. His inquiries were prompted not only by the question why religious rituals generally do take place but also by the question why a particular ritual is being performed in a particular form at a particular time and place.

Turner's work can be said to have evolved around four main topics: processual analysis, symbol theory, the dual concepts of structure and anti-structure or communitas, and the analysis of liminal and liminoid phenomena. It is important to recognize two different though related periods in the development of his thinking. At first Turner focused mainly on traditional societies and the way ritual functioned to maintain order. Ritual functioned to integrate society by stressing the central values of society. In this period Turner developed his own particular research-method, his concept of ritual performance as 'social drama' and his concept of the 'ritual symbol'. In his later work Turner focused more on the processual character of rituals, on the dynamic and transformative aspects of what he called the ritual process. He not only developed a theory of ritual, but also a theory of society. When earlier he stressed the integrative function of ritual - its capacity to resolve conflicts and restore equilibrium - in later works (of which *The Ritual Process* (1977a (1969)) is the cornerstone) he stressed the transformative qualities of ritual, its capacity to change not only individuals but social structure itself. Though not in direct contradiction, his earlier ideas and later theories show some discrepancy.

2.1 The social function of ritual

In *Schism and Continuity in an African Society* (1957), *The Forest of Symbols* (1967) and *The Drums of Affliction* (1968b) Turner describes Ndembu village life and shows how the ritual system of the Ndembu functions as the central social mechanism to resolve conflicts, to restore social equilibrium and to enhance group solidarity. "Ritual performances", according to Turner, are "distinct phases in the social processes whereby groups adjust to internal changes and adapt to their external environment" (1967:20). By conceiving social life as a 'process', the temporal sequence of social events came to be a crucial tenet in his analyses. Social life evolves in time and in its course *processual units* can be discerned, of which the *social drama* is a species (1974a:33). In *Schism and Continuity* Turner regarded the social drama as the principal unit of description and analysis in the study of social processes (1957:xvii). The social process which constitutes the social drama is divided into four major phases. First a *breach* of regular norm-governed social relationships occurs. Following this a phase of mounting *crisis* supervenes. In order to limit the spread of breach, certain adjustive and redressive mechanisms are brought into operation. Following this third phase of *redressive action*, the final phase ensues, which consists either in the *reintegration* of the disturbed group or in the social recognition of irreparable *schism* (1967:91-2). The mechanisms coming into force in the third phase of redressive action vary in character. They may range from personal advice and informal arbitration, to formal legal procedures, or to the performance of public ritual. In Ndembu society, which lacks a centralized political system, ritual constitutes the primary means to uphold the bond between people and groups. Turner shows how in the various types of ritual the common values and priorities of Ndembu village life are made explicit and receive dramatic form. As such, ritual has a direct bearing on social life and therefore has to be examined in relation to its bearing on the functioning of the social system.

So far Turner's interpretation stands clearly in the Durkheimian functionalist tradition. Durkheim was of the opinion that rituals enhance social cohesion because they convey the collective values of society to the ritual participants. Turner advanced a more differentiated view. Based on his Ndembu experience he maintained that in reality there is no cohesion or consensus; social norms are often mutually opposed and for that very reason often give rise to conflicts. According to Turner, one of the important functions of Ndembu ritual is that it enables the Ndembu to enact some of the tensions and conflicts inherent in the structure of social life, ensuring continuity by

3

pressing conflict itself into the service of affirming group unity (1957:129).

In *The Drums of Affliction* Turner once again elaborated his views concerning the cohesive social function of religious ritual. He posited

> "that rituals performed by societies that possess a considerable degree of cohesion - whose members, moreover, feel their unity and perceive their common interest in symbols - are rituals pervaded with affect. People derive emotional satisfaction from the observance of secular customs which ensure the maintenance of the social structure. Any threat to this continuity arouses strong emotions" (1968b:235).

Ritual mobilizes strong emotions in support of the social order. But, according to Turner,

> "ritual also recognizes that the psychic nature of man is not infinitely malleable with respect to the forces of social conditioning. To make a human being obey social norms, violence must be done to his natural impulses. These must be repressed or re-directed" (235-6).

For instance hate and illicit sexual passion may be repressed beneath customarily prescribed behavior. It is highly possible, Turner writes,

> "that individuals will be subliminally aware of these psychological pressures that menace social cohesion ... A breach in the continuity of socially prescribed relationship, whether caused by the social process itself or by the action of individuals, brings to the surface what has hitherto been repressed by external social pressures and by internal psychic mechanisms of defence against illicit drives ... Such breach is contagious ... From the members of a disturbed group there may be a 'feed-back' of disruptive drives into the social system ... [Ritual] must give expression to these illicit drives ... in order that they may be purged and exorcised" (236).

"In ritual", Turner continues,

> "... society reappraises its ideology and structural form ... The expression of conflict [is] allowed and sometimes even prescribed, to release energies by which social cohesion can be renewed. But social cohesion is the outcome of a struggle to overcome cleavages caused by contradictions in the structural principles of the society itself. Struggle may also arise from the resistance of human nature to social conditioning" (237).

4

Turner adds with emphasis "that ritual is first and foremost a *social* phenomenon, a system of social facts" (238). As such ritual portrays typical or stereotyped kinds of conflict:

> "Whether in any particular case individuals have in fact come into conflict or not is irrelevant in the ritual situation .... The conflicts of society are the same as those dramatized and symbolized in its ritual. Because people are deeply concerned emotionally about such conflicts, they are moved when they see them ritually portrayed. And when they are ritually resolved, they feel emotional catharsis" (238-9).

These quotations reveal several of the issues important to our discussion of the psychological implications of Turner's theories. It will be clear to any reader familiar with psychoanalytic theory, that Turner's views on ritual echo many of the theses this school of thought has brought to the fore. Not only much of his terminology (like 'internal psychic mechanisms of defense' and 'repression and/or redirection of illicit drives') derives from depth-psychology, but also such important notions as the idea that violence must be done to man's natural impulses to make him obey social norms, or the notion that the explicitation or expression of conflictuous drives can remedy or alleviate existing tensions. However, most important in this context is perhaps Turner's view that implicit conflicts find a symbolized expression in ritual. The ritual symbolic representations refer to existing social and/or intrapsychic tensions, which are normally subconscious and repressed. From this it follows that the interpretation of ritual necessarily coincides with the analysis of ritual symbolism. To this end Turner developed an elaborate methodology in which his concept of the 'ritual symbol' figures prominently, a concept which has several important psychological connotations.

2.2 The analysis of ritual symbols

According to Turner, ritual has to be examined in its actual historical field-setting because of the temporal structure of social life and the direct relation of ritual to social processes. He defines ritual as "prescribed formal behavior for occasions not given over to technological routine, having reference to beliefs in mystical beings or powers" (1967:19). Interpretation of the symbolism expressed in ritual, necessitates the study of the form as well as the actual content of ritual symbols, which he defines as "the smallest units of ritual which still retain the specific properties of ritual behavior" (id.). More generally he endorses the definition given in the Concise Oxford

5

Dictionary, which says that a symbol is "a thing regarded by general consent as naturally typifying or representing or recalling something by possession of analogous qualities or by association in fact or thought". Empirical observation of ritual symbols in a field situation will present objects, activities, relationships, events, gestures or spatial units as bearers of symbolic meaning (id.).

As Turner states, the ritual symbol is a factor in social action; its structure and properties are those of a dynamic entity. The symbol is an independent force which itself is the product of many opposed forces. This conception of dynamism, of generating action, is central to Turner's symbolic analysis. Symbols entice action, generate strong emotions. The question how they manage to do so, is certainly relevant to the psychological study of religion. According to Turner, a symbol is the expression of a relatively unknown fact. It is the task of the anthropologist to uncover its hidden meanings. Turner points out some crucial analytical distinctions to assist analysis.

There are two categories of ritual symbols: dominant and instrumental symbols. The meaning-content of dominant symbols possesses a high degree of constancy and consistancy throughout the total symbolic system. They also posses considerable autonomy with regard to the aims of the rituals in which they appear. They may be regarded as ends in themselves, as representative of the axiomatic values of society (1967:31-2). Instrumental symbols must be seen in terms of the system of symbols within a particular ritual. They serve as a means to attain the explicit goal of the respective ritual.

Ritual symbols, especially the so-called dominant symbols, bear the characteristics of *condensation* or *multivocality, unification* of disparate meanings in a single symbolic formation, and of *polarization* of meaning. The property of condensation or multivocality indicates that many things and actions are represented in a single formation: A symbol may stand for many things. These different meanings are connected by virtue of their common possession of analogous qualities or by association in fact or thought. This is what Turner calls the property of unification. The third property of symbols is polarization of meaning. Ritual symbols possess two clearly distinguishable poles of meaning. One is the *ideological* or *normative* pole. Here a cluster of meanings can be found that refers to moral values and principles of social organization. The other pole is the *sensory* or *orectic* pole. Here the meaning-content is closely related to the outward form of the symbol. This pole of meaning refers to natural and physiological phenomena and processes. Here Turner links the social aspect to the biophysical dimension, which according to him are both equally important in our understanding of ritual symbolism. The emotions generated by a symbol's association with human physiology (like blood, or milk) or natural processes (such as death or birth), serve to 'energize' the social order, thus making the 'obligatory' desirable (1977a:49). In this way it is possible to overcome the fundamental conflict between repressive social exigencies and natural individual impulses. In an elucidating article Turner explicitly describes how psychoanalytic theory had a strong formative influence on his conceptualization of ritual symbolic processes. Especially the concept of 'sublimation' enabled him to picture the process of Ndembu ritual as involving a 'deflection' of impulses and of their 'energy', on to the abstract notions which form the normative pole of a symbol's semantic field, thereby making the obligatory desirable (1978:575). Here too Turner stresses the difference which exists between the sublimation process going on within an individual and the process of 'sociocultural sublimation', as the latter is directed to a collectivity rather than arrising within an unconscious 'psyche' (id.). He warns several times that it is theoretically unacceptable to explain social facts, such as ritual symbols, directly by concepts of depth-psychology (1967:36-7; 1978:576). Implicitly acknowledging the universality of unconscious psychological processes as underlying symbolic ritual behavior, Turner explicitly treats the sensory pole of meaning as a constant factor. It is the variable social and ideological aspects whose interdependencies he seeks to explain.

In his analysis of symbols Turner distinguishes three fields of meaning: the *exegetical* meaning (the indigenous interpretation of the ritual symbols; i.e. the explanations provided by the ritual participants themselves); the *operational* meaning (the way the symbol is utilized within the ritual context); and thirdly the *positional* meaning (which is the meaning of the symbol as determined by its relationship to the other symbols, by its position in the total symbolic system). Turner criticizes anthropologists for whom only the indigenous interpretation of ritual has significance. According to him many ritual symbols have no apparent meaning and cannot be adequately explained by the ritual participants themselves. It is therefore up to the anthropologist to discern the latent meanings of ritual symbols by observing their operational and positional meanings. Turner is equally critical of psychoanalytic approaches to ritual, which often compared 'primitive' religious customs to the symptoms of neurotic patients and regarded indigenous interpretations as irrelevant. As he writes:

7

"For those interpretations that show how a dominant symbol expresses important componants of the social and moral orders are by no means equivalent to the 'rationalizations' and the 'secondary elaborations' of material deriving from endopsychic conflicts. They refer to social facts that have an empirical reality exterior to the psyches of individuals" (1967:35-6).

The preceding discussion is not relevant for the psychology of religion just because of the explicit psychological dimension which Turner takes into account, or because of both his use of psychoanalytic concepts and his criticism of psychoanalytic interpretations of religious ritual. Turner's message is clear: There is more to ritual than the social or individual motivations such as can be verbally explained by ritual participants. Ritual also has to be *observed* while *in motion*, to discover its latent meanings, which cannot be recovered by means of questionnaires only. Ritual performances also cannot really be 'measured' or 'quantified'. Whether people attend sunday-masses frequently or seldom, whether they go on pilgrimage or not, whether they pray both individually and collectively or not at all, is just one side of the matter. Ritual also has to be observed from within. Furthermore, it's not only the verbal aspects of ritual, or the verbal explanations of ritual participants, that make up ritual. Ritual is more than a conscious, cognitive affair, as it is more than a behavioral affair. Affective dimensions are involved which are frequently too elusive to capture. In this context Turner provides a framework which draws explicit attention to the expressive or aesthetic aspects of ritual performances. It should also be stressed that Turner has a positive view of ritual. To him it is a universal and potentially wholesome phenomenon, which need not be overcome in order to be really 'civilized' or 'sane'. This positive impact of ritual lies at the heart of the theoretical framework he developed in *The Ritual Process* (1977a (1969)) and subsequent writings.

Another important message is the explicit link between ritual and social process. Ritual shouldn't be studied without taking the social field in which it takes place into account. The performance of ritual is foremost a collective affair referring to wider social processes. Ritual experience as such is closely bound up with social experience, which has an ever changing historical character. In his later work, at which we arrive presently, Turner still links ritual to social experience, but in a very different way. In these later writings ritual experience is the source of innovation, social criticism, and 'communitas', which is an experience said to transcend socio-structural (i.e. specific contextual) boundaries. It is to these themes we turn at present.

2.3 The processual structure of ritual
As we have seen, in the course of his study of Ndembu ritual Turner found ritual performances to have a socially integrative function. Not only conflictuous situations appeared to be ritually contained, also change was being ritually controlled. Change, in Ndembu society, however, was of a repetitive kind, concerning individual transitions from one social position to another or cyclical transitions of social life. Change in this respect did not involve structural change of the social system itself.

In *The Ritual Process* Turner examines the processual structure of tribal ritual itself, concentrating on its transformative qualities. Turner states, as an aside, that the term 'ritual' applies to forms of religious behavior associated with social transitions, while the term 'ceremony' has bearing on religious behavior associated with social 'states' (a 'state' being a "relatively fixed and stable condition" 1967:93)), where politico-legal institutions also play an important part. Ritual is transformatory, ceremony confirmatory (1967:95).

Van Gennep's concept of *rites de passage* (rites of transition) serves as starting-point. Van Gennep (1960 (1909)) defined rites of passage as "rites which accompany every change of place, state, social position and age" (Turner, 1977a:94). These rites of transition are characterized by a distinctive temporal structure of three successive phases: the *preliminal* phase (accompanied by *rites of separation*), the *liminal* phase (accompanied by *rites of transition*) and the *postliminal* phase (which is accompanied by *rites of incorporation*) (Van Gennep, 1960:11). According to Turner the rite of passage involves a transition between two fixed 'states', between two 'relatively fixed and stable conditions'. His basic model of society is that of a 'structure of positions'. Accordingly, *liminality* must be regarded as an interstructural situation (id.). Essentially, liminality is an ambiguous condition. The state of the ritual subjects (called 'novices', 'liminars' or 'liminal personae') during the liminal phase is "betwixt and between all fixed points of classification. They pass through a symbolic domain which has none of the attributes of their past or coming state" (1974a:232). From the viewpoint of social structure liminal personae are 'invisible'. Much of the symbolism of the liminal phase of transition rites is derived from human biological processes. Ritual subjects may for instance be treated as 'dead' or 'newly-born'. During liminality role reversals may occur, normal social obligations being suspended. Behaviour may be allowed that normally would be considered immoral or indecent. Often the symbolic separation from normal social life is accompanied by the actual spatial seclusion of

9

the ritual subject(s). Furthermore, during the liminal period novices often have to submit to an authority that is nothing less than that of the total community. The ritual elders represent the generic authority of tradition, their moral authority being absolute (1977a:103). A crucial aspect of liminality in this context is the learning process. The liminal personae experience an essential transformation. Their previous social status being symbolically demolished, the ritual subjects are being prepared for their new, postliminal station in life.

2.4 Social structure and anti-structure: the concept of communitas

Because of their classificatory or even physical seclusion from the social structure, ritual subjects tend to develop among themselves intense comradeship and egalitarianism. Thus liminality engenders *communitas*. Communitas, according to Turner, is a vital aspect of human relationships. It is a dimension of all societies past and present (1977a:130). In this context he develops a dual vision of society, in which communitas is contrasted to social-structural relationships. He defines social structure as "the patterned arrangements of role-sets, status-sets, and status-sequences, *consciously* recognized and regularly operative in a given society. These are closely bound up with legal and political norms and sanctions" (1974a:202). However, social structure is not a static entity. Social relations have a dynamic character. The 'social' is not identical with the 'socio-structural'. There are other modalities of social relationship (1977a:131). Beyond the structural lies communitas. Essentially, Turner says, communitas is a relationship between concrete, historical, idiosyncratic individuals. These individuals are not segmentalized into roles and statuses, but confront one another as total human entities. Along with this direct, immediate confrontation, arises a model of society as homogenous, unstructured communitas, whose boundaries are ideally coterminous with those of the human species (1977a:131-2). The bonds of communitas are *anti-structural* in that they are undifferentiated, equalitarian, direct, nonrational (though not *ir*rational) (1974a:46-7).

In this rendering of social structure and communitas, Turner sketches a rigid contrast between these two modalities of social relationship. In fact he ascribes to social structure a static character. Structure is all that holds people apart, defines their differences and constrains their actions (1974a:47). Communitas on the contrary is likened to spontaneity, freedom, universality, openness. Turner emphasizes that social structure and communitas, though in contrast, are nonetheless closely connected:

10

"Communitas is the _fons et origo_ of all structures and, at the same time, their critique. For its very existence puts all social structural rules in question and suggests new possibilities" (1974a:202, emphasis in the original).

Social processes, it can thus be concluded, derive their dynamism from communitas. To survive, people have to create structure, but without communitas this structure would be static, arid, suffocating. Still, the spontaneity and immediacy of communitas can seldom be maintained for long. Communitas itself develops a structure, in which free relationships between individuals become converted into norm-governed relationships between social personae. Thus Turner distinguishes three types of communitas: _existential_ communitas (as it originally emerges), _normative_ communitas (where existential communitas is organized into a perduring social system) and _ideological_ communitas (which applies to utopian models of society based on existential communitas) (1977a:132).

Communitas, says Turner, is hard to pinpoint. It emerges there where there is no structure (1977a:126). Three conditions appear to be especially conducive to engendering communitas: liminality, marginality or outsiderhood, and structural inferiority. While liminality is 'betwixt and between' structure, marginality and inferiority are connected to structure, that is to say, to its margins and bottom.

2.5 Comparative analysis; from liminal to liminoid

Turner first developed the concept of liminality with reference to the liminal phase of rites of passage, such as performed in tribal society. Later on he applied the concept to different kinds of phenomena, like pilgrimages, religious orders, or hippies. In the later stage of his career Turner devoted himself to the comparative analysis of the ways in which "social actions of various kinds acquire form through the metaphors and paradigms in their actors' heads (put there by explicit teaching and implicit generalization from social experience) and, in certain intensive circumstances, generate unprecedented forms that bequeath history new metaphors and paradigms" (1974a:13). Living action, he maintains, is not the result of a 'program' (of 'structure' so to speak), but of the processual structure of social action itself.

As his attention gradually shifted from small-scale preindustrial societies to large-scale industrial societies and his methods as a result became more comparative, Turner developed the concept of the liminoid. In small-scale preindustrial societies ritual still has a collective character, whereas in large-scale industrial societies the religious domain has considerably 'contracted'. In these societies religion has become a matter of individual choice, no longer involving everybody or

11

encompassing society as a whole. Such societies are characterized by religious pluralism. Symbols that once were central to the mobilization of ritual action, tended to migrate directly or in disguise, into other domains, esthetics, politics, law, popular culture, etc. (1977b:36). In this large-scale, complex context, liminality is no longer a self-evident condition. 'Pure' liminality hardly exists any more. Analysing what had happened to liminality, Turner noticed that some aspects of liminality had become detached from the religious domain and had become secularized, like music, art, dance, drama, sports, poetry, etc.. He called these forms *liminoid genres*. Liminoid is like liminal, but is not identical with it. Liminal phenomena tend to be collective, concerned with natural or sociocultural processes. Liminoid phenomena are characteristically produced and consumed by individuals; they are not cyclical, but continuously generated. Liminal phenomena are centrally integrated into the total social process. Liminoid phenomena develop outside the central economic and political processes. They are plural, fragmentary and experimental. Liminal phenomena tend to have a common intellectual and emotional meaning for all members of society. Liminoid phenomena tend to appeal to specific individual tastes. Although considered potentially dangerous from the viewpoint of social structure and therefore hedged around with taboos, liminal phenomena are functional for the continuity of the social system. Liminoid phenomena on the contrary have a more subversive character. Often they express radical criticism and propagate alternative models (1977b:44-5).

3. Turner: his significance for the psychology of religion

Having presented a bird's-eye view of Turner's theoretical achievements, we must now return to the psychological implications of his work. Zadra (1984) has voiced some of these with perfect clarity. As he writes, Turner does not offer a theory of mental structures, but provides an extensive phenomenology of the mental features of the symbolic process. Symbols are directly related, not only to structures of cognition, but also to affectivity. As such they have an experiential character related to the mental life of the individuals who participate in the ritual process. They do not, however, define individualistic dimensions of experience but have reference to ethos and morality as they are generated and specified within the liminal condition. Ethos, moreover, is related to the condition of the social bond.

The symbol may be a function of meaning for the individual actor, but when the public dimension is taken into consideration, it is clear that the significance of a symbol may not be described simply in psychological terms. According to Zadra, the understanding of the public symbol in its operation as mental function for the individual presents a special difficulty for the study of religion (1984:88-9). This issue, of course, is of immediate importance to the psychology of religion. In this respect Turner's discussion of liminality has provided us with important insights. Somehow the symbolism of the liminal phase affects the individual in such a way as to transform his inner experience. Collective ritual symbolic action results in destructuring and subsequently rebuilding the individual's image of self and society. While Van Gennep outlined the general processual structure of ritual, Turner added greatly to our understanding of it by his vivid analyses of the symbolic imagery of liminality.

With reference to the concept of the ritual symbol (with its properties of multivocality and polarization) and the social cohesive function of ritual, the influence psychoanalytic theory had on Turner's thinking has been mentioned before. It is interesting to note, and probably not surprising, that the concepts of liminality and communitas in their turn have inspired others concerned with depth-psychology, such as Ross & Ross (1983). In their article they attempt to demonstrate the shortcomings of traditional Freudian approaches of religious ritual. They link the concepts of liminality and communitas explicitly to Winnicott's conceptions of 'transitional object' and 'potential space'. According to them, the capacity for symbolization, arising in infancy, matures into the ability to generate and use artistic creations, religious beliefs and imaginative ideals in later life. Religious ritual, they say, includes all these things. The qualities that originate in the potential space between mother and infant, which begin as the overcoming of the mother-infant separation through the transitional object, are transformed in due time into communitas, which is the overcoming of separation between ritual participants through ritual symbols. As they put it, rituals present an ideal order in the real world in the same way that transitional phenomena present an ideal state of presence in the real world of absence. While Turner is not concerned with causal psychological explanations, Ross & Ross use his concepts, among others, in order to do just that. Others have used Turner's concepts with similar intentions, that is, to criticise psychoanalytic theory and/or practice and to specify particular mental processes. (See also in this volume H.G. Heimbrock, *Ritual and transformation: a psychoanalytic perspective*, for his critical remarks on Ross & Ross).

Gay (1983) makes use of Turner's discussion of liminal and liminoid forms of communitas in relation to Kohut's analysis of narcissism. According to Gay egopsychology can help explain the ubiquity of ritual actions in all cultures, preindustrial as well as industrial. One task of ritual institutions, he says, is to help shape a homogeneous and coherent sense of self and worth. Recognizing that Turner had tried to illuminate an interpersonal phenomenon, i.e. communitas, not an intrapsychic one, like self-esteem, he maintains that Turner's remarks on the interpersonal aspects of ritual are pertinent to our understanding of psychoanalysis and narcissism alike. As Gay puts it, Turner's distinction between native liminality and modern liminoid states is a social-psychological theorem: the more 'equal' one is to fellow participants in communitas, the more individual one may be. This paradox, he says, is only apparent, for with the experience of communitas each ritual actor is reminded of his or her place in the group. While liminality may evoke terror, dread or despair, it does not evoke 'anomie', alienation or 'angst', which are precisely the feelings that dominate the inner experience of the narcissistic personality. Gay partly accounts for the recent increase of narcissistic disorders by noting how liminal forms of communitas have given way to liminoid forms. Both narcissism and its psychoanalytic treatment are liminoid, he adds. And liminoid forms of communitas, like those in the analytic relationship, secure self-esteem less adequately than liminal forms do.

When using Turner, psychologists of religion have concentrated mainly on the concepts of liminality and communitas, as the aforementioned examples of Gay and Ross & Ross demonstrate. This is understandable, because these are general concepts with a universalistic character. When Turner's ideas are, however, incorporated in this way in psychological (or rather psychoanalytic) theory, one serious deficit comes to the fore, due in part to Turner's own general treatment of the concept of communitas: the contextuality of ritual symbols gets obscured. The actual meaning-content of symbols again is under-exposed. The explicit teaching that ritual symbols are connected to social experience and to morality in fact is accepted as a general statement only. The same holds true for the professed importance of the expressive dimension of ritual symbolism.

Though he too neglects emphasizing the actual analysis of meaning-contents, Moore (1984b) has given more specific attention to the theme of morality and to the function of ritual in transmitting collective values (also see Reich, *Rituals and social structure: the moral dimension*, in this volume). In relation to ministry and theological education he stresses the importance of ritual leadership in the liminal phase, the moral authority of the ritual elders being of paramount significance in this transitional 'space/time pod', as he phrases it. Bonding and identification (essential to moral education) are complex ritual processes; they do not take place, says Moore, without adequate ritualization. Ritual involves a process of deconstruction and reconstruction in a ritually constructed 'holding environment' (a term

14

taken from Winnicott) or liminal space/time. It is Turner's great merit, according to Moore, that he gave us to understand that transitional space/time can and does exist in contemporary culture. His work helps us to ask fundamental questions about the ritual significance of the congregation. Moore thinks these questions should be considered seriously, because liturgy in most contemporary worship resembles what Turner calls 'ceremonial'. Holmes (1973) is of the same opinion. He applies Turner's concept of liminality from a pastoral point of view. As he puts it, the task is not so much as to create new structures by historical and theological research, but to allow archaic realities and symbolic power to find expression, which requires a willingness to risk the freedom of anti-structure and a faith to live with the ambiguity of mystery (1973:397).

Elsewhere Moore (1983, 1984a) argued that contemporary psychotherapy can fruitfully be considered as a ritual process through which a small segment of modern society receives leadership in times of crisis. Similar observations have been made by Van der Hart (1981, 1984) and Canda (1988). Explicitly referring to Turner, they plead for the construction of therapeutic rituals in order to help individual patients make succesful transitions. Here Turner's processual theory of ritual transformation is put into practice. In the context of this article however it leads too far to discuss the differences between religious and therapeutic ritual. (For a discussion of religious and therapeutic rituals, see Vandermeersch, *Psychotherapeutic and religious rituals: the issue of secularization*, in this volume).

Unfortunately Turner's qualitative research methodology has seldom if ever been practiced by psychologists of religion. As has been said, they concentrate primarily on the concept of communitas, which is understandable, since it is a powerful 'meta-concept' with very positive connotations. It is not surprising that the concept has been used to back-up pleas for liturgical innovations. As such its analytical potential possibly gets obscured in favor of its ideological appeal. Evidently, communitas is more than an analytic concept; it is an ideal. It embodies western values of equality, fraternity and brotherhood, of creativity, universality and openess. We should ask ourselves which positive standards we apply to the notion of communitas. Do we really use it analytically by measuring its concrete effects or manifestations? As Reich points out in his contribution to this volume, rituals per se are morally neutral and the communitas experienced within a certain community may have very damaging effects outside its boundaries. It seems to me the concept has primarily been used as a programmatic pointer, which, if we aren't careful, distracts us from the actual

15

analysis of ritual liminality. Still, though communitas is an elusive and problematic concept, it does indeed seem to refer to an important socio-psychological dimension of community-experience, which need not be restricted within certain community borderlines, but can transcend these. Exactly how this is being achieved remains to be examined, the more so since Turner himself presupposes a strong connection between social structure and anti-structure, the liminal context in which communitas is engendered.

In connection with this it should be mentioned that there seems to be a tendency to call every situation in which we recognize the presence of communitas or the innovative power of creation or criticism, a liminal or liminoid condition. Here we touch upon some issues that have been raised by anthropologists. As Morris (1987) pointed out, Turner treats structural relationships as being entirely pragmatic and as lacking any symbolic dimension, whereas reciprocity and patterns of mutual cooperation, and social relationships that do not involve hierarchy, are left entirely out of account. Informal, egalitarian interpersonal relationships that are part of everydaylife - and that embody the notion of community - are ignored. All structural relationships are assumed to be unequal, impersonal and alienating. Some crucial distinctions between different social structures get obliterated (1987:258-9). Morris goes on to say that Turner's concept of communitas is misleading. Turner essentially suggests that religion and ritual are liberating aspects of human culture. He not only leaves out of his analysis any explanation of the intimate relationship between religion and political authority but he also ignores the hierarchical nature, in thought and structure, of religious institutions themselves. He fails to recognize the ideological status of religious symbolism and pays no attention to the fact that ritual behavior, being highly structured, involves patterns of authority and specific role expectations (259-60). What follows is that the rigid dichotomy between social structure and communitas is untenable. (This gives us an idea of the reason why so many phenomena appear to be liminoid).

A related criticism is voiced by Austin (1981). She examines the nature of the communitas generated in the rituals of Jamaican Pentecostalists and shows that communitas, far from being a force for social change in the believer's lives, is indicative of their subordinate social position. She argues that the locus of social change cannot be found in man's capacity to symbolize. This, she says, only appears to be the case when symbolic and structural realms of social life are conceived of as a simple dichotomy. Sallnow (1981) essentially states the same. Examining Christian pilgrimage in the central Andes, he questions Turner's model of the pilgrimage process, which is based on the concepts of liminality and communitas. Sallnow demonstrates how the universalistic cosmology attached to the focal shrines is belied by the endemic competition and conflict which characterizes the devotions of Andean pilgrims. Moreover, this divisiveness is shown to be a direct consequence of pilgrimage itself.

The idealistic mould of the concept of communitas has been touched upon by Walker Bynum (1984) from again a different angle. She questions the universality and prescriptiveness of Turner's notion of liminality. This notion, she says, is applicable only to men. She argues that Turner's ideas concerning liminality and communitas describe the symbols of men better than those of women. Only men's stories are full 'social dramas' and only men's symbols are full reversals. Women are fully liminal only to men. According to her, Turner's theory of religion is inadequate because it is implicitly based on the Christianity of a particular class, gender and historical period, the problem being that the dichotomy of structure and chaos, from which liminality or communitas is a release, is a special issue for elites, for those who *are* the structures. A model which focuses on this need for release as *the* ultimate socio-psychological need may, as Walker Bynum says, best fit the experience of elites. This view raises of course interesting questions when compared to Austin's criticism of the concept of communitas. According to Austin communitas is an expression of the subordinate social position of Jamaican pentecostalists; according to Walker Bynum it is the expression of the experience of the elite!

These criticisms being what they may, should warn psychologists of religion for adopting Turner's theories unquestioningly. Having been devised in process, they need continuous elaboration, as Turner himself would have been the first to point out.

Inevitably, many issues touched upon by Turner, have been omitted here, such as his analysis of pilgrimage (Turner & Turner, 1978), his writings concerning the biophysical basis of the human capacity to symbolize (1983), his use of the psychological concept of 'flow' (1974b) or his discussion of modern drama and festival (1982, 1986). Still, it will be clear from the foregoing that Turner was a creative thinker and versatile anthropologist. His ethnographic accounts of Ndembu ritual are rich in detail and are a must for anyone who wants to embark upon qualitative psychological research of ritual performance. As to his theoretical writings: they are rich in metaphor and show imaginative erudition. This account can only be a pale extract in comparison.

AN INQUIRY INTO THE MEANINGS OF RITUAL SYMBOLISM: TURNER AND PEIRCE

Henri Geerts

1. Introduction

When rituals are seen as ways of conduct in which religious references and meanings play an important part, it is obvious that an empirical inquiry into ritual experience must also study the meanings which participants assign to them.

The study of the nature and content of signs has now become established practice not only in linguistics but also in disciplines concerned with film and architecture. Accordingly, elements of a ritual can, as vehicles of meaning, also be defined and classified in concepts derived from semiotics. Such a classification is particularly interesting if it enables us to draw up questionnaires by means of which we can examine various types of signification given by participants in religious rituals. Do all participants assign the same meaning to the different elements of the ritual? Do they see the ritual as being related first of all to their personal life, to the life of the group, or to the religious content which is realized during the ritual? Which background variables determine the giving of meaning during a ritual? Such questions can only be adequately dealt with through empirical research. It goes without saying that researchers in this field must be familiar with the culture and religious traditions in which the rituals concerned take place. This condition appears to be met by a researcher who comes from the religious culture in which the experiences he examines occur. Next, for his research to be more objective he must employ concepts which sufficiently abstract from the religious culture in question. The standard abstract term that is used in this field of investigation is the concept of 'symbol'.

For my inquiry into the experience of the Celebration of the Eucharist by Dutch Roman Catholics I have looked for those aspects of the concept of 'symbol' that can be translated into terms which are operationally meaningful in the context of an empirical inquiry into the meanings participants in this ritual assign to it. They may be found in semiotics.

One of the first who argued in favour of a close analysis of the various aspects of the symbol as a vehicle of meaning in rituals with the help of semiotics was Turner (1974c). In his view, semiotics can, as a theory of signs, offer some definitions and distinctions that may be useful to the study of symbols in religious rituals, especially when such symbols are being approached from an empirical angle.

This article describes a number of Turner's divisions of meanings relating to religious rituals. His concept of 'symbol' underlying these divisions is disputable, however. Here the theory of signs developed by C.S. Peirce may, as a philosophy of the giving of meaning, provide an additional theoretical contribution to an anthropological or socio-scientific approach of our problem. Thus, through a comparison and combination of Turner's and Peirce's ideas I intend to design a theoretical framework within which it is possible to give an empirical description of the various meanings which participants assign to religious rituals, particularly to the Celebration of the Eucharist.

2. The ritual symbol in a semiotic perspective (V. Turner)

The significance of Turner's contribution is twofold. Not only did he clarify the importance of proceeding from semiotic distinctions, also he has been the first to point out that research into the meanings given by participants in rituals should make use of empirical methods (as an example he mentions the scale of Osgood).

In his essay *Symbols and Social Experience in Religious Ritual* (1974c) he argues that ritual is the frame of reference of his concept of symbol. A ritual is composed of symbols, which are its 'units' or 'molecules'. Thus a symbol is an element of ritual. Next Turner compares and positions the concepts of symbol, sign and signal within a semiotic framework. Central to his article is the question how symbols are connected with social situations and relationships which also play a part in religious rituals. To trace this connection he describes the characteristic features of a symbol in semiotic terms. He then examines how such symbols fit in with the life of the group that performs certain rituals.

A symbol within a ritual is a sign which for its practitioners has at least two components. First, as a sign a symbol can be perceived by the senses. Secondly, it refers to a content. In order to specify this reference Turner cites an article by Weinreich on semiotics and semantics. That which refers, the carrier of the meaning, is called the 'vehicle' or in French the 'signifiant', whereas the meaning referred to is called the 'designatum' or the 'signifié'.

According to Turner an important characteristic of symbols within rituals is what he calls their 'iconicity' - that is to say, the quality which distinguishes a symbol from a purely conventional and arbitrary sign. In his view a symbol directly affects one's 'sensory nature', one's sensorium. Symbols hardly require any explanation; it is by what they are that they give access to what is being referred to. Essential for

20

this iconic aspect are analogy and association, because both transcend the convention and arbitrariness that play an important role in most signs.

Turner then mentions a specific element of the study of symbols within rituals. The scientist engaged on this kind of anthropological research comes across symbols that always convey several meanings at the same time. He gives an example from the society of the Ndembu in Zambia. The muyombu or tear-tree secretes a certain kind of gum. The similarity of this gum to tears emerges in funeral rituals when in the eyes of the next of kin the tree is a symbol for their sorrow and respect for the deceased ancestor or ancestress. But this tree 'collects' several other meanings as well. When a member of the tribe falls ill a new muyombo tree is planted if the illness is attributed to the fact that a deceased relative has not been sufficiently 'remembered'. Such a tree refers to and 'replaces' the deceased relative, and also makes it possible to restore the bond with him or her in symbolic form. So in a way the tree 'preserves' the dead, keeps them 'alive' in the community. The tree can also play a ritual part when the mutual relations between kinsmen are disturbed. Apart from its 'tears' the muyombo tree has other properties as well which play a part in rituals. Thus, one of these - the capacity of cuttings from the tree to regenerate quickly after replanting - refers to the notion that the memory of an ancestor will for ever remain. So when a village moves to a new site cuttings are taken from one ore more trees and then replanted in the new village to maintain the bond between the living and the dead. Also the white wood of the tree which appears after its top has been cut and pared, has a symbolic function. Within the ritual of circumcision the white wood refers to the purifying effect of the operation.

It is evident that in different ways and at different times this particular tree has an important function in the life of the Ndembu. As a 'symbol-vehicle' the tree conveys several meanings that attribute to its 'power'. Of the qualities inherent in all the rituals in which the muyombu tree has a symbolic function Turner stresses the social component:

> "Since the tear-tree is central to impressive rites that are performed many times in the experience of the individual it tends to absorb the total quality of the social situations it focusses..." (Turner, 1974c:6).

Equally important for Turner is the conclusion that generally symbols do not refer to a single meaning (denotatum, designatum) but to several meanings simultaneously. He terms such symbols 'multivocal' in contrast to 'univocal' symbols, which refer only to one meaning. For Turner 'multivocality' constitutes the characteristic feature of symbols within a ritual context. Therefore, he finds that a simple 'sign' model is inadequate to describe symbols within rituals. They have a rich semantic content attached to them, as appears from his definition: a symbol within a ritual is multivocal,

> "a thing (object, .. person, .. activity) regarded ... by persons of the same <u>culture</u> as 'naturally' ... representing something by possession of analogous qualities or by association in fact or thought" (Turner, 1974c:7).

Turner clearly pays much attention to the directly perceptible or analogous representation of symbols. He emphasizes that the term 'natural' for this set of symbols is rather unfortunate because all signs and symbols must be regarded as 'cultural'. The meanings of symbols are fixed only within a group. Nevertheless, Turner seems unable to choose from the different elements that form part of the symbol as he himself has outlined it. In my opinion his concept of symbol remains ambivalent since its meaning is directly perceptible to the senses on the one hand and confined to one particular culture on the other hand. Meanings do not exist outside contexts, and that goes for symbols too. This ambivalence poses a problem which Turner cannot solve. The tension actually makes itself felt, for example, in the many possible meanings individuals may assign to identical symbols. Symbols within rituals can have a meaning which participants in that particular ritual interpret in their own individual way.

Also a tension exists between the directly perceptible meaning and the culturally mediated meaning in a group of observers. In the mentioned article Turner pays attention to the difference between the meaning given to a ritual by members of the culture performing it and the meaning of the same ritual for anthropologists. What is characteristic for either of them?

As to the meaning given by the performing community, Turner distinguishes two categories. First, this meaning has a functional quality in that the ritual strengthens the bonds of the group. This is illustrated by the rituals concerning the tear-tree, which in the experience of the Ndembu not only strengthen the bond between the living but also form "a set of structures of thought and feeling about the relationships between the living and the dead" (1974c:6). The second category refers to the traditional character of the meaning assigned by the group. As far as the individual participants are concerned, the meanings of a ritual are pre-given. For the group the ritual is therefore the opposite of a unique event. Especially typical is the fact that unlike language the meaning of non-verbal ritual "is limited in its capacity for flexible and varied expression" (1974c:7). Thus, the meanings of symbols are more or less fixed.

In order to explain the tension noted above it is helpful to cite Turner's conviction (which is based on his studies of African rituals) that symbols within rituals (i.e. multivocal symbols) show 'a polarization of reference'. This means that some of a symbol's denotations or connotations ('their senses') refer to 'physiological objects and processes' and others to 'cognitive, moral and ideological factors and influences' and even to 'results of valid experience and experiment' (1974c:8-9). Since they do not share the participants' cognitive-ideological reference, 'out-siders' (like anthropologists and other observers) assign other meanings than the participants to the ritual, which, as we have seen, is characterized by its bonding function and traditional character. It is evident that the elements of rites do not for all human beings 'naturally' refer to 'something'. The references in rituals are susceptible to different kinds of explanations or significance.

In conclusion of this survey it is necessary to discuss, however briefly, another distinction made by Turner, namely his important classification of symbols into three major dimensions of meaning (1974c:11 ff.). The first of these is the exegetic dimension. It consists of all the explanations of a symbol's meaning provided by indigenous informants. These explanations may take the form of myths, doctrine and dogma. Three semantic fields are the bases of these explanations, i.e. the nominal, substantial and artifactual semantic bases of a symbol. In the case of a nominal basis, the symbol is referred to by name in a ritual context, in a non-ritual context, or in both. The substantial basis relates to objects used as symbols and consists in their natural and material properties. The artifactual basis is represented by the symbolic object which as a result of human activity has become a cultural artifact.

In the second dimension, the operational dimension, a symbol's significance derives from its use - from what ritual participants *do* with it rather than what they say about it. Certain investigators analyse this aspect in particular. On the one hand, they focus on the structure and composition of the group performing the rites, asking who are absent on these ritual occasions, and why. On the other hand, they concentrate on the affective quality of the acts expressed during the rites (Turner mentions aggression, sorrow, joy, etc.).

In the third dimension of significance, the positional dimension, the meaning of a symbol depends first of all on its relationship to other symbols. According to Turner anthropologists who follow Levy-Strauss consider the meanings of symbols to be defined by their interdependent structure and positioning rather than their content. They usually see symbols in terms of binary oppositions, which enables them to distinguish sharply between the meanings of symbols. For that reason, says Turner, they are inclined to regard symbols as univocal. Consequently these writers seem to him to overlook the 'latent senses' which symbols may have. The three dimensions, however, enable observers to collect data about the structure as well as the content of symbols in rituals.

2. Turner's theory applied to the Eucharist

When the insights of Turner are applied to the central ritual of Roman Catholic religion which is celebrated all over the world and in many diverse cultures, we must take note of the following points.

The first remark concerns the concept of symbol. For Turner a symbol is part of a ritual. As elements of ritual designation symbols have a number of properties relating to the designation of meaning. These properties derive largely from the fact that the symbols analysed by Turner are non-verbal. An important feature of most elements of the Celebration of the Eucharist, however, is that they are verbal in character. This is definitely true of the liturgy after the second Vatican Council. Prayers, hymns, Bible readings and sermons are elements of the celebration which cannot be termed 'things' in the broad sense in which Turner describes symbols (object, event, person, relationship, activity, place, period of time, etc.). This is not to deny that (the breaking of) the bread and (the drinking of) the wine, the furnishings of the place of worship, the vestments of the celebrant, and suchlike, can be regarded as things in Turner's sense. Viewed from this perspective the concept of symbol employed by Turner to define the elements of rituals can be applied to the Celebration of the Eucharist only in a limited sense. It is not unlikely that acts like singing and reading, in which the text plays an important part, also have several meanings for the participants. Their content may be just as multivocal as the elements of the ritual that are directly perceptible to the senses and have several meanings at the same time. That would result not so much from an analogous relationship between sign and content which is perceived in a natural way by the participants, as from agreement within the culture of faith about the verbal content of various elements of the ritual. This kind of agreement would of course leave room for individual significations.

The difficulties concerning the concept of symbol can be resolved by distinguishing between non-verbal and verbal symbols. The concept of the former coincides with Turner's idea that apart from other characteristics a symbol may have, it is primarily sensorily perceptible, as we have seen above. The second category comprises the verbal elements of a ritual. On account of their metaphorical character it would be justified to assume that they are multivocal as well. Turner's classification of symbols into three dimensions of meaning has an important part to play in the study of both types. The first of these, the exegetic dimension of meaning, consists of the explanations given by indigenous informants. With regard to the Celebration of the Eucharist in the Roman Catholic Church explanations of the meaning of the various elements are given at three levels. The first level is that of the participants. Two groups can be distinguished here: the group of the churchgoers (those attending the Celebration of the Eucharist regularly and those attending irregularly) and the group of the celebrants or ministers. Since the latter are responsible for the selection of hymns and prayers and for the content of the sermon, they are important with respect to the form and content of the celebration. Presumably there is a considerable difference between the two groups as to their theological and liturgical knowledge. The second level is that of the ecclesiastical authorities in the different church provinces and Rome who are responsible for texts and usages within the Celebration of the Eucharist. Third level information is derived from the study of liturgy as a theological discipline which specializes in the interpretation and structure of liturgical celebrations, especially the Eucharist. Its approach to the liturgy is chiefly historical or historico-systematical.

In Turner's view explanations in the exegetic dimension may take the form of myths, doctrine and dogma. In addition to the nominal, substantial and artifactual semantic fields of Turner it is necessary to mention the historical as a fourth source of explanation, precisely because it is extremely relevant in the case of the Celebration of the Eucharist. In Roman Catholicism tradition and history have always played a prominent part in explaining the form and content of rituals. Later Turner has added the historical explanation as a basis for understanding the meanings of some phenomena in Christian culture (Turner & Turner, 1978).

The nominal basis of the Celebration of the Eucharist is 'to give thanks', to thank God for his Son. Latin and Greek terms provide the nominal explanation for the various elements of the celebration (Kyrie, Gloria, Credo, etc.). There are a number of substantial elements, e.g. the water that is used for the washing of the hands. The gestures performed during the celebration are examples of artifactual foundations. To mention just a few: gestures of prayer, the spreading of the arms, kneeling and the kiss of peace.

In the operational dimension of significance operations or actions taking place during the ritual are investigated in order to discover their meaning. Here we may also consider the structure and composition of the performing group at any phase of the ritual; also we pay attention to the group which is absent. Canon law plays a part in questions like which group may take part in the Celebration of the Eucharist and which group may go to Communion as well. From the socio-religious point of view however, it is probably more relevant and interesting to examine how and why the group of churchgoers - for example in Holland - has dramatically decreased during the last thirty years. Which part of the Catholic population has decided to attend the Eucharistic Celebration no longer, and which part has decided to go on doing so?

In the third dimension the meaning of a symbol derives from its relation to other symbols, from the particular positions which elements of a ritual, in this case the Celebration of the Eucharist, occupy in relation to one another. In terms borrowed from structuralism, liturgical studies speak of a paradigmatic or syntagmatic connection between the elements of a ritual (Scheer, 1985; Carminati, 1988). The term 'paradigmatic' refers to the content of the elements of a liturgical celebration; 'syntagmatic' refers to the sequential process of these elements.

Summarising it can be concluded that the study of the Celebration of the Eucharist can certainly benefit from Turner's analyses. However, for a better understanding of the assignation of meaning by the participants (their) language seems to provide a more congenial approach. Particularly Turner's concept of the symbol as a category allowing the observer to distance himself to some extent from the ritual is problematic. Also it is difficult to see how Turner's notion of a symbol as 'naturally typifying or representing something' can be reconciled with his proposition that a symbol conveys meaning due to 'general consent' by persons of the same culture. It is even more difficult when that general consent is subject to various kinds of interpretations by various subgroups.

Turner emphasizes the iconic or analogous sign value of a symbol, which means that the 'sign vehicle' has a perceptible impact on the sensory nature of the participant in a ritual. But, as we have seen above, he has given no indication of how the analogous sign value is connected with the cultural aspect of the meaning assigned to a ritual symbol. After all, a symbol also has meaning by virtue of the socio-psychological world view of the group concerned. Neither has Turner resolved the question how the analogous sign value of a symbol is connected with the life and personal history of the individual who uses it.

An empirical inquiry into the interrelations between these different forms of assignation of meaning may enable us to gain insight in symbols that cannot be clearly understood from the study of ritual symbols that refer to or derive their meaning from myths, ideologies or religious convictions. Psycho-religious research may shed some light on the meaning of symbols in so far as they refer to the extra-ritual reality of the individual participants. This particular sign value offers the possibility of examining the meanings which participants in rituals assign to certain symbols on the basis of their personal life history. Thus there will be room for a broader concept of symbol, so that a symbol within a ritual need not be confined to the sign that is rich in iconic quality, but may in principle be equated with any element of a ritual - such as readings, sermons, hymns and prayers, which aren't just meaningful on account of other meanings they may have for the participants.

The proposition put forward in this article is that in comparison with Turner's understanding of symbols the theory of C.S. Peirce, which will be discussed presently, can be of greater help in describing the empirical reality of meanings ascribed by participants to the Celebration of the Eucharist. The choice for the semiotic theory of Peirce is based on two arguments. In contrast with other semiotic theories, Peirce's approach is characterized by the premise that there is a connection between sign and reality. Naturally this is important for an empirical inquiry which is intended to examine the interrelationship of liturgical celebration and the everyday reality of those taking part in it. The second argument is that the formal tripartition of Peirce admits both the analogous and the cultural aspect of Turner's concept of symbol.

3. The classification of the assignation of meaning (C.S. Peirce)

What is the theory of Peirce about? It starts from the assumption that through signs humans try to bring order into the chaos of reality. Signs, reality and human subjects form a triangle of forces influencing one another. For anyone perceiving a sign, its meaning is not restricted to one's inner life but also extends to one's behavior. Thus, a sign is capable of initiating a new interpretation of reality and new behaviour as well. A succession of such perceptions is a process which in principle may again and again induce new contents and forms of conduct.

From the relations between sign, reality and subject, Peirce derives a distinction between different kinds of signs, resulting in three distinct categories (van Wolde, 1989). According to Peirce a relation that greatly depends on a physical-causal connection between sign and reality is an indexical relation. If the connection is mainly due to the sign, Peirce calls the relation iconic; if the connection is primarily due to the subject and answers to a rule (this will be explained below), he speaks of a symbolic relation.

An indexical relation between sign and reality supposes there is something pre-given in reality (or in other signs) which makes the relation possible. This causative influence is based on what Peirce calls the principle of indexicality, and the index then stands for the sign that is thus influenced. So indexical signs are indicators pointing to something in reality. A classic example of this is a weathercock or weathervane.

An iconic sign, on the other hand, is quite independent of reality but has the potency of becoming linked with it. An example is a strangely formed calebash which, if it happens to resemble a certain politician, turns from a potential into an iconic sign when carried on a stick in a demonstration (van Zoest, 1987). The calabash is no longer a potential sign but has become an actualized sign of a predominantly iconic character. Stories abound in possibilities that help listeners to interpret reality in general but also their own reality. Due to their likeness to something else most pictures are iconic signs. The sign itself brings about the link with reality. The iconic sign has a power of its own which is actualized, as Peirce says, by the the subject, i.e. the person perceiving it. At this point it is worth noting that Turner's concept of symbol is not so very different from Peirce's definition of iconc signs.

For Peirce a symbol is a sign whose relation to what is referred to (the designatum or denotatum) is determined by a universal rule. In the case of a symbol the assignation of meaning is entirely or mainly dependent on the subject and because of its conventional character conditioned by the social group. In our culture shaking hands is a sign which according to general agreement or conventional rules has to do with saying hello or saying goodbye, or with offering congratulations. To prevent confusion it might be a good thing to substitute 'conventional sign' for the term symbol.

Indexical, iconic and conventional signs form the division by means of which it is possible to distinguish different aspects in the giving of meaning by participants in rituals. With regard to the Celebration of the Eucharist the question may then be asked how the elements can be understood as a collection of interrelated signs which are interpreted by the participants in different ways.

A participant's perception of a ritual or liturgical celebration is said to be indexical when, and in so far as, he or she experiences something that for him or her refers to a pre-given reality. Elements of the celebration may, for example, refer to names of relatives or situations from the present or the past that are familiar to the participants. Indexical relations are established when the celebrant or other functionaries refer, for example, to events from the life of the parish. References to history may be indexical signs too; think of the participant who finds a reading from the gospel interesting or important precisely because it refers to some historical event.

The second kind of meaning assignation is mainly determined by the intrinsic quality of the sign itself. An iconic sign in a ritual can therefore be discribed as an event brought about by the power of a sign or an image evoked by it, through which a participant realizes more fully or experiences more deeply some significant aspect of his personal existence. Characters from the scriptural readings, for example, may stimulate the imagination of the listener and encourage him to compare their way of life with his own.

Finally, an example of the category of signs which owe their existence to agreement or convention is what the faithful experience when they recite the Creed rather mechanically during the weekend liturgy. They experience the Creed whichever way it is recited as a matter-of-course part of the service, since it is agreed that this element should refer to and express the faith of the congregation (while individual members when asked point-blank may make some reservations about their personal beliefs). The link between what people believe and what they openly confess is not necessarily strong. The force of habit, on the other hand, may be very strong indeed.

4. A design for empirical inquiry into the meanings assigned to the Celebration of the Eucharist

Research into the ideologies and religiosity of groups within other cultures often employs ritual as an important source of evidence. In our culture rituals seem to play only a minor part in research. This is probably based on the supposition that religiousness is rather to be found in opinions, values and actual forms of religious conduct such as the frequency of churchgoing and the extent to which people use the media to be informed on religious matters.

Consequently, little or no research has been done on how churchgoers in our culture experience and appreciate the rituals in which they participate, how their experience and appreciation are related to their ideas as believers, which elements of a celebration appeal to their imagination, and if, and to what extent, they make themselves familiar with the content of the ritual. It follows that empirical research of the experience of participants with respect to the Celebration of the Eucharist must of necessity be exploratory in character.

However, before carrying out such an inquiry, or any empirical inquiry for that matter, it is essential to decide first on a conceptual framework appropriate for it. Peirce's classification was chosen provisionally to serve as the frame of reference of an inquiry into liturgical experience, which was conducted in ten parishes in Holland. This choice was based on the consideration that this theory meets the following two conditions. First it can be put into operational terms that are in keeping with the language and traditions of the participants. Secondly, it embraces the concept of symbol which is employed by Turner in his research on rituals, as we have explained above. Translating the classification of Peirce into operational terms implies-certainly in this exploratory phase - that it is necessary to choose from the many diverse elements of which the Celebration of the Eucharist consists.

An accurate description of the Celebration of the Eucharist as a whole requires that it should be divided into as many small elements as possible. On the other hand, there is of course the danger that such a division might become unwieldy as well as irrelevant. Next, it is important to note that the term element is here understood to refer exclusively to actions, and not to objects. Objects used during the ritual derive their meaning from the use made of them in actions, so that bread or wine, for example, are not elements in themselves but part of the actions of blessing, breaking and eating, pouring out and drinking which take place during the service of the table. The Celebration of the Eucharist as a whole is to be distinguished into four levels of action. At the first level it consists of twenty-five elements, at the second level of five parts (rite of introduction, rite of the word, in-between rites, rite of the table and final rite), at the third of two principal parts (the service of the word and the service of the table) and finally, at the fourth level, the liturgical service as a whole.

For the purposes of our inquiry two elements - "reading from the gospel" and "table prayer" - were selected from the two principal parts of the service. They constitute central elements within the Eucharistic Celebration as far as their meaning is concerned. In addition, they can be put into operational terms in accordance with the three categories of Peirce's classification.

The four gospels are read in the course of three liturgical years. In 1989 it was the turn of the gospel of Luke. On the day of our inquiry (the first sunday of october) the part of the gospel to be read was Luke 16:19-31. Accordingly our measuring instrument had to be formulated in terms of the parable about the poor man Lazarus who would have been glad to satisfy his hunger with the scraps from the rich man's table but actually received nothing. After they had both died the rich man asked Abraham if Lazarus might be sent to his relatives to warn them for a fate like his own, but his request was refused.

Participants in the weekend liturgy in question were asked to respond to the reading by answering a number of propositions which are in fact operational definitions of the three categories of Peirce. To each proposition participants could react by choosing either one of two alternatives ("No, I do not agree with this statement." or "Yes, I agree with this statement.").

In the final section of this article some examples are given to illustrate how these propositions reflect the indexical, iconic and conventional categories of meaning. The indexical questions are formulated in such a way that they reflect the historical reality referred to by certain elements of the celebration. The following examples are related to (a) the scriptural reading and (b) the table prayer:

    a. "The story shows that the belief in Abraham, Moses and the prophets was very important in Jesus' time."

        "Since this story is about a time over and done with, it means little to me." (This proposition indicates a negative indexicality).

    b. "For me the Eucharist refers to sacrifices that nowadays are made by people for their belief in God."

        "The Eucharist or table prayer reminds me of the Last Supper of Jesus Christ."

        "I see the Eucharist as a repetition of the last gathering of Jesus with his disciples today."

        "During the Eucharistic prayer I think of Jesus' suffering, death and resurrection".

Participants are said to derive meaning for their own life from certain elements of the celebration when they experience the content of these elements as an image or representation of their own situation. A few examples of iconic meanings related to (a) the scriptural reading and (b) the table prayer:

    a. "The story has made me think of what the difference between rich and poor means for me personally."

        "This story makes me think what it means that God chooses the side of the poor."

        "That the rich man in the story regrets his behaviour has made me think this weekend about my own behaviour."

b. "The sacrifice of Jesus challenges me to live a life in the service of others."

"That Jesus Christ gave his life inspires me to lead a life that is centred on God."

"The celebration of the passion, death and resurrection of Jesus helps me to live through difficult situations in my own life."

When the assigned meanings are such that participants say that they are familiar with them, they are conventional meanings. Examples are again related to (a) the Bible reading and (b) the table prayer:

a. "This story bears out my belief that there is justice in God after death."

"This story confirms my belief that God does not value people because they are rich."

"This story is important because Jesus Christ has told it."

"I have heard this story about Lazarus many times, so I know it quite well".

b. "The most important aspect of the eucharist is for me that we celebrate the sacrifice of Jesus."

"The celebration is holy to me because at that moment the sacrifice of Jesus takes place."

"The prayer of the table during the weekend liturgy made me give thanks to God for the salvation by Jesus Christ."

In distinction from the categories used by Turner these three types of meaning assignation are expected to detect or trace some ways in which the Celebration of the Eucharist is experienced by those taking part in it. Do they experience the weekend liturgy, or rather some of its elements, first of all as a stimulus to reflections on their own life, or do they still interpret it traditionally (with the emphasis on its sacrificial character), or do they rather see it as a reference to historical events? It is very well possible that in the experience of the participants there is something of each.

Translation by W. Bisscheroux

RITUAL AND TRANSFORMATION
A psychoanalytic perspective

Hans-Günter Heimbrock

1. Theories of rituals in social sciences
Studying ritual symbolic activities from the perspective of modern psychology of religion immediately raises severe theoretical problems. These problems could be indicated with two crucial questions:

a) To what extent is the theoretical framework suitable to give a differentiated analysis of relevant phenomena, i.e. a framework that is not preoccupied by underlying negative stances against ritual symbolism anyhow?

b) Are we able to work out a psychological complement to prominent theories of cultural anthropology with special regard to the analysis of ritual symbolism as a process of transformation?

As to the first question, for generations of scholars there existed a kind of hidden coalition between psychodynamic and cognitive approaches towards human ritualism. Freud (1972 (1907), 1973 (1912/13)) and his early followers - among whom Reik (1919, 1964) should especially be mentioned - interpreted relevant phenomena as the more or less unconscious repetition of the infantile past. In their studies, they recognized religious rituals as being similar to neurotic symptoms, that is unsuitable means to overcome underlying emotional conflicts. Although this pattern of analysis leads to unexpected but in many respects nevertheless fruitful results, one cannot overlook its underlying axiomatic values. More or less in line with E. Durkheim (1912), ritual behavior was taken by the early psychodynamic psychology of religion as an important element of religion that should be converted into rational behavior. Rituals, according to this view, present dominantly infantile starting points or even regressions of individual as well as social patterns of human life.

I think it was a coincidence not purely by chance, that Piaget - in his famous studies on the development of individual conceptions of the world outside - came to similar conclusions as Freud (Piaget, 1926). Although being cautious about too narrow a parallelism between ontogeny and phylogeny, he discussed rituals, especially magic rituals, as premature forms of reasoning.

Being sympathetic to Freud's notion of the infantile "Allmacht der

Gedanken", Piaget in his cognitive structural theory also had a sceptical look at rituals. Because of his focus on the development of natural causality concepts and on account of growing insights in the boundaries between the individual and the outside world, he estimated rituals as underdeveloped forms of cognitive capacity.

We are not quite out of the woods, if we turn to an entirely different theoretical position, presented by Jung (1952) and his psychological school. To me this rather speculative view on human ritualism seems nearly the other side of the coin. Because here, rituals are rather uncritically seen as positive and most helpful means for personal and cultural "individuation" and growth (Neumann, 1978 (1951)). Also in this theory I miss the necessary criteria to give a suitable, that is a differentiated interpretation of ritual experience in all its psychic ambivalence.

As to the second crucial question, in the field of cultural anthropology during our century there has been made quite an impressive progress from older Durkheimian analyses towards other positions. Well-known in Durkheim's analysis is the functionalistic intention of what he called primitive and elementary forms of religion. Behind all those phenomena, and also behind rituals, he tried to unmask society and social forces as the hidden core. Of less interest to sociologists however seems to be his incidental psychological explanation of ritual phenomena. At least once he did not hesitate to identify them as follows:

> "...the real function of the cult is to awaken within the worshippers a
> certain state of soul, composed of moral force and confidence, and ...
> the various effects imparted to the rites are due only to a secondary
> and variable determination of this state" (Durkheim, 1912:386).

Two generations later the perspectives have changed as far as functional dimensions of rituals are concerned. Especially Turner, who elaborated A. van Gennep's views on "rites de passage" (van Gennep, 1909), has provided us, by means of extensive field-studies and cross-cultural comparative analysis, with important insights in the transformative symbolic language of ritualism. Given the methodological progress from structural-functional analyses of religion towards C. Geertz's interpretative position (Geertz, 1966), Turner draws attention to the functions as well as the expressive meanings of religious rituals in tribal societies (Turner, 1977a (1969); see also Boudewijnse, *The ritual studies of Victor Turner: An anthropological approach and its psychological impact*, in this volume). Well-known is his central thesis, that rituals provide society with the possibility of changing temporarily from normality to "liminality" in order to experience the basic social values of "communitas" (Turner & Turner, 1978).

In later studies he envisaged, without any naive nostalgia, similarities as well as differences of ritual symbolic behavior in modern industrial societies as compared to ritual behavior in tribal societies (Turner, 1984). Under the conditions of social differentiation and in times of secularization, participation in religious rituals is more or less reduced to superficial experiences, comparable to other activities of leisure time. Instead of a deeper experience of social or individual transformation, there often remains nothing but a 'reduced' liminality, called "liminoid form of transformation" (Turner, 1974).

Meanwhile, exactly this contemporary theory of cultural anthropology has been applied to give new insights in the nature and meaning of encounter workshops (Holloman, 1974) and of psychotherapeutic rituals (Moore, 1983, 1984; see also Vandermeersch, *Psychotherapeutic and religious rituals: The issue of secularization*, in this volume).

The psychology of religion should take Turner's legacy as a challenge to give further attention to psychological interpretations of psychic transformative qualities of ritual experience. On the other hand, Turner's implicit psychology should certainly be a challenge for psychological investigations in cultural anthropology. In a later autobiographical article Turner admitted to what extent his own analysis of social ritual symbolism was stimulated by Freud's interpretation of personal symbolism (Turner, 1978). Obviously he didn't just follow the psychoanalytic path in focussing on hermeneutics, especially on unconscious meanings of rituals. He also identified them as processes of collective regression to basic social forces, an interpretation most similar to what psychoanalysis would call "primary process". Furthermore, by means of his central term "communitas" Turner developed a kind of "meta-anthropology" comparable to Freud's meta-psychology.

For generations of psychologists of religion one of the main topics of study was the ideological religious transformation called "conversion" (James, 1903; Gordon, 1967; Loofland, 1977; Richardson, 1978). An attempt to study cognitive conversional processes has been lined out recently by J. van der Lans in his article on Christian liturgy seen through Sundén's perspective of changing roles and changing the frame of reference (van der Lans, 1984; Sundén, 1966b). In the present article, I would like to enlarge his attempt by following another theoretical path of modern psychology. It is my opinion that this in at least some respects does not lead to competitive views but rather to complementary insights in the psychic nature of ritual transformation.

2. On the psychodynamics of transition

In what follows, I will try to reconstruct the psychodynamic concept of "transitional objects" as a suitable theoretical framework to explain religious ritual phenomena. Originally, this concept was developed by the British paediatrist and psychoanalyst Winnicott in order to explain certain infantile steps of self-development in contact to reality (Winnicott, 1986a (1951); see also Coppolillo, 1976). But sometimes even he stated his impression that en passant some fundamental roots of cultural experience on the whole are being touched upon.

Given the general theoretical progress of psychoanalysis after Freud towards a psychosocial and a more empirically related theory of human development, I first present a short outline of Winnicott's notion of the 'intermediate sphere' of transitional objects and transitional phenomena. A further step will be directed to reformulate this for the interpretation of religious rituals.

Winnicott had a triple process in mind as he studied early infantile development. He described the psychic need to build up "the capacity to be alone" (Winnicott, 1958), as well as the necessity for the child to get into contact with what we call "reality", and, last but not least, the growth of the symbolic function. All three inner capacities must be taken as different theoretical perspectives of one entire process, the process during which the individual establishes a more or less suitable shift between the self and the outer world, between 'me' and 'not-me'.

Initially, Winnicott had certain well-known and rather common phenomena in mind, as he talked about 'transitional objects': early habits of the young baby to get oral satisfaction by means of a thumb, a fist or another available object such as a teddy or a piece of blanket. In some cases, even the mother or some babbling may be used in the same function. On the basis of direct observation he gave a fourfold characterization of the childish manipulations of these objects (Winnicott, 1986a:2):

a) The infant's capacity to recognize the object as 'not-me';
b) the place of the object - outside, inside, at the border;
c) the infant's capacity to create, think up, devise, originate, produce an object;
d) the initiation of an affectionate type of object-relationship.

Placed in a structural vision on early dynamics of world experience, those transitional objects fulfil an important step for the infant. They indicate that the separation between a growing self and the world outside cannot take place all at once. The transformation of the initial mother-child unity - experienced as an undifferentiated primary harmony -into an inner and an outer sphere, the motoric, cognitive and emotional acceptance of a rudimentary self as separated from things 'not-me', are related to a special mode of experience.

This transitional sphere is a necessary and creative process, through which the child elaborates more or less playfully a rudimentary image of the self as well as an early notion of 'reality'.

The concept of 'transitional objects' describes in fact aspects of the well-known symbolic function. Transitional objects are representatives, connected with an inner symbolic meaning. But compared to mere inner images their specific quality must be understood as tied to a reality outside, to things that do not only exist in pure inner fantasy. They are part of the child, but at the same time the initial point of getting into contact with the world outside. They stimulate reality testing:

> "The transitional phenomena represent the early stages of the use of illusion, without which there is no meaning for the human being in the idea of a relationship with an object that is perceived by others as external to that being" (Winnicott, 1986a:3).

Genetically looked at, transitional objects fulfil a very important function in the growth of illusions. They represent a bridge between the early omnipotence fantasy of controlling everything and a balanced disillusion which leads to realistic images of the self as well as of the outside world, predominantly the mother.

In another context Winnicott described the specific qualities of transitional objects, distinguishing between 'object relations' and 'the use of objects'. The former point at the cathexis of subjective meaningful images; they are directed to inner processes such as projection or identification. Theoretically they can be described as inner dynamic phenomena. As to the later 'use of objects', there is a certain growth at hand, a specific decline of control, an awareness of not being able to manipulate the object entirely:

> "In the sequence one can say that first there is object-relating, than in the end there is object-use; in between, however, is the most difficult thing, perhaps, in human development; or the most irksome of all the early failures that come for mending. This thing that there is in between relating and use is the subject's placing of the object outside the area of the subject's omnipotent control; that is, the subject's perception of the object as an external phenomenon, not as a projective entity, in fact

37

recognition of it as an entity in its own right" (Winnicott, 1986b (1969):105).

Obviously this concept of transitional objects points first of all to infantile developmental tasks, as I just lined out. The first objects of transformative quality such as the thumb or the teddy lose their value when the child is growing up. However, one fundamental task, linked to these objects, does not disappear: "the task of reality-acceptance". Winnicott puts a strong emphasis on this task, stressing

> "that no human being is free from the strain of relating inner and outer reality, and that the relief from this strain is provided by an intermediate area of experience ... which is not challenged ... This intermediate area is in direct continuity with the play of the small child who is 'lost' in play" (Winnicott, 1986a:15).

By formulating these ideas Winnicott has implicitly and explicitly pointed out a central problem for the psychology of religion because he relates phenomena of artistic and religious meaning strongly to the transitional sphere. When focussing on religious rituals, this idea must be elaborated.

3. Rituals as transitional objects
The application of Winnicott's concept to ritual experience surely follows from studies already set up by others. As to religious symbolism in the function of transitional objects I only have to mention the famous study of Rizzuto (1979). Furthermore Pruyser in his psychodynamic interpretation of culture presented a most stimulating vision of phenomena like art, literature, music, religion and even science as cultural equivalents to Winnicott's "transitional objects" (Pruyser, 1983). Both of them, Rizzuto and Pruyser, by means of Winnicott's ideas developed a differentiated view on the dynamics of human illusion processes. Fantasy may be an unconscious invitation to return to the infantile "Allmacht der Gedanken" (Freud), neglecting reality outside. But it might also be our most productive ability to build up a creative balance between inner emotional experiences and the perception as well as the construction of outer reality (Heimbrock, 1977).

In those studies the concept of transitional objects is used to illuminate predominantly inner mental symbolism as God images or visions about biblical figures (see also Meissner, 1984; Grünewald, 1982).

Personally I believe this concept to be even more valuable in describing the fundamental psychodynamics of symbolic activities in ritual behavior. Looking at some of the most prominent rituals in nearly all religions in their cultural variety - such as rituals of blessing and of prayer, rituals related to nature such as funeral customs, rituals of holy meals or holy fasting, not to forget ritual music - one can identify at least one fundamental common ground: through ritual means individuals and groups try to elaborate an experiential space between the self and reality analogous to the early transitional sphere. A combination, moreover: a playful balance between active disposal of the world on the one hand, and getting in touch with the very other - with the 'not-me' in its deepest religious meaning, i.e. with God - on the other hand, is expressed symbolically in ritual activity. Following this perspective, I would like to advance the thesis that, psychologically looked at, religious rituals enact the difference between the subject and the object "as an entity in its own right" (Winnicott) and at the same time represent its transgression.

To put this somewhat more concretely, I'll try to illustrate the idea by focussing on specific rituals. Central to most world religions are rituals of holy meals. The process of incorporation presents as a central theme the physical and metaphysical transition between 'inside' and 'outside'. Religions by means of ritual eating reenact the infantile oral transitional mode, the longing for an unseparated unity between the self and its protecting and feeding cover, as well as the basic human recognition that there is a split between the subject and the cosmos. Most important to me seems to be the fact that rituals present all the mentioned (and of course other) elements of experiencing in a perceptible way. People can see, hear, touch, smell and move something. It is not merely an inner illusionistic process.

Another example could be the gestural ritualism of blessing. Typically this takes place in the context of a separation, such as in situations of farewell and of critical biographical transitions. The fact that in many cultures a benediction is looked upon as having magic power - once spoken and administered, it has its own reality, cannot be drawn back- corresponds exactly to the pattern of Winnicott's concept.

Taking the concept of transitional objects as a useful theoretical framework to study rituals in the psychology of religion, however, will not be succesful, if we don't take into consideration, that we are dealing with psychic phenomena of quite diverse qualities. Transitional objects are rather ambivalent phenomena. They don't always solve the above mentioned fundamental task of relating inner and outer reality in an adaptive manner. In order to follow my initial criterion to present a theoretical framework which is suitable for a differentiated analysis of ritual experience, it seems necessary to look at the various ways in which different individuals elaborate the transitional sphere.

In their feminist study on the psychodynamics of the catholic mass Ross & Ross use Winnicott's concept of transitional objects and come to a rather unambiguous conclusion: "The 'making present' of the transcendent through the Eucharistic symbols is a creative act in which every worshipper participates" (Ross & Ross, 1983:38). But unfortunately the authors, while focussing on an analysis of official liturgical texts, overlook the significant and crucial difference between an official ritual and its reception in the experience of various individuals. Without further knowledge of personal emotional backgrounds however it is impossible to say anything about the creative or regressive inner use of official symbols by even one worshipper. Otherwise one would run the risk of merely using a psychological concept for uncritical and apologetic purposes of sustaining certain speculative theological interpretations of liturgies. (For an alternative feminist perspective on ritual experience, see E. Ouwehand: *Women's rituals: Refelections on developmental theory*, in this volume).

Critical reflection on the relation between the transitional sphere and religious rituals must therefore take into consideration what Volkan & Corney described as the 'satelite state' of the defective self (Volkan & Corney, 1968). Their clinical studies point out that people don't always succeed in establishing a tolerable balance, but that due to a certain infantile deficiency of the individualization process there remains a life-long tendency "of maintaining a satelite relationship with the mother or some other source of ready gratification" (ibidem:284). As far as grown-up patients are concerned, in later life a partner or even a religious group may function as such an "instant mother". In this context we have to conduct more studies on several new cultic movements as the "unification church", "the People's temple cult", but also studies on the specific use of traditional Christian churches.

Given the actual ambivalence of individual and cultural forms of elaborating a state of individualization, it might be even more fruitful for further theoretical and empirical research to apply a typological structure of defects concerning the transitional sphere to ritual experience. With regard to infantile development this structure has been proposed in a fourfold manner by Ogden (1985). With almost logical evidence he states four possibilities of defective illusionistic processes dealing with the balance between the "reality pool" and the "fantasy pool":

a) reality is subsumed by fantasy (i.e. illusions are taken without reality-testing as facts; subjective feelings seem objective facts; play becomes compulsive);

b) reality is taken as defence against fantasy (i.e. the individual is not capable to see more than facts, reality-testing is over-developed as a result of protection against dangerous insights in the meaning of the situation);

c) the dissociation of the reality and fantasy poles of the dialectical process (i.e. a tension to avoid meanings, fetishistic behavior, a certain 'splitting of the ego');

d) the foreclosure of reality and fantasy (i.e. merely a schizophrenic position, perception without experience and attribution of meanings as the result of the complete collapse of other defense mechanisms).

Transposing this structure to ritual experience may lead to a more differentiated interpretation. In a tentative way we could identify the first position ("reality is subsumed by fantasy") as the pattern of classical neurotic obsessive behavior. But I think other phenomena also belong to this category: for instance with regard to funeral rituals, a certain conduct accepting the ceremony only up to the point when the coffin actually should be led down into the earth. Also rituals that are more or less restricted to dealing with verbal symbolism or even with the pure interpretation of meaning instead of partly relating to realities, belong to this first category. In a certain sense one could even say that European white Protestant upper class religiosity with elaborated liturgies concentrating on (internal) dogmatic interpretations instead of other (external motoric) activities runs the risk of destroying the balance between the realistic and the fantastic pool, putting a sharp emphasis on the inner events of the "word of God".

As to the second position ("reality as a defence against fantasy") people take rituals, if there is any ritual practice anyhow, in a rather magic sense. These rituals are supposed to function without an individual process of attributing meaning, quite by natural power; they are looked at in an instrumental sense as technical behaviour rather than as expressive symbolic activities. The inner experiences of rituals are neglected by the participants. With reference to funeral rituals, one rather concentrates on the purely materialistic and well done burying than on the spiritual dimension of handing over the dead person to a transcendent power. Certain forms of healing rituals and of manipulating pendulums also belong to this second category.

As to the third pattern ("the dissociation between the realistic and the fantastic") I suppose we could identify at least some tendencies, even in traditional ritualism, for instance if we imagine the inability to return from the ritual context to an every-day-perspective, as it takes place in the official interpretation of the Catholic Eucharistic doctrine: once the bread is consecrated, it never will return to normal bread and has to be treated as holy.

4. Conclusions

Summing up the results of my article I would like to strengthen the possibilities the presented path opens for the psychology of religion.

1) By concentrating on the transitional qualities of ritual behavior we follow the contemporary methodology of qualitative analysis of religions. 'Ritual and transformation' aims at the general anthropological focus on rituals, in which they are looked at as enactments of meaning in an individual direction. This kind of psychology of religious ritual experience overcomes some sweeping statements of older interpretations. It remains open to further developmental and clinical studies.

2) Based on psychological concepts of human experience the attempt does not follow or even repeat an uncritical interpretation of rituals given by some experts of a religious community in speculative liturgical theories. Rather the theory provides a suitable instrument to work out a critical interpretation of ritual experience. At once it aims at a further differentiation of the individual use of fantasy and illusions. However, this contribution likes to be useful even for religious communities, who are interested in scientific analysis of their religious life.

3) The psychodynamic approach broadens the perspective of the psychological interpretation of religious ritual aiming at both the interdependence between actual experience and biographical past and the interrelations between official ritual symbolics and personal processes of interpretation. It might be a challenge to other studies of rituals, especially in its concentration on emotional qualities of ritual experience.

THE MEANING OF RITUAL IN THE LITURGY

Heije Faber

1. Introduction

A few short examples may indicate the phenomenological world we are entering when discussing ritual. The first is the remark of a psychologist in debate: "Human beings are just collections of habits". The second is an observation made in a Protestant rural parish in the Netherlands, where the whole congregation was upset when the new minister, before beginning with the Sunday service, stood at the foot of the chancel and said a short prayer to himself. People were upset because they weren't accustomed to their minister doing this. The third of my examples is another observation, this time from a Dutch family whose members were accustomed to begin the St. Nicholas celebrations with the ringing of the front doorbell and to find a basket with presents outside, put there by a secret hand (the neighbour). When the children were older and nearly adult, the family still celebrated the feast, but one of the sons felt it was not a real St. Nicholas celebration unless the doorbell rang and a basket appeared.

Much has been written about ritual. Three things strike me when examining the literature. In the first place: in the early psychoanalytic publications, especially those of Freud and Jung, ritual has a negative connotation. Freud (1972 (1907)) associated rituals with obsessions and Jung (1940) saw them as defence mechanisms in threatening encounters with the numinous. Secondly, psychotherapy has, in recent decades, given more attention and approval to ritual. And thirdly Erikson, in a well-known essay *Ontogeny of Ritualization in Man* (1966), has developed the vision that ritual forms an essential element in a person's achievement of "basic trust", which he believes is essential to a person's sense of well-being.

2. A change in our culture

We may wonder whether the changing view on ritual represents a fundamental change in our culture. There is certainly an element of obsession in ritual. Rituals arise in a community and try to give direction to and set boundaries for the behavior of human beings. So, in Freud's time, ritual was being condemned: ritual was regarded as playing a part in "das Unbehagen in der Kultur" of which Freud (1982 (1930)) had written and which was so typical of his view of human beings. Meanwhile society was struggling with the problem of an unconscious which was repressed. In a society which was characterised - to use Paul Tillich's (1926) phrase - by a spirit of finiteness, particularly sexuality and death were being deeply repressed. Jung maintained that the unconscious, as a numinous kindler, alerted the human consciousness, which in its turn sought a defence in particular rituals. From the attitude towards ritual we can infer that people, at the beginning of the twentieth century, experienced freedom as a necessary element in opposition to the pressure of society, and so viewed ritual negatively.

When we hear ritual being defended as a positive phenomenon, especially by psychotherapists, we can assume that there has been a change in our culture. It seems that people in their freedom need the support of society and find this support in rituals. It is remarkable how the need for ritual reveals itself. Especially in the field of so-called mourning processes, the absence of ritual makes it difficult for the bereaved to deal with their feelings of loss, as psychotherapists have discovered. When someone has lost a loved one, for example a spouse or a child, one is vulnerable in one's freedom, and experiences society not as a pressure but as a support. In such situations, rituals acquire a positive significance. Mustn't we therefore come to the conclusion that human beings in the modern world experience their freedom not only as a good to be defended, but also as an domain where they are vulnerable?

Ritual is ascribed positive qualities in other areas too. Wherever we see people trying, in their vulnerability, to entrust themselves to a community which may accept them, we see scientists studying ritual. We see a renewed interest among theologians in liturgy. We see psychotherapists developing rituals in their dealings with their clients. And we even see undertakers paying great attention to the form of burial or cremation.

But what is the role of the unconscious? Can a positive view of ritual be discerned here, related to a changing valuation of society? Or, in other words: does the community contain a space where the unconscious no longer threatens, but instead nurtures and gives direction? If this is true, we have gone a step forward in our culture. Freedom isn't just something towards which we strive simply because we cannot live under compulsion; nor is it a field in which we feel vulnerable. Instead freedom is a possibility to become a human being and to be guided by the unconscious. It is Erikson who, in the above-mentioned article, raised this issue. We will return to his article later on.

3. Human needs

I have tried to show that rituals have their basis in particular needs which are essential to human beings. For example:

a) *The need for life to be structured*. The psychologist's remark as well as the son's reaction to proposed changes in the St. Nicholas celebrations, show how difficult people find it to see life as an improvisation. The German sociologist Gehlen (1964 (1956)) developed the hypothesis that people create rituals to avoid the burden of constantly having to make decisions. Certainly rituals have this advantage. I think however that the need for ritual lies deeper. It seems to me that it is the need for sameness (Erikson) and coherence (Kohut, 1977) which forms a necessary basis for the growth of the concept of identity (with Erikson) and the development of a self-consciousness (with Kohut). Rituals form an essential part of this.

b) *The need to be freed from a straitjacket*. It was Freud who again and again showed that ritual, as an essential element in religion, holds people in a straitjacket. (Paul W. Pruyser has written a good overview of this in an instructive article in *Beyond the Classics* (1973)). But human beings have a deep-seated need for freedom, and rituals are always in tension with this need. In the tradition of the Enlightenment Freud emphasized the liberating effect of knowledge in a society which is kept in a state of tutelage.

c) *The need for safety*. On the other hand ritual provides a certain sense of safety at points where life "breaks through the walls of the prison", particularly where human beings are being confronted with the irrational and therefore threatening aspects of the numinous. Fear of death, fear of demons, fear of unknown depths in sexuality, fear of the boundlessness of the divine, in short, the fear of loss of control as against Nothingness creates the need for rituals to exorcise these fears and to provide the person concerned with the safety of a firm structure. In the first years of psychoanalysis, especially Freud and Jung showed that the need for security lies at the basis of life.

d) *The need for disclosure*. We touch upon the reality of ritual when we state with Erikson that rituals have a function of disclosure: they contain a source from which human beings are being nourished. Ritual somehow arise out of a mystery, perhaps THE mystery. Ritual is an answer to the fundamental danger that threatens our life, the danger of becoming nothing, of being swallowed by Nothingness. Ritual provides, so Erikson says, basic trust.

e) *The fixed form of rituals* is important precisely because changing them puts the reliability of the mystery at risk. If we lose the old rituals we may also lose the navel-string to the world where we belong and which we need. Then we fall into emptiness.

4. Our purpose

The purpose of this article is to consider the liturgies which we use in our churches in the light of the above. The liturgy of a church service, at a burial or cremation for example, is a planned ritual event. Therefore, a reflection on the phenomenon of ritual such as we try to give in this article, can throw light on what we actually do in our forms of liturgy, as well as on the problems which we encounter there.

Even a superficial glance shows that there is a clear difference between Protestants and Roman Catholics in their regard for liturgy. Roman Catholics give a great deal of attention to their liturgy, make careful studies about it and see to it that it is carried out correctly. For many Protestants the sermon is by far the most important part of the service, in fact to such a degree that they consider the liturgy - that is the ritual form of the church service - as being subsidiary. In recent years things have improved a lot, but the difference with Catholic practice is still tangible. In the past these differences have again and again given rise to irritation: Protestants often rejected changes in liturgy as being Catholic intrusions. Can we clarify these problems by a closer examination?

In the second place, in our times we see an obvious decline in the value that is being attached to the practice of ritual by the decline of participation in baptism, communion, and churchgoing itself. We also observe a lack of understanding of the old rituals which accompany death and mourning, and a consequently slipshod execution of those rituals. Most people attribute this decline to secularization but show little insight as to the connections.

In the third place we have to ask whether new rituals are developing, since rituals do fulfil a function and meet a need, and whether we can say something about the viability of these new rituals.

In the fourth place: do we have any idea of the role the pastor plays in the notion of ritual in her or his own parish? For instance, can the pastor influence the parishioners' attitudes towards change? During the changes within the Roman Catholic church, the role of the priest has been very important. Can he also contribute to the development of new rituals? And does it make any difference whether the pastor is a man or a woman?

5. Erikson

The best entry to the meaning of ritual is the article *Ontogeny of Ritualization in Man*, which Erik H. Erikson contributed to a collection in honour of his psychoanalytic colleague Heinz Hartmann, titled *Psychoanalysis - A General Psychology* (Erikson, 1966). Consistent with his psychoanalytic view of psychic development, Erikson demonstrates here how in the very first contact between mother (or nurturing person - H.F.) and child, rituals do exist which form the basis for a later notion of ritual. He examines what it is that the nurturing person and child experience in the ritualising of their contact and demonstrates what people experience in the rituals in which they participate.

Erikson's argument is built on the foundations of the theory that human development - and therefore the concept of ritual - takes place in clearly discernible stages. Rituals, as well as the need for them, arise in the contact with the nurturing person, but also play a role in the following stage with the father-figure, and later in the contact of a child with his friends, as they play together. This stage is followed by that of the school years, when learning is organised according to fixed ritual patterns. Finally there is the stage of adolescence which is characterised by initiation rituals. In this process the individual is absorbed into the group into which he or she is born, i.e. the tribe, clan or class. The rituals followed by the first nurturing person lead the child into the society, whereas animals are led by instinct. At the same time, rituals guarantee that the growing child achieves a certain independence (that is, its own identity), which is confirmed by the group's initiation rituals at adolescence. In this way the young woman or man is integrated into the life of the group.

Against this background Erikson's argument is clear. First he analyses what happens between nurturing person and child and shows how this influences that which happens in the following stages. What is essential, according to Erikson, is that the actions, words and touch of the nurturing person, and gradually also of the child, are formalised or, in other words, ritualised. According to Erikson, human beings are born with "a need for regular and mutual affirmation and certification". In the Netherlands the psychiatrist Anna Terruwe has founded her theory of psychotherapy on this need for affirmation. She was one of the first people in the Netherlands to observe the particularity of the mother-child contact.

In this contact, the child passes through this affirmation experiencing what Erikson calls a numinous element. One might compare it to Rudolf Otto's well-known description of the religious experience as an experience of the numinous. He describes it more precisely as "the sense of a hallowed presence". Through the presence of the nurturing person, which is like a numinous presence, the child experiences a sense of separateness transcended but of distinctiveness preserved. Also it is important that, in contact with this holy presence, it feels that it is no longer separated from the nurturing person (for it is received into a deeper union), and at the same time, that it is separate and as such may be there.

In the rituals which develop between nurturing person and child, this presence is revealed and preserved. This is essential for the psychic development of the child. Erikson also establishes a clear link with religious rituals: they are fashioned in the same way. Equally important for our argument however is that Erikson, in the sequel to his article, in which he pursues the development of the concept of ritual in later life, does not mention religious rituals again. It appears that he has forgotten all about it and one has to ask: Why?

But let me first continue summarising his article. Erikson as a psychotherapist is interested first and foremost in the meaning of rituals for mental health, while we are interested more in their meaning for religious practices in general and for the liturgy of religious gatherings in particular. Erikson gives us important indications.

According to him, ritual has to do with "the reciprocal needs of two quite unequal organisms and minds". Erikson is thinking of mother and child, whereas we may mention the worshipping community and the individual worshipper. In both cases, rituals are important and give structure to life. On the one hand, rituals are a highly personal matter, but at the same time they are "group-bound". As a result, ritual heightens the sense of belonging and of personal distinctiveness at one and the same time. In and through the rituals of the liturgy, the worshipper knows that one belongs to a worshipping community, but also that one is a separate individual. In the same way a child feels that it belongs to the nurturing person and yet is a separate being. Erikson makes an important point when he says that ritual marks out a path in a person's life. "Becoming familiar through repetition, (the ritual) yet renews the surprise of recognition which provides a catharsis of affects."

Repetition inspires us with confidence in the rituals and the liturgy, but this doesn't mean that our emotions are any the less involved. On the contrary: just like nurturing person and child may, time and again, experience spontaneity and surprise in the repetition of touch and caress, so worshippers experience, as Erikson puts it, the surprise of recognition in liturgy if it is well conducted. Their emotions are involved: they want to express them in song (as we do in the West) or in movement (as among Africans). And these emotions reach the deeper levels of our existence: they work cathartically. This means that people become more authentic, more in touch with their own nature, more themselves.

Erikson looks more closely at the emotions which play a role in the ritualised contact between mother and child, and therefore between worshipping community and worshipper. He presumes (and produces evidence to show) that the conquest of ambivalence is an important goal of human ritualising behaviour. "For what we love or admire is also threatening, awe becomes awfulness." When the nurturing person refuses contact or perhaps even leaves the child alone, the child must feel that the sun has disappeared. It feels itself deserted, betrayed, rejected. This experience arouses strong emotions of alienation, abondonment, anger. In the contact between nurturer and child there is always an element of uncertainty, because the child is dependent on the adult and is therefore afraid of being let down. The child as a consequence has ambivalent negative and positive emotions towards the nurturing person.

Erikson maintains that in rituals, this ambivalence is overcome. The rituals are, he says a periodic reassurance of familiarity and mutuality. He adds, "Such reassurance later remains the function of the numinous, whether it is dominant, as in the religious ritual, or subsidiary, as in all ritual." In other words, people receive in the rituals of liturgy the reassurance of their contact with the "numinous", with a hallowed presence. We can also say: in rituals the central secret of human existence is revealed, that we - with Heidegger (1972 (1927)) - are thrown into this world but are enclosed in it "by a deeper bond". This bond has, Erikson says, the traits of a face turned towards us; as human beings we can only speak and think in images about it. We speak of God's smile, of His hands, of His voice, which calls us by name and evokes traces as it were of the first experiences which we have had of the mystery of a love which carries and strengthens us.

Herewith the most important aspects of what Erikson has said about the meaning of ritual are summarized. In the rest of the article he explains how rituals contribute to a human being's growth towards adulthood. He argues that people gain their identity only through a process in which ritual in different ways plays a decisive role. A person's free will is formed in a learning process in which one learns what one has to do. Games and learning at school are unthinkable without ritual and also contribute to the growth of a deeper identity, by which freedom, recklessness, guilt and sacrifice appear. The process is completed in adolescence when the adult has the task of educating the new generation in the concept of ritual.

Although Erikson says that the essential elements of the previous stage are always embodied in the next, it is evident that the numinous actually disappears in the course of growth. Has Erikson no place for it? We need here to define the problems more closely. It is not true to say that Erikson's view of human development has no place for religion. On the contrary. As I have shown in an article on the meaning of presentday psychoanalysis for insight into religion (Faber, 1988), Erikson is one of those psychoanalysts who has valued religion. His famous book on Luther (1958) shows this. But the place he confers to religion is not entirely clear. In his book on Luther he sees religion as an important part of the ideology which a person - Luther, for example - needs in order to reach identity. He says, for example, that "One basic task of all religions is to reaffirm that first relationship" (1958:119), namely that with the nurturing person. And on page 21 this is said in other words: Religion "translates into significant words, images and codes the exceeding darkness which surrounds men's existence, and the light which pervades it - beyond all desert or comprehension." It is a repetition of the child's first experiences with the person who cares for it. At the end of the book Erikson summarizes it well:

> "The original faith which Luther tried to restore goes back to the basic
> trust of early infancy ... it is the smiling face and the guiding voice of
> the infantile parent images which religion projects into the benevolent
> sky ..." (1958:265-6).

One could also say: "Religion is in essence 'basic trust' and different symbolic systems are given to this 'trust'".

All this notwithstanding, there is no mention of rituals in the book on Luther. This suggests that Erikson accords rituals only a subsidiary place. The reader of the article on ritualization has the same impression. At the outset Erikson puts all the emphasis on the numinous element in the mother-child relationship, which he says continues in the religious relationship, so that one can learn from an analysis of the first many of the essential elements of the second. But when showing how the need for ritualization - and therefore the contribution of rituals - are to be seen in all important aspects of human development - he says nothing about religion. It would seem that religion is no longer interesting to him as a psychologist. Religion is apparently only of interest as a way in which certain people hold on to a basic trust which was created in their youth, and give it a form. When he thinks of ritualization he thinks about games, school, youth groups; but not about religion.

6. Religion in modern culture

Here we can see the central problem of our modern culture. Erikson's treatment of the phenomenon of ritualization reflects the way modern people regard religion and the way religion - perhaps - still has meaning for them. Religion is something which plays a role in the "archaic" layers of our emotional lives. At least, that is a view we often find among psychoanalysts. To this extent human beings are religious beings. But the ways in which religion is realised are not only culture-bound: indeed they are, in many ways, also random and dangerously one-sided. As young people grow into adulthood and in the later stages of human development, the "basic trust" which is formed in the first relationship lives on concealed. From the reactions of W.C. Smith (1978) or a developmental specialist like Fowler (1981) - with their views about "faith" as the central element in religion, separated from its varying manifestations - we can infer how this view of religion gains ground, even among theologians.

When considering Erikson we must make it clear that two aspects distinguish the contemporary view of religion as a phenomenon. First, for many people the search for their own identity - or the problem of mental health - apparently is so urgent that they do not achieve an interest in a more comprehensive or deeper view of humanity. Religion comes within their range of thought only in so far as it is of importance for their mental health. Therefore, the question of the truth of religion - and therefore the question whether the rituals, stories and symbols which are essential to religion, rest on a reality which reaches out above human beings - is not relevant to many people. They do not get beyond a certain scepticism or agnosticism.

7. Problems of liturgy

I want to consider the question of how far the presented material sheds light on some problems concerning liturgy as it functions in contemporary church life. We have mentioned four such problems:

First, the liturgical differences between Protestants and (Roman) Catholics. Catholics emphasize the celebration of the Eucharist; this celebration is always carried out with ritual care. Protestants consider the exposition and proclamation of the biblical message to be central. Certain rituals are involved, but much less the care is given to them. Interestingly we have in the Jewish religion a comparable difference between the temple service on the one hand and the gathering in the synagogue on the other hand. It is a contrast which has for a long time attracted attention. One of the most interesting studies is that of Samuel Terrien, *The Elusive Presence* (1978), in which he shows how

51

two tendencies can be discerned in the Old Testament. One, which he calls that of the Name, and the other, which he calls that of the Glory. The first tendency embraces prophecy, which Terrien associates first and foremost with the north of Israel and which lays all the emphasis on the word. The second tendency is that of the temple service, which has its centre in Jerusalem and which attributes essential importance to the sacrament and the priest. The link with Erikson's remarks is not hard to establish. The second tendency is that of the relationship of the child to the mother or nurturing person, where the mother with her "hallowed presence" gives the child the reassurance which it needs to survive. It is the priest who in the sacrament, which he celebrates carefully with the prescribed rituals, mediates the "hallowed presence" of God. The doctrine of transsubstantiation aims to show that, and in what way, God is present in this sacrament. The fist tendency is that of the relationship with the father, who is present with his children particularly through the word. Lacan shows that the father, through the word, divides the relationship between mother and child and releases a new dimension in the child's existence. This division indicates that his presence has a different character of that of the mother; seen from an emotional point of view the father reacts through his word and from a greater distance. Terrien, for example, mentions the elusive presence of God. And dialectical theology, with its emphasis on the fatherhood of God, emphasizes the distance in the relationship between God and human beings. Karl Barth even speaks about the "Todeslinie". Rituals therefore play a lesser role in Protestantism than in Catholicism. They only play a role in the sphere of spirituality, where the distance between God and human beings is bridged by the experience of the Holy Ghost in singing and praying during the church services, when there is a certain "presence" of God. One may ask whether the anxiety of the Dutch congregation, which I mentioned at the beginning of this article, was aroused because they were afraid that the sermon was being removed from the free sphere of exposition into the protected sphere of a "hallowed presence".

Secondly, an important point is that of the decline of rituals in the church and in religious life. This decline is serious. I have already mentioned the decline of participation in ritual events such as baptism, communion, and churchgoing, and in rituals at the time of death and mourning. But we need to look also at family life, which, for centuries, has handed down religious traditions from one generation to the next. I am thinking for example of the telling of biblical stories, of evening prayer, of bible reading and prayer decades. In most places, but especially in the big towns, these customs have   - with certain exceptions - disappeared. The whole problem of the transference of tradition is one of the most important aspects of the question of the survival of church and belief in our modern society.

What is the explanation for this crisis of religion in our modern culture? Social scientists, especially sociologists, have looked for an answer to this problem. The answers vary, but can be summarized under the heading of 'secularization'. The experts don't agree however on the content of this concept. It seems that during the last decades, several factors have contributed to the crisis and have invited the experts to add more and more aspects to the concept. Some of these are: modern knowledge and its influence on the religious world view; urbanization and its effects on communities; conflicts between generations and consequent failure to transfer religious traditions to younger people; the influence of modern communication and the superfluity of information concerning views on the deeper issues of life, often expressed in a certain relativism on the one hand or in aggressive fundamentalism on the other hand; the individualization of life for many modern people and, connected with this, an existential philosophical atmosphere which expresses itself in "basic distrust" as one's deepest conviction.

When I consider the decline of ritual as an element in this crisis, I come to the conclusion that the erosion of community life is a very important factor. We have learned from Durkheim (1912) that religion, especially through its rituals, fulfils an integrative role in society. From Erikson we learned that rituals originate in the mother-child relationship; that, later on, in the community in which a person lives, rituals disclose and hold fast the "hallowed presence", the binding mystery of the community. Thus, without community there is no ritual and there are no rituals without a community. Where the community withers, as in our modern society, rituals decline. The decline begins with so-called initiation rites (like baptism and confirmation) and - since mourning can also be considered to be a sort of initiation rite- with mourning customs. Rituals survive best in church services where the congregation is united in a central experience which is considered holy.

One may also ask how rituals can be re-established. Is it possible, by means of new or perhaps renewed rituals to bring people to religious convictions or experiences? In some cases, such as experimental church services or new forms of religious communities, like church days or foot marches, we do see phenomena which resemble new rituals. What significance do these rituals have? I think Erikson can help us here. He notices certain characteristics of rituals. When rituals originate, in the contact between nurturing person and child, and later with "real" and spontaneous rituals, there is the experience of a "hallowed presence" and of "affirmation and certification, a sense of separateness transcended and yet also of distinctiveness confirmed, which provides a catharsis of affects..". In other words: genuine rituals are rooted in the deepest experiences of our lives. We may speak here of existential experiences. Heidegger points out that we are "thrown into the world". Because of that we need confirmation that we are, on the one hand, individuals, separated from our ground (mother or nurturing person), and on the other hand that we are at the same time held in love which surrounds us. Our deepest feelings, of anxiety, hope and disgust are thereby purified. I doubt whether people gain these deep existential experiences from the experimental church services or the new forms of religious community. New rites are most likely to arise, as they have previously done in times of crisis, during a pastoral visit to a deathbed or at a celebration of communion at the end of an impressive consciousness-raising process at a conference or training session. Experience also teaches us that presently the old rituals fulfil their function better than the new ones. The "hallowed presence", which is concerned with refuge and salvation, is disclosed with difficulty through new rituals.

It is important to ask what role the pastor plays in the experience of rituals. Rituals are living elements in a community. They arise there, but they are also subject to changes or meet with resistance to attempts to change them. Yet every community has its authority figures which can help to encourage or discourage change. If the priest gives an example or approves changes in the celebration of the Eucharist, (for example in the way the Host is being received), it is easier for the congregation to accept the changes. To the congregation the priest represents the church, which lives in these rituals, and sets the example to show that a change in the external form of the inner meaning does not represent damage.

When experiments with new rituals are being carried out, a similar process can play a role. This is not, however, essential because usually the group itself has accepted some responsibility for the experiment and so the priest just underlines the significance. In such circumstances there will sometimes be occasions when the group dares to make a renewal against the advice of the priest.

An interesting and for some people difficult problem, is that of the female priest. For the Roman Catholic curia in Rome, it is unthinkable that a woman should be a priest. The argument used is that Jesus only had men as disciples, which is understandable given the historical circumstances in which He lived. But this argument avoids the question

54

of how far the cultural patterns of His time should influence us today. Jesus also healed a sick person with saliva and no theologian will recommend following this example. There are indeed many cultures where women wield priestly power, just as there are many Christian churches where women may become priests. Now that we recognise that there was a great deal of discrimination against women in Jesus's time, the pressure on church authorities is becoming so strong that women will increasingly be admitted to posts in the church. Another argument is that where women do hold such positions, they usually do their work very well indeed. It should make no difference whether women or men are involved with rituals.

Finally I want briefly to consider the role the priest generally plays when rituals are solemnised, especially in the liturgy. In other words, what is the nature of the mediation which the priest provides in the liturgy? There are many rituals where a priest plays no part at all. Erikson shows that our whole life is ritualised: there are burials, marriages and many different gatherings. It is not without reason that psychologists say that a human being is a collection of habits. One can also regard society as a group of people united in rituals and customs.

In the church liturgy however the priest plays an essential role. Which role? I think we come close to the truth if we say, in Erikson's words, that in ritual the priest discloses a perspective on the "hallowed presence" with which the assembled community feels itself linked in belief - the hallowed presence being the mystery which, as a spiritual reality establishes a link between people in a group, and between people and God. On the one hand the priest represents the community and on the other hand the mystery, God; in this double function the priest can so to say form a bridge and thus disclose that other reality into our human reality.

There still remains another problem which seems to me to be of central importance for the future of the church community and its rituals. This problem is: is there always a real disclosure of the "hallowed presence" and therefore a real experience of the mystery? Heidegger (1927) has told us of his view of 'das Mann' who drags along human beings in his wake and prevents access to the self. We live, says Heidegger, in a world which flees from reality into a remarkable kind of superficiality. We say the words and we attend the rituals but they no longer have any meaning for us. On the contrary: they hide reality. Church and world know the longing for, and also the anxiety about the life of the self, real communication, and about opening oneself to the mystery. Life will return to the liturgy and its rituals when we can help ourselves and each other to find the way to true communication. We shall need to look together at our anxiety and to open ourselves to the spirit: in the bible this is called Love.

RITUAL STUDIES IN THE HISTORY OF RELIGIONS
A challenge for the psychology of religion

Owe Wikström

1. Introduction

The question of the morphology and ontological status of the religious experience was, in spite of its complexity, for a long time understood in terms of a "religious predisposition". Terms as *tabu* and *mana* were understood as having explanatory value. R. Otto for example described religiosity as a kind of inherited feeling or sensorium in relation to the "Holy". He claimed that a common trait in the experiences of the religions was a particular "numinous" quality. It was generated through the meeting with a frightening and appealing reality, "tremendous and numinous" (Otto, 1917). Others, like F. Schleiermacher, thought that a feeling of absolute dependence was the main ground of the religious experience.

M. Eliade (1988) assumes that there is a unique content in the religious experience which is transculturally similar and valid. But it is not possible to reduce, translate or describe the experience in terms of social, cultural or psychological processes without atomizing and destroying it. On the contrary, there is a *sui generis* quality in the religious faith. Through the centuries and in different religions he observes what he calls the "homo religiosus". This "religious constant" seems to survive throughout generations.

Phenomenologists of religion observe and describe these qualities but don't discuss their psychological and sociological conditions nor their ontological status. In spite of their effort to be close to the phenomena and only report observations, these "sui generis theorists" nevertheless give causal explanations.

But these types of "explanations" of the religiosity of man are problematic. The concepts one uses to explain things are so to say built-in in the data one wants to explain. Explan*ans* contains explan*andum*. The theoretical effort and explanatory value is weak. The question "why is man religious?" is answered by saying that man is religious because man is religious, which is a vicious circle. To a behavioral or social scientist this is of course not sufficient. One does not leave the phenomenological phase and go further on to causal explanations, but one ends up on a descriptive level of the research process. This may be the aim of a historian or a scientist of comparative religion. However, social and behavioral scientists dealing with religion are concerned about the conditions, i.e. the social and psychological processes which determine the religious experience and are maintained by means of rituals. For a psychologist these forces are understood in terms of the motives and needs of ordinary man, i.e. in terms of psychology.

The problems of the sui generis quality are solved in very different ways, depending upon whether the researcher assumes a transcendent God or suprahuman subject that is intervening in reality or - on the other hand - if he sees man's experiences or religious feelings as consequences of social or psychological forces which are working "through", "with", "in", or in the course of the empirical reality. The most common answer seems to be that these questions cannot be answered from a scientific perspective. I agree with this view. My point here is, however, to stress the psychologist's need to be conscious of his implicit assumptions about the ontological status of the concepts and images in a religion. This meta-theoretical elaboration is especially important in a field where the informants in their own selfunderstanding have a selfevident relation to the truth claims of their religion.

The object "God" as experienced by a subject is of course not accessible to a scientific investigation. But on the other hand, the social and psychological genesis, function and maintenance of religious experiences can be described and analyzed. Cultural artefacts, holy texts, buildings, myths, traditions, songs and particularly rituals, are accessible to the researcher. Rituals are particularly important as a generating, cultivating and facilitating factor for the religious experience. In rituals the religious faith is passed on in a total manner; as a Gestalt. Ritual can be described as a fusion of social, emotional and esthetical experiences in a communicative field. But, is it necessary to assume that this fusion implies a *sui generis* quality of the experience that is provided?

The researcher can - of course - from separate theological or philosophical preferences - postulate or argue that there is a real divine power "behind" the tendency to exceed the borderline of the ritual process. This, however is not an empirical question accessible to scientific investigation.

How a researcher interprets the ontological genesis and the value of ritual experience depends in its turn upon the fundamental apprehensions of reality, which the scientist sees as true or important. Scholars interpret the religious man's experiences in materialistic, Jungian, Christian, agnostic, ambivalent, marxist or atheistic frameworks. The psychologist uses, among others, a psychoanalytic theory, an attribution theory or social psychology. How does his use of psychological theories affect his answer to the question of the sui generis problem? With this question we approach another problem concerning scientific psychological studies of religion in general: the question of reductionism.

2. Reductionism and perspectivism

Any attempt to explain religious rituals in terms of just *one* fundamental psychological or sociological cause or factor often demonstrates a deadlock. Some assert that *all* ritual behavior is a result of ordinary socialization, others claim that it is an archetypical need generated by the collective unconscious; others again assert that all religiosity basically develops as a result of hidden emotional needs stemming from early age.

All these propositions concerning religious ritual as *nothing-but* must be dismissed. Instead there is a built-in prerequisite in all scientific activities researchers choose: a perspective through which to perceive the world. Psychology provides a number of methodological tools and theoretical glasses by which religious experience and behaviour is made visible (Barbour, 1984). But of course, the framework is not the religious reality itself.

Let us illustrate this with two perspectives. Religious persons use a mythical linguistic code in order to understand their internal or external world. The verbally transmitted religious systems of myths are legitimized and strengthened by dramatized rituals. Rituals are then understood in terms of a cognitive or *attribution* theory (Spilka, Hood & Gorsuch, 1985). But of course, this is not a sufficient explanation. It must at least be completed by a theory that takes the individual's emotions into consideration.

Some psychoanalysts claim that religious ritual makes it possible for an individual to feel comforted in a mythological world where God is described as a cosmic parent. God or Allah or a Boddhisattva provide-psychologically speaking - a compensation for deprived and supressed naive feelings. The ritually legitimized regression during a service or mass, reactivates the participator's hidden memories of his father or mother, it gives the individual access to primary processes. These are *psychoanalytic* perspectives (see Heimbrock, *Ritual and transformation: a psychoanalytic perspective*, in this volume).

Theoretically, religious ritual behavior and experiences are supported by *both* emotional and cognitive processes. But evidently these are just *two* out of an endless amount of perspectives. A lot of variables are left aside a priori through the perspective used by the researcher. Let us therefore link the question of perspectivism with the problem of reductionism.

I would like to underline that it is important in all social sciences of religion to be aware of the necessity of methodological reduction while at the same time understanding that this scientifically motivated reduction cannot provide answers to ontological questions. To be more precise: a methodological reduction means that the researcher reduces the phenomenon (in this case the ritual experience) - for a specific purpose - in terms provided by the theory. However, as soon as the researcher claims that his perspective is the One and Only, then his methodological reduction has lapsed into an ontological reductionism. It has become a "Wissenschaftsaberglaube".

All scientific perspectives are fundamentally provisory. The claim that it is possible to describe ritual in just one or a combination of theories must be false because man is too complex and above all, different religious rituals have too many different dimensions. Instead I think it is necessary to speak about different perspectives which
are complementary to each other, and from which psychological connections can be deduced which do justice to the individual's ritual experiences.

3. The ritual generates a "symbiosis" of individual, symbol and group

As I see it, the psychological studies of ritual fall into two main areas. The first has to do with careful investigation of the social, cultural and linguistic context of ritual. The second seeks to understand the participator's emotional way of understanding himself in terms of a socially transmitted symbolic universe. These two fields - social psychology and psychoanalytic theory - must be kept together as a dynamic whole.

To study a ritual solely as a historical, social or cultural phenomenon makes it difficult to understand which role the individual's experience plays in the maintenance of the ritual. On the other hand, to only study the individual's "internal experiences" in psychodynamic terms and disregard the cognitive content of the religious traditions would imply that the researcher is not faithful to the object under study: the ritual.

I propose that it is the *interaction* between a socially transmitted and given worldview and the individual's emotional needs, deprivation or outlet that must be at the center of study.

3.1 The individual's perspective

The images and symbols legitimized and mediated through religious rituals are linked to the participators very early preverbal memories. The ritual process intrinsically leads to a "symbiosis" between existential individuation/separation experiences and the religious systems of language and symbolic expression. To combine psychoanalytic theory with the attributional possibilities provided by the mythical images-especially the personalized God image - leads us to a functional perspective (Wikström, 1987).

The individual's representation of God, which is activated and cultivated during the ritual process is psychoanalytically spoken a creation which consequently has at least four distinctive features; it contains memory images of the individual's real parents, it is filled with other qualities like security, firmness and tenderness, it is filled with those omnipotent fantasies which brood in the individual's unconscious and it is, above all, influenced by the conceptions and images that are promoted by religious traditions and submitted through primary and secondary socialization (Rizzuto, 1979; Meissner, 1984, 1987).

Now, to complete my perspective, the cognitive role of religious traditions and their myths and conceptions often isn't taken seriously by psychoanalytic theorists. The religious myth with its narratives and images of deities must be understood not only as a container of regressive projections, but also as a creative and important promotor of religious experience in rituals. The socially provided myth must be understood as a generating factor in of its own. Therefore, social psychology or psychology of culture must be seen as a determining complement to the one-sided emotional accentuation of the individual's perspective.

3.2 The cultural perspective

By understanding ritual in its cultural setting, one immediately questions the reasonableness of interpreting the individual's ritual experiences independent of the symbolic environment. Social psychology stresses among other things the importance of language systems. (Sidenap, 1989; see also Geerts, *An inquiry into the meanings of ritual symbolism: Turner and Peirce*, in this volume). To be socialized into a religious tradition means that the culture provides a verbal network which not only helps to interpret or attribute experiences in a meaningful way but it also is a prerequisite for a perceptual awareness. On the whole, research in the psychology of religion can to a great extent adapt to Geertz's classical volume *The Interpretation of Cultures* (1973b).

With regard to Christianity, it is of course the Bible and its interpretations of reality which is in focus for a cultural understanding of Christian ritual. Accordingly, the individual does not create its own meaning giving patterns, but adopts them from Significant Others.

Religious rituals offer possibilities for a person not only to think about God, but also to experience oneself in a real meeting with a partner. According to Sundén (1966b), the religious roles are not only fixed in religious traditions and texts, they are even dramatized in liturgy and rituals and therefore make it possible for the participator to have a real "meeting with a partner". Within culturally given frameworks and institutions, these socio-psychological requisites for the religious dialogue are being cultivated. The individual, joined with others during the ritual, orients himself/herself towards a symbol of the invisible reality: an altar. In the liturgical calender a person annually repeats the opportunity for identification through the sacralization of time.

Through the ritual role-playing there also arises a kind of changing of time in the sense that the profane time temporarily seems broken and is replaced by a realization of the mythical or the original time. In the Christian liturgy one realizes these time-changing moments by the words which accompany the sacramental eating of the bread: " ...in the same night in which He was betrayed, He took the bread, thanked God, broke it and gave it to His disciples and said... ". To observe this behavior, to go to the altar, to kneel, to eat the bread, facilitates the individual's dedication to the described partner role in the tradition. Music, olfactory and esthetical noncognitive languages in combination with symbols, images and religious texts act as intermediaries for conditions which make it possible for the religious person to be identified regularly, year in and year out, not only with the many-faceted world, but also with the invisible, yet present (Sundén, 1966b).

There is a link, however, between Sundén's view regarding the function of the mythical role as it is described in religious traditions and Geertz's views. Common to the social perspective is the view that language not only represents reality, but actually creates the reality about which it speaks. Geertz maintains that religious myths and traditions constitute a cluster of different symbols. These theologies function in their turn as a kind of verbal net which captivates particular elements in reality:

> "Sacred symbols function to synthesize a peoples ethos - the tone, character, and quality of their life, its moral and aesthetical style and mood - and their world view - the picture they have of the ways things in sheer actuality are, their most comprehensive ideas of order" (1973b:89).

Religion according to Geertz is

> "1) a system of symbols which acts to 2) establish powerful, persuasive and longlasting moods and motivations in men by 3) formulating

conceptions of a general order of existence and 4) clothing the conceptions with such and aura of factuality that 5) the moods and motivations seem uniquely realistic" (1973b:90).

The religious symbols by which a group or a subgroup interprets its experiences, provide models for understanding the world as a totality:

"The importance of religion lies in its capacity to serve, for an individual or for a group, as a source of general, yet distinctive, conceptions of the world, the self, and the relations between them, on the one hand - its model of aspect - and of rooted, no less distinctive "mental" dispositions - its model for aspect - on the other. From these cultural functions flow, in turn, its social and psychological ones" (1973b:123).

Consequently, religious language is not merely passively "existential-interpretative". The models which are described within the myths also give feed back to those who live by them. They provide to the religious person a special way of perceiving himself. Simultaneously, as the ritual participant understands himself to be in relation to the deity he himself becomes an object for the deity's power. Myths and roles in the religious traditions consequently also contain components for self-understanding. Religious experiences

"...do not merely interpret social and psychological processes in cosmic terms - in which case they would be philosophical, not religious - but they shape them" (1973b:124).

A religious symbol (the Cross, the Bread, the Light) which is spoken of or functions within the ritual, summarizes in itself an existential quality. It creates a feeling of facticiousness about itself. There occurs a reification. Questions of meaning and purpose of life can be "contained" within the symbol. Therefore whole meaning-systems

"are stored in symbols: a cross, a crescent, or a feathered serpent. Such religious symbols, dramatized in rituals or related in myths, are felt somehow to sum up, for those for whom they are resonant, what is known about the way the world is, the quality of emotional life it supports, and the way one ought to behave while in it. Sacred symbols thus relate an ontology and a cosmology to an aesthetic and a morality: their peculiar power comes from their presumed ability to identify fact with value at the most fundamental level, to give to what otherwise merely is actual, a comprehensive normative import" (1973b:127).

4. Ritual, symbols and the sui generis character of religion

Let us summarize and link our arguments back to the question of the sui generis character.

The individual's perspective of the ritual process points to the emotional genesis of the belief in a personal God. From this extreme individual oriented perspective it is maintained that people become religious because:

* they have a memory from an early symbiosis with the mother and this memory lingers as a spiritual void
* the religious myths, symbols and images are connected to and express, interpret and assimilate primary needs
* religious imagination and expression turns out to exist in a kind of transitional space as neither objective nor wholly subjective (Pruyser, 1982; Müller-Pozzi, 1975; see also Heimbrock in this volume).

However, this explanation as to why a person is religious is narrow and one-sided, since it aims only at emotional processes. It must be supplemented. Therefore, from a cultural or social perspective man is religious because:

* he assimilates himself in a special reality-map
* among other frames of interpretation, the religious ones are in focus
* the religious tradition in a culture is the basis for the experience of a cosmic Thou.

One observation however, which links both perspectives, is the relation between persons, emotional experiences and the religious languages. In other words we could maintain that the interaction between emotions and cognitions during the ritual experience moulds into a unique original character. But to make this claim, is something else than to say that this observation implies a sui generis quality that can't possibly be reduced and stems from "another world" or which is not reducable to general psychological categories.

The "religiousness in religion" has probably something to do with the functional character of the religious language. The ritual creates a fusion between existential threats, emotional reminiscences or longings and the religious language and expression.

One way to come further in the elaborating of this theory is to extend our points with a few words on the role of symbols in general. Images and symbols are both products of and at the same time constitute stimuli. They are - as one used to say during the medieval times - multivalent and evokative. There are experiences in connection with symbols which a more exact, logical analysis cannot reveal. A symbol conveys not only more than a thousand words, it conveys something different than a thousand words.

Tillich in his turn claims that religious language must by necessity become symbolic rather than scientific. Religious truths can only come into conflict with science if both misunderstand themselves and try to replace each other (Barbour, 1984). But why should truth or belief be expressed symbolically instead of being expressed directly? Tillich argues that it lies in the nature of things that the truth or a belief must be expressed symbolically since the transcendent, absolute or infinite, which is not a thing among other things, cannot be formulated in concepts. Both art and religion are therefore compelled to work with images and symbols. Contrary to the sign, the symbol itself has a share in that to which it points. It points to a level of reality which otherwise is inaccessible, it opens up dimensions within man's own psyche that correspond to these levels and are inaccessible to conceptual knowledge.

Eliade (1988) has studied the role of symbols in the rituals from the perspective of the history of religion. His main thesis is that in archaic societies, religious symbols defined the "true reality" and that which is fundamentally durable in life. When these cultures talked about hierophanies, that is to say, when the Holy was manifested in this world, it occurred at the same time as the ontophanies. Reality and the Holy were mixed in the revelation of origin. Eliade asserts that this means that religious rituals are built around an ontological essence.

It can be said, from a phenomenologist's point of view, that a religious symbol in a ritual constitutes a kind of "language" which mediates between this trivial world and a reality which can only be expressed in symbols. Eliade, like Tillich means that religious symbols perform two functions at the same time; in the first place they give a person access to this "true" world, through or via the observable world. Bread used for communion is commonly made from flour. Yet this bread points or refers to another world. Secondly, the symbols (in theological terms: the sacraments) touch man's ground of being. Thus the symbol is multivalent; it has many options. It is associated with many different "layers" in a person and at the same time it mediates something. A symbol

> "translates a human situation into cosmological terms, and reciprocally more precise, it discloses the interdependance between the structure of human existence and cosmic structure" (Eliade, 1988:29).

If we finally turn to our own field, the psychology of religion, Batson & Ventis have observed the fusional character of religious symbols. They describe man's use of symbols in relation to what they call the "facilitating factor". Rituals are among such processes:

"...(symbols)... in kernelized form are an expression of both the existential question that provoked the creative religious experience and the new vision that allows the subject of experience to see this question in a new way. Because they kernelize a way of making sense of seemingly conflicting concerns we shall call such symbols synthetic. All major world religions seem to have developed one or more supreme synthetic symbols. These kernelize a new vision that deals with a range of existential questions simultaneously ... We suspect that these supreme synthetic symbols have assumed a role of centrality in their respective traditions because they contain, in a capsule, the basic existential questions and new visions" (Batson & Ventis, 1982:128).

Thus, according to Batson & Ventis, the symbols in rituals evidently have a double role; they "descend into the depths of existential crisis and they subsequently ascend to a new perspective on the crisis-provoking question" (ibidem:129). Or in our terms they are a fusion or symbiosis of emotional conflicts and interpreting symbols.

5. Conclusions

Religious rituals create a very specific experience. There are at least two main scientific perspectives that can shed light upon the psychological processes. These perspectives are joined together in the way they describe religious experiences, as a fusion or symbiosis of two dimensions. On the one hand the individual's emotional experiences (of separation, longing for unity, the need for meaning, or standing in the presence of the totality, etc.) and on the other hand the religious traditions and their symbols and mythological roles that are cultivated and provided by cultural artefacts and dramatized during the ritual.

Therefore the sui generis character of religious rituals must be taken seriously; a formation of interaction or reciprocal interplay between the individual's experiences and the language of the myths.

Let me conclude. In order to describe the psychological conditions during rituals one must pay attention to at least two dimensions: the participator's internal *emotional* dynamics and the participator's interaction with the surrounding religious *culture*. To simply describe the religious person from internal emotional points of view draws our attention away from the fact that the religious person is placed in a cognitive context. On the other hand, to explain only in terms of socially given structures or symbolic universes impedes us to see how emotional drives and forces interact with those religious interpretative schemes that are provided by society.

Therefore the cooperation of dynamic psychology, social psychology and cognitive theory may offer the most productive perspective for interpretation and description of the multidimensional religious ritual.

This does not, however, solve the problem of the sui generis character of the experience, but it does make one point clear: the effort to understand the religious experience - whether in ritual or otherwise - in terms of just one or a combination of two or more theories must be seen as a necessary methodological or theoretical reduction. But even if this reduction points to an original or interesting fusion of different psychological processes as a kind of "sui generis quality", it does not answer the question of the ontological status of this very quality.

EMPIRICAL STUDIES:
A SELECTION OF CHRISTIAN RITUALS

PRAYING AS AN INDIVIDUALIZED RITUAL

Jacques Janssen, Joep de Hart and Christine den Draak

1. Introduction

Recent research shows a steadily declining participation of youth in institutionalized religious rituals. Furthermore a decreasing amount of young people agree with the different religious prescriptions, commands and attitudes (for an indication of this process in different countries consult: Fuchs, 1985; Helve, 1989; Hutsebaut & Verhoeven, 1989; Evenshaugh & Hallen, 1989; De Hart, 1989a and 1989b). In the Netherlands one can even observe a conspicuous decline in church-affiliation, especially among young people. While in 1960, 20% of the population had no religious affiliation, this percentage is now estimated at about 50; for youth this percentage is 60 (Doorn & Bommeljé, 1983, 1987). The prognosis seems crystal clear: in the future religiously affiliated people will be a minority in the Netherlands. Finally the enlightened philosophers who predicted the end of religion in western society, get substantial empirical support. Contemporary social scientists, when discussing religion, even use the term 'explosion' (Felling, Peters & Schreuder, 1982). The Christian house still exists, but is severely damaged and surrounded by ruins.

Among contemporary youth the future is already visible: all the studies mentioned above indicate that secularization among adolescents is at its highest level. At the same time there is an indication that praying-practices are considered to be of substantial value, also for young people. The Gallup-report (*Religion in America*, 1985) shows that about 90% of the American people 'sometimes' pray and that this percentage hardly changed since 1948. Meadow & Kahoe (1984) state that "various surveys have shown that as many as 87% of youth pray". Greeley (1979) refers to a NORC-study which reveals that 54% of the Americans pray daily; for youth (20-29 years) the percentage is considerably lower (37%). Fuchs (1985) reports that 36% of German youth prays regularly; for the parent-generation this percentage is 43. In a national Dutch survey (*God in Nederland*, 1967), 69% considered it useful to pray. In 1979 (Goddijn et al., 1979) this percentage has dropped to 53 and for young people (17-24 years) it was even lower (42%). In a study of 5000 Dutch high school pupils (mean age 16.8 years), De Hart (1989b) found that 29% prays regularly. At the same time he observed that these pupils more often pray alone in private than with others in their parental homes.

It is hard to reach a definitive conclusion. The figures we mentioned cannot be compared in a direct way. Praying-activities seem to be declining, but at the same time a substantial percentage of young people keeps praying, even if they do not go to church, or do not consider themselves to be church-members. The impression is that in a secularizing society praying-practices have more importance for young people than one should expect (see also: Nieuwenhuis, 1978a and 1978b). In our research, which combined qualitative and quantitative research-techniques, we have tried to clarify this general impression.

2. Theoretical background and hypotheses
Some interesting (empirical) studies about prayer have been undertaken, but their number is low indeed and there is a lot of confusing argument (cf. Finney & Malony (1985) for a recent review). Moreover, hardly any research has been done on praying practices as such. Greeley (1979), after stating that prayer is widespread and associated with psychological well-being, added: "we do not know how Americans pray, why they pray, when they pray, to whom they pray; and we cannot even explain why prayer seems to make them happier!". Analysing the answers of Dutch youth to similar (open-ended) questions, we have tried to give a preliminary answer.

There is no clear-cut theory of prayer; there is not even agreement about definitions and basic concepts. Gill (1987:493) concluded that there is no precise definition; the word just serves as "a general focusing device". Definitions and theories of prayer will be mentioned, but our research did not start from a preliminary concept. We simply asked our subjects to describe how *they* would define prayer. Consequently the main data are spontaneous, written, self-formulated answers to questions about definitions, motivations and ways of prayer.

In putting these questions to our subjects, we focused on the core topics which can be found in the literature about praying: 1. why do people pray? 2. how do they pray?, (focusing on praying as such), 3. to whom do they pray?, 4. what effects do they obtain?

1. Finney & Malony (1985), when reviewing several pieces of research, stressed the importance of a motivation or *need* as the impetus to prayer. Already in the classical studies of Tylor (1958 (1871)) and James (1982 (1902)) needs were a central topic. Also in the classical work on prayer by Friedrich Heiler (1921) needs to receive special attention. It appears to be essential that something is being asked for, when people pray. Capps (1982) called petitionary prayer "the heart of prayer".
2. Gill (1987:490) interpreted prayer primarily as an "act of communication" and "an act of speech". Sabatier's concise statement that "prayer is religion in act", is well known. Heiler (1921:3) mentioned this phrase as coined by Thomas Aquinas: "oratio est proprie religionis

actus". In most research this view is supported, explicitly or implicitly. Since prayer is essentially an *act*, we prefer the verbal form 'praying'.

3. The direction of prayer is mentioned by Tylor (1958 (1871)): there has to be a 'Thou', as he called it. However, Gill (1987:491) and Heiler (1961:306) included non-theistic, meditational forms of prayer.

4. The effects of prayer are a major point of discussion. Pratt (1910/11) provided a list of subjective benefits of prayer by quoting the subjects whom he interviewed:

> "calming influence upon the nerves; spiritual uplift; self-confidence; the substitution of love for hate and courage for fear; an increasing of strength, both physical and moral; help in resisting temptation and in thinking clearly; joy, relief from care and the sense that all's well."

Johnson (1945) proposed a similar list of effects of and motivations for prayer, including

> "awareness of needs, emotional catharsis, peace of mind, broader perspectives on problems, decisions, emotional renewal, social responsiveness, joy, gratitude, acceptance of one's losses, loyalty, perseverance, and integration of the personality."

Finney & Malony (1985:107), quoting Johnson's list of subjective effects, added that "Johnson's speculations have not yet been empirically investigated".

The four core topics that are discussed in literature, can be summarized in one sentence: "because of some reason (need) people address themselves (action) to someone (direction) to achieve something (result/effect)". Leach (1968) speaks of the grammar of ritual, thereby understanding ritual as a cognitive category. We studied the grammar of prayer, similarly understanding prayer as a cognitive category. We consider this to be the *structural* aspect of prayer.

Subsequently we analysed the *content* of prayer. The content of prayer consists of the different kinds of needs, methods, directions and effects. We also examined whether there is a difference between our subjects in the *completeness* of the praying-structure and the content of prayer, according to denomination and praying-experience. A major issue refers to the *relation between needs and effects*. If prayer is mostly petitionary prayer and instigated by a need, it seems quite logical that needs and effects are homologous. Nevertheless, James Pratt (1910/11) argued that such a homology is not necessary and not even likely. Finally, can one maintain that prayer is always based on a *communication* to a (personal) God? Capps (1982), amongst others, argued that this is indeed the case. Gill (1987:491) and Heiler (1961:306) include non-communication forms of prayer. We will introduce a constructivist perspective of praying, that accounts for both ways of praying.

3. Sample and method

In 1983 a national survey was held among 5.000 Dutch highschool pupils (mean age 16.8 years), who were asked 'closed' questions about political and religious matters (De Hart, 1989b). In 1985 a group of 192 of these pupils were asked to give answers to an extensive questionnaire, which partly consisted of open-ended questions. This sample was stratified according to religious affiliation to ensure that each major denomination would be substantially represented. The sample consists of 61 Not Religiously Affiliated, 60 Catholic and 71 Protestant pupils (34 Dutch Reformed and 37 Calvinist). Three of the open-ended questions concerned praying: 1. "what does praying mean to you?", 2. "at what moments did you feel the need to pray?", 3. "how do you pray?". Our results are based on a content-analysis of the answers to these three open-ended questions and two 'closed' questions (on religious affiliation and praying-frequency).

A computerized system (called TexTable) was used to transform the open-ended answers into analysable units (Janssen, Bego, Van den Berg, 1987). The TexTable-procedure involves three steps. Step 1 results in the construction of two kinds of data-sets. The first one is the usual set of information obtained from the closed questions (consisting of numbers); it will be referred to as the closed data-set. We used SPSS-x to analyse the data-set. The second data-set (open data-set) is made up of the literal answers to open-ended questions (consisting of text). We used TexTable as the analytical device. Both sets were connected by a common subject-number for each subject. We began the analysis by converting text into numbers (step 2). The program offers several possibilities. Here we applied a semi-automatical way of coding. For each question the program offers a listing of all the words that are used by the subjects (at the top of the list the words most often used, etc). After eliminating words of no significance (e.g. articles) we had a picture of the main ideas the subjects used. We gained an impression of the way categories should be constructed and synonyms should be taken as one. Obviously, any computer-decision has to be controlled. It is one of the advantages of the TexTable-procedure that all decisions can be continuously controlled and changed if necessary. The category-system one finally decides to use, consisting of several strings of synonyms, can be filed and used again in continued research. The coding then proceeds automatically, although it has to be controlled because changes in time, place and subjects can result in new category-systems.

After this procedure the numbers for each category were transmitted to the closed data-set. However, at each moment in the analysis it remains possible to return to the original answers (step 3). So TexTable offers the possibility for an interaction between open and closed information-processing.

4. Results

The analysis we made of the three open-ended questions mentioned above, could be summarized in a rather simple structure. Most of the elements of this structure were discussed in the literature we referred to. Our subjects describe praying as an *action* (predicate), emanating from a motivation or *need* (conditional clause), directed to *someone or something* (indirect object), having some *effect* (direct object). They also specify this activity to *time, place and method* (adverbial phrases). (See Figure 1).

Figure 1

The Focusing Device of Praying

1. Need ------------->   2. Action ----------->   7. Effect
   (conditional clause)   (predicate)   (direct object)

---

3. Direction   (indirect object)
4. Time   (adverbial phrase 1)
5. Place   (adverbial phrase 2)
6. Method   (adverbial phrase 3)

Each subject was given a score on each structural aspect. The mean score totalled 3.5 (the scale ranges from 0= no elements mentioned, to 7= all elements mentioned). For non-prayers the mean score was 2.1, for prayers 3.7 (no affiliation: 3.3, Roman Catholic: 3.6, Dutch Reformed: 3.6, Calvinist: 4.4.). We further established a correlation of .45 (Pearson-r, $p < .001$) between the number of structural elements mentioned and praying-frequency (the scores range from 1= never, to 5= daily).

An interpretation of the denominational differences will be given below. Here it is important to observe that competence and experience indeed have an influence upon the self-formulated answers. If people pray and if they pray more regularly, their description of prayer is more complete and more extensive.

The TexTable-program offers the possibility of leaving the numbers and of returning to the original answers (step 3). In this way we could detect the people who pray most completely (subjects whose answers include all structural aspects). Six subjects offer a complete praying-structure. In a literal and unshortened quotation of one of them, all the structural aspects (indicated in parentheses) can be recognized which were distinguished in the focusing device: "Talk (2) to God (3) and ask (2) Him (3) for help (7) and blessing (7); when I feel unhappy in a love-affair (1), had trouble at home or at school (1); at night (4) in bed (5), quietly, hands joined and eyes closed (6)".

So far the formal structure has been discussed. But what do people really do? What is the content of the formal structure? We distinguished 45 categories. As mentioned before, each category is the label for a string of elements (e.g. synonyms) that are summarized together. Table 1 gives the final results.

Let us summarize the main results:
(1) *Needs*. Praying was generally motivated by problems: personal problems, sickness, death (of others, mostly relatives), war/disaster, examinations, problems of others, and sin, totalling 81% of all the needs that are mentioned (124/154 = 81%). Only 13% of the needs (20/154) were related to happiness; other needs (10/154) totalled 6%.
(2) *Actions*. Only 33% of the actions consisted of asking or wishing something. Given the vast number of problems people pray for, one should expect a larger number of petitional actions. Our data indicate that there is no direct relation between needs and actions. A classical issue, as Gill (1987:492) puts it, is whether "prayer is a monologue, dialogue or neither". The scholars do not agree, neither did our subjects: the latter mostly defined prayer as being a monologue (especially if we include meditation as being a monologue), but almost as many talk of prayer as a dialogue. Thanksgiving and praise, well-known traditional types of prayer, were only mentioned by 14%.
(3) *Direction*. The direction of prayer is a related, regular topic in the literature about prayer. Our research showed that most prayers are directed to a being, mostly called God (60%). However, further analysis made it clear that God is regularly not described as a personal being. Most subjects use abstract words (e.g. 'love', peace', 'hope') or describe

Table 1

Percentage of Content-References to Each Structural Category

1.Need	personal problems (60)	sickness (23)	happiness (20)
(85%)	death (16)	examinations (10)	war/disaster (6)
	problems of others (6)	change (6)	habit (4)
	sin (3)		
2.Action	tell/monologue (38)	talk/dialogue(36)	ask/wish (33)
(83%)	meditate (22)	thank/praise (14)	
3.			
Direction	God/Lord (80)	Spirit/Power (13)	
(60%)	Someone (11)	Mary/Jesus (2)	
4.Time	evening/night (90)	at day (8)	
(20%)	dinner (8)	anytime (5)	
5.Place	bed (86)	home (11)	
(34%)	church (11)	outside (9)	
6.Method	Posture:hands joined(36)	eyes closed (26)	kneeled down (4)
(55%)	alone (39)	prayer-formula (17)	
	low voice (19)	aloud (4)	
7.Effect	help/support (38)	favour (34)	remission (13)
(37%)	rest (10)	trust (9)	blessing (4)
	comfort (7)	protection (6)	strength/power(6)
	reflection (6)	understanding (1)	advice (1)

Note. The percentages of the structural aspects are calculated in reference to the whole group (n = 192). The percentages for the content-categories are calculated in reference to the number of subjects that mentioned the structural aspect (n = 85% of 192, 83% of 192, 60% of 192, etc.). Because each subject could mention several aspects, the total number may exceed 100% (e.g. needs: 154%).

the activities of God ('helping', 'inspiring', 'forgiving').

(4) *Times* and (5) *Places*. If our subjects mentioned time and place, they were almost unanimous: young people pray at night, in bed (86%). Surprisingly few (11%) mentioned the church. These results are similar to those of Nieuwenhuis (1978a and 1978b) who interviewed young people a few years ago. He also mentioned that young people often pray in bed. In our conclusion we will argue that the importance of this finding should not be overlooked as being merely interesting or curious.

(6) *Methods*. The methods of praying included some traditional procedures (hands joined, eyes closed, using prayer-formulas). Others preferred to pray in silence and alone.

(7) *Effects*. The results show that 'help/support' and 'favour' were considered to be the most important effects. Most striking, as we see it, was the rather abstract, psychological terminology people use to describe the effects, especially in relation to the more concrete definition of needs. Above we observed a rather weak connection between needs and actions; now we can add the weak relation between needs and effects.

We have shown that there are differences in the completeness of the open-ended answers related to experience and competence. It is to be expected that there will also be differences between the denominations. Table 2 contains all significant content differences.

Table 2

Significant content-differences (Chi-square, p < .05) in
praying-practice for religious affiliation in percentages
for each structural category (n = 192)

Content Elements		Non-Prayers	Prayers 1.*	2.*	3.*	4.*
		(n = 27)	(n = 34)	(n = 60)	(n = 34)	(n = 37)
1.Need	happiness	0	7	18	21	32
2.Action	dialogue	27	17	33	38	59
	meditate	9	25	33	9	9
3.Direction	God	89	62	80	88	82
6.Method	hands joined	0	33	22	61	42
	eyes closed	0	17	17	50	29
	prayerformula	0	21	32	6	4
	aloud	0	0	3	0	12
7.Effect	help/support	75	33	24	60	56
	favour	25	20	47	30	11
	remission	25	20	12	20	0

* 1.No affiliation 2.Roman Catholic 3.Dutch Reformed 4.Calvinist

These results are not easy to interpret. It seems that non-prayers tend
to define praying in a rather traditional way: they often mention the
categories 'dialogue', 'God' and 'help/support'. Closer analysis reveals
that they refer to the prayer of others or to practices in former days
at home. For the rest their answers are rather incomplete, as we have
already shown. The differences between the praying-groups can partly
be understood as influenced by the traditions of the denominations and
their specific cultures. Former research in the Netherlands made it
clear that traditional opinions about religion follow the line: no
affiliation -> Roman Catholic -> Dutch Reformed -> Calvinist (for a
recent example see: Schreuder & Peters, 1987). The content-elements
'happiness' and 'dialogue' run parallel to this line and can be

interpreted as typical for traditional religious behavior. The completeness of structural elements and praying-frequency also follow this line, which indicates that traditionally oriented people have more praying-experience and are better informed about the subject. In one case the main difference is between the three religious groups and those not affiliated: the latter mentioning God to a lesser extent. Roman Catholics attract attention because they often mention 'meditation' and 'prayer-formulas'. Protestants prefer to pray with 'hands joined' and 'eyes closed', to ask for 'help' and 'support', but hesitate to mention effects (as shown in Table 2). The Calvinists pray aloud more often and do not pray for 'remission'. Without speculating too much, some of the traditonal (spiritually and theologically inspired) differences between Roman Catholic and Protestant practices can be related to these results: Roman Catholics more often use prayer-formulas, Protestants more often pray aloud, eyes closed, hands joined, and direct themselves personally (not by formula) to God. It could further be argued that their theological convictions (e.g. belief in predestination) prevent Protestants from being too specific about effects of prayer in general.

Finally we return to the original texts. By specifying the characteristics for each group, mentioned in Table 2, we can find the typical praying-practice for each group as represented in the original answers. For instance, we had the computer search for the texts of Roman Catholics, who meditate, refer to God, use prayer-formulas and ask for a favour. After specifying similar 'if-statements', we found the literal answers optimally fitting the characteristics of each group. Table 3 gives the results.

We have now completed the cycle of the TexTable-procedure: after having analysed the coded texts, we returned to the original answers. The texts we presented were the result of a methodological procedure. They were not chosen because they fit our preconceived ideas, but because they illustrate a carefully prepared and statistically derived conclusion.

Table 3

TexTable for individuals who optimally fit the characteristics
mentioned in Table 2, containing literal answers to the open-ended
questions: 1. What is praying for you?
2. At what moments did you feel the need to pray?
3. How do you pray?

Non-Prayers
1. Talk to God in thoughts to get something or to give thanks.
2. (In former times) when I was scared, for example when my parents had a quarrel.
3. I don't pray anymore; in former times I told a complete story to ask for help.

Prayer: No Affiliation
1. A kind of meditation: to let the strength in head and hands go together: a real pleasure.
2. With fears of examinations, but especially with relational problems.
3. Press one hand in the other: raise the pressure in your head.

Prayer: Roman Catholic
1. Trying to arrange your thoughts, mostly to ask a favour for other people.
2. When my brother had to undergo an operation and was in the hospital for a long time.
3. Tell in thought why and for what you pray and thereafter an 'Our Father' and a 'Hail Mary'.

Prayer: Dutch Reformed
1. Asking for remission of sins and support for me and others.
2. When I have done something terrible or something happens.
3. Eyes closed, hands joined and thinking, and mumbling a prayer.

Prayer: Calvinist
1. To share your cares with God, eventually asking Him for help for yourself and for others.
2. When I felt guilty because I behaved badly after good intentions.
3. Alone, sitting, lying and talking, eyes closed and hands joined.

81

5. Conclusion and discussion

Empirical research on prayer is primarily focused on the study of effects. Since theories about prayer pay special attention to the 'petitionary prayer', their main focus is also on effects. Typological studies show that petitionary prayer is the most widespread and thought to be the oldest form of prayer (Gill, 1987:489). Tylor (1958 (1871)), anticipating modern developmental studies, introduced a stage-model of prayer and argued that in the earliest stage prayer is unethical: "the accomplishment of desire is asked for, but the desire is yet limited to personal advantage"; at later and higher moral levels "prayer becomes an instrument of morality" (1958:450). Nevertheless, Tylor's final conclusion is that there is "throughout the rituals of Christendom an endless array of supplications unaltered in principle from savage times - that the weather may be adjusted to our local needs, that we may have victory over all our enemies, that life and health and wealth and happiness may be ours" (1958:456).

Of course, an empirical study based on a specified sample of, on average, seventeen year old Dutch youth, has its limitations. The richness of possible praying-practices, as for instance described by Heiler (1921), cannot be expected. Nevertheless, our results do allow for some tentative conclusions. If we confront the above reflections with the data we presented, there seems - at first - to be a major fit. Our respondents also pray when they are in trouble, when their trouble is rather incurable, for the health of others, and some even pray when the weather is bad or their dog is ill. There is no need common and childish enough to be excluded. The endless array of supplications stands as before. So the observation made by Dorothee Sölle (1965), that "prayer in the case of ultimate need is vanishing in a secularizing society", is not corroborated and her perception "that this can be positive, because prayer does not belong to borderline situations but to the centre of life", seems premature. Our subjects pray almost exclusively because of need: it seems that nothing has changed since the days of Tylor.

However, there is an important difference between the classical petitionary prayer as described by Tylor and James, and the petitionary prayers our subjects utter. In short: Tylor and James talk of people praying for health and for fine weather; our subjects pray when they are ill and when the weather is bad. The effects they aim at are not directly derived from their needs, because - as we observed - these needs are caused by concrete moments and feelings of unhappiness, whilst the effects are formulated abstractly and in general terms (help/support, favour, rest, trust, remission, blessing etc.). For example, when being ill they don't pray for immediate cure; they pray for help, trust and blessing. So, praying seems primarily to be a way of coping with inevitable, incurable unhappiness. Pratt (1910/1911) concluded that there is "a simple human impulse to pray, to cry out for the help we need, for the good we want". According to Heiler (1961:307), the elementary form of prayer is a cry, as shown in old praying-formulas like Hallelujah and Kyrie eleison. So there is ample argument to stress the importance of petitionary prayer as an involuntary cry for help, not mitigated by the real availability of real help. It could be argued that people tune the intended effects to the experienced effects, accepting a basic discrepancy between needs and effects.

The main conclusion can be summarized by applying Geertz's definition of religion (1966) to a definition of prayer. Geertz interprets religion as a semiotic device: religion is the technique people use to bring together the picture they have of the world 'in sheer actuality' (the worldview) with the picture of the world as they think it should be (the ethos). In line with Geertz, prayer is the act of attuning worldview and ethos. This process can take two directions. Either assimilation: making things acceptable as they are, or accomodation: changing them according to our wishes. Because praying, according to the definition of our subjects, is very often stimulated by incurable and insoluble problems, it mostly functions as a coping mechanism. Empirically speaking, this function of prayer is by far the most important, although praying as a concentrated motivation to change should not be forgotten. Our subjects refer to it when they are praying for examinations. The sociobiologist Wilson, when trying to grasp religion, emphasized the function of ritual as 'anticipatory action' (1978). So praying can be understood as a concentrated preparation to change or rearrange elements of everyday life. Pratt (1910/11) referred to "the praying athlete", a phenomenon which, "if it is to be taken seriously, will be on psychological rather than on theological grounds". We think it should indeed be taken seriously.

So prayer can be seen as a way of constructing reality, as a way of making sense in a multi-interpretable world. This idea, which originated from symbolic interactionism (e.g. Berger & Luckmann, 1966) and influenced Geertz's definition of religion, is also held by modern psychology (Gergen, 1985). People constantly have to shape and reshape the world they live in. Praying-practices function as a psychological mechanism to do so. Fowler (1974), in presenting a developmental perspective on faith, defined faith as "a verb", as "an active mode of being": "faith is a way of construing or interpreting one's experience". We defined praying as a verb, as an activity: praying is a mechanism to construct and interpret one's experience.

The place where young people construct and interpret experiences is in bed; the time is at night, before sleeping. More research is needed to understand the meaning of this phenomenon. We think it could be worthwhile. In psychological research the mode of consciousness of prayer and meditation is located between active thougt and deep sleep. People who pray experience this mode as being 'turned inwards' (Spilka, Hood & Gorsuch 1985:165-6). Our hypothesis is that, when the institution of prayer is fading away in secularizing society and when praying - as we maintained - indeed has important psychological functions, people will reconstruct a mode of praying on their own. It seems understandable that this non-institutionalized reconstruction will take place at the moment most suitable from a physiological point of view. At night in bed people are finally on their own and have an opportunity to contemplate the day in silence and alone. The paramount reality of everyday life is interrupted; brain activity is reduced. A mode of passive receptivity prepares one to meditate the contradictions of daily life.

The individualized prayer of modern youth should not be overlooked. But can we speak of an individualized 'ritual'? Ritual can be defined as "those conscious and voluntary, repetitious and stylized symbolic actions (including verbal behaviour such as chant, song and prayer) that are centered on cosmic structures and/or sacred presences" (Grimes, 1987). In our opinion one can speak of a ritual indeed. As we showed, the grammar of the prayer of today's youth is structured in a rather traditional way: all the elements discussed in literature could be demonstrated. The ritual is individualized and minimal in its form, but complete in its structure. It could be the prototype of a new way of praying. "In our contemporary religious situation", as Van Ouwerkerk (1984) argued "apparently an uninhibited dealing with praying is only possible if we have returned to it from a critical distance". The 'distant' praying of contemporary youth seems to entail the rediscovery of meditational prayer. In contrast with several institutionalized religious practices (e.g. church-attendance), praying might have essential practical and psychological significance for youth.

The general structure of praying - containing seven elements and pointing in two directions - can be applied to different theological or metaphysical contexts, as was demonstrated by the differences between the denominations. Effects are more abstract or more concrete according to the philosophy one supports, but are formulated and experienced anyhow. He/she who believes in a personal God will define prayer rather as a dialogue; he/she who believes in an undefinable power will prefer definitions of meditation. Both define an act. As we mentioned above, Capps (1982) considered petitionary prayer to be "the heart of prayer". Our data support his contention insofar they show that a kind of petitionary prayer is empirically prominent. Capps' interpretation of petitionary prayer, however, in terms of transaction and communication (which function psychologically by co-orientation and role-taking) is interesting but seems to be a specific characteristic of those who pray to a personal God. In the sample we studied most people indeed pray to God, but only a small minority uses personal attributes to describe God. So we see communication as a specific cultural translation of a more general construction-process. Augustine already stressed the constructivist perspective. One has to pray, he says, "ut ipsa (mens) construatur, non ut Deus instruatur" that is: "to construct the soul, not to instruct God" (Epistola CXL, caput XXIX, 69). Of course there are important contextual and theological differences between Augustine's conceptions and the conceptions of our subjects, but there is a related psychology of praying.

A previous version of this contribution was published in the Journal of Empirical Theology, 2/1989/2. The investigations were financially supported by the Radboud Foundation and the University of Nijmegen.

2.2

THE IMPACT OF THE LITURGICAL SETTING
An empirical study from the perspective of environmental psychology

Jan van der Lans & Henri Geerts

1. Introduction
In psychology, the basic assumption is that human behavior is determined by genetics, intrapsychic (cognitive and emotional) processes and by social and physical characteristics of the situation. Research in psychology, then, is the search for antecedents of our various behaviors. In studying religious behavior, psychologists of religion have paid little attention to situational factors, so far. Only a small number of studies is known, in which the question whether and under which conditions situational characteristics can evoke a religious experience has been the focus. Hood (1978), Hood et al. (1981) and Van der Lans (1980) may be seen as examples of this approach.

In this chapter we will pay attention to a specific religious situation. Assuming that a religious ritual may be conceived as a situation which is meant to generate religious behavior in those who participate, we will investigate whether the liturgy of the Eucharist in Roman Catholic churches is indeed one of the factors explaining the variance in behavioral effects, which are reported by participants.

First, some arguments will be adduced in support of the conception of ritual as a situational factor. Secondly, some questionnaire-data will be analyzed which in several churches were obtained from people who participated in the celebration of the Eucharist.

By the 1940s, some scholars in psychology began to take a close look at the effects of environmental conditions on human behavior. In the 1960s, the term 'environmental psychology' originated to decribe this focus. Now, this has become one of the prominent branches of psychology. Its distinguishing mark is the approach of human behavior as a dynamic interchange of personal and environmental factors. Sometimes, the study is restricted to the effects of the physical environment on behavior, e.g. the relationship between the design of psychiatric hospital wards and therapeutic progress (Proshansky & Altmann, 1979). However, according to others, limiting the field to physical surroundings is too narrow. Canter & Craik (1981) define environmental psychology as that area of psychology which brings into conjunction and analyses the transactions and interrelationships of human experiences and actions with pertinent aspects of the sociophysical surroundings.

Although it has not been a subject of investigation by environmental psychology untill now, the systems approach which is characteristic for environmental psychology seems to be very useful for the behavioral scientific study of religious ritual. Environmental psychology approaches the behavior setting as an environmental unit. Theoretically, it is possible to unravel this unit into a lot of distinct components, each with its own effect on human behavior. In reality however, a behavior situation is not the sum of separate stimulus-response relationships, but an integral whole with characteristics that distinguish it from other environment-behavior systems. Liturgy is a ritual situation, in which a group of believers, who came together in a sacred place, share symbolic actions, symbolic objects and symbolic language. A lot of elements could be distinguished: burning candles, smell of incense, organ-music, singing of psalms, liturgical vestments, prayers, listening to bible-lecture and sermon, holy communion, bodily positions. It may be presumed, that, next to these intrinsic liturgical elements, it also depends on characteristics of the physical context whether the intended effects will come into existence. Numerous historical examples demonstrate that the physical environment in which the ritual takes place has always been carefully selected and organized: entrance, the architectural design of the building, statues, light falling through stained windows, and so on. These examples show the complexity of the behavior situation, in which the ritual takes place. It implies physical components (building, visual and auditory stimuli) as well as social interaction. A complex whole of environmental elements, affecting all the sense-organs of the participants, construct this behavior setting as a liturgical one. Not the distinct elements, but the environment as a structural unit determines which type of behavior will occur in this setting. To understand the environment-behavior relationship that is typical for liturgy, a system approach is necessary instead of investigating distinct stimulus-response relationships separately. All the same, environmental psychologists will investigate how fluctuations in the environmental setting affect the behavioral response. As Turner (1967:277; 1974a:55) has pointed out, the meaning of symbols may vary from situation to situation as well as from one individual to another. An environmental-psychological approach will be the most adequate one to investigate this interdependency.

Here, not the standing pattern of collective behavior that characterizes a liturgical setting will be the object of study. Instead, we will focus on two aspects of this behavior pattern which in contemporary Roman Catholic pastoral theology are considered to be principal aims of the liturgy: to enhance community-consciousness and to stimulate the

88

participants to reflect upon their faith. The problem to be treated here is whether these two variables are affected by fluctuations in liturgical settings.

2. Dependent variables

2.1 Community-consciousness

The strengthening or regeneration of community-feelings has always been considered to be a principal function of rituals:

> "A real effect of cult is the periodical recreation of the society on which we depend and which depends on us. [...] The essential function of rituals is that individuals feel together and act together" (Durkheim, 1912:495/553).

Rituals actualize the community's experience of the ultimate basis of its existence. Men have always experienced a tension between the everyday reality of social life, with its conflicts and unequalities, and the ideal of community. Rituals serve to transcend this discrepancy. According to Turner (1974a) it is a common cultural characteristic of rituals that differences of social status are ignored during the ritual. People between whom a big social distance exists in everyday life, mix with each other in an egalitarian way during the ritual "to ensure what is believed to be the maintenance of a cosmic order which transcends the contradictions and conflicts inherent in the mundane social system" (1974a:238). During the ritual, the social-structural relations of the workaday world are replaced by 'communitas' (Turner, 1974a:238; Randall Nichols, 1985). The description of the Christian community as "God's people on its way", which has been emphasized by the Second Vatican Council, may be seen as the wording of this same idea. According to art. 14 of the Constitution on the Liturgy, proclaimed by this Council in 1963, "active participation" is a key-concept. In all its aspects, the liturgical renewal aimed at the creation of facilities to realize a fully active and conscious participation of the laity in the liturgy. Active participation is proposed in the Constitution to be "the first and necessary source of the real Christian spirit".

As far as we know, there is only one investigation so far, that has tried to verify empirically the assumption that liturgical participation enhances community feelings. Frundt (1969), after having selected two parishes, which were similar with respect to geographical, demographical and social-economical factors, concluded from interviews with members, that differences between the two parishes in community bond could only be explained by the fact that one of the parishes had a history of active liturgical rite involvement. "Liturgy forms community if liturgy is enjoyable and frequently (weekly) experienced" (1969:99). He describes this outcome as "a discovery of enormous implications for the future of parish life" (1969:95). A weak point of Frundt's research design however is that, allthough starting from a causal theory with respect to the impact of liturgical involvement on community, his conclusions are based on zero correlations between items of both categories. Correlation coefficients do not allow interpretations with respect to cause and effect. Further, it is remarkable, that Frundt assumed a one-way causal relationship between characteristics of the liturgy and community experience instead of considering the possibility that the latter might be an effect of interaction between the liturgical situation and individual characteristics of the participants. Frundt paid attention to individual differences (age, sex, education level, income, ethnic background, political background, recreational interests, length of parish membership, perceptions of the pastor) as control variables only in order to test the similarity of the parishes in these respects.

2.2 Mental reflection
Besides the strengthening of community and with fewer emphasis, cognitive change has been mentioned as an objective of ritual. Rituals embody the religious perspective of a culture, as Clifford Geertz (1973b) has pointed out. In the midst of ritual, the participants are transported into another mode of existence (1973b:119-20). The enactment of the myths, which takes place during the ritual, makes that the mythical figures are experienced as being present and that the metaphysical conceptions, of which they are the symbolic representatives, are reinforced. The ritual presents "not only models of what [the participants] believe, but also models for the believing of it" (1973b:114). Geertz quotes a statement of Santayana, in which this philosopher says that the power of a healthy religion consists in its message that there is another world to live in (1973b:87). A major objective of the ritual is the actualization of the religious perspective, that usually is suppressed by the common-sense perspective of the everyday world. The enactment of the ritual should work out a reinforcement of the religious world view so that it will become the reference frame for the participants' selfperception and for their choosing of life-goals.

In the description of the aims of the Roman Catholic liturgy, the importance attached to cognitive renewal has been growing during the last decades. The Dutch bishops, in their pastoral letter on worship in 1975, said that it is the objective of liturgy "to make the mystery of redemption" recognizable. In this way, liturgy can "deepen faith and keep it alive". And one decade earlier, they mentioned as an objective of liturgy "the renewal of our views on God, the world, ourselves and others". This same intention characterizes the Constitution on the liturgy of Vatican II. It emphasizes that the liturgy should be comprehensible for the participants. The Fathers of this Council seem to have considered it of great importance that the message, which is implied in the liturgical verbs and acts, should be understood by the participants. This also suggests that conscious assimilation is an intended effect of liturgical participation. The ratio of the liturgical reform, that has taken place in the seventies, was to improve the visibility of the worldview and ethos of Christianity for those who celebrate the ritual (Greeley, 1971).

As far as known, empirically derived information regarding the impact that liturgy as such has on the religious consciousness of participants is missing until now. Some empirical studies have focused only on the impact of the sermon on religious thinking and values (Pargament & Silverman, 1983; and indirectly Daiber et al., 1980). Leege, Welch & Trozzolo (1986) found a significant but low relationship between frequency of Mass attendance and socio-political attitudes, and concluded that Mass attendance does not insure that Catholics will internalize the teachings it transmits.

3. Method
3.1 Design
To assess whether and to what degree people have experienced community and have come to reflection when they participated in the celebration of the Eucharist is not difficult. However, to proof that the liturgical rite itself has contributed to these effects, is very complicated. First, one needs a point of comparison. However, a pre-post design with a matched control-group, as it is used for instance in evaluation-research with respect to psychotherapy or educational strategies, would not be adequate here. For, when community consciousness and reflection with respect to liturgy are the object of research, the investigator has to question people about the liturgy they have participated in. Secondly, it is not self-evident that the ordinary weekly liturgical celebration will bring about the intended psychological effects to such a degree that they can be noticed by an observer or investigator. Academic studies on effects of rituals that we have cited above, primarily apply to occasional rituals like "rites-de-passage". In contrast with these, for the majority of participants the weekly celebration of the Eucharist is part of an acquired behavior-pattern. They don't visit it on the occasion of a life-crisis. Although people generally don't visit the church involuntary nowadays, as has been the

case previously, this does not mean that they are in a disposition to undergo a conversion-experience each time. Methodologically, for an investigation into the impact of participation in liturgical rites, a longitudinal study would be the best procedure. Because of the practical difficulties we would encounter, such as loss of respondents and high expenses, this method has not been used, however. As an alternative we have chosen the research-design which is analogous to the one used in environmental psychology. In order to investigate what are the typical patterns of behavior they evoke, psychologists like Barker compared several behavior settings with each other. Here, we will compare the impact of the Eucharist, celebrated in the same weekend in several parish churches and investigate whether several cases of this kind of environment have a similar bearing on the behavior of participants or not. When differences in behavior of participants will appear from one liturgical environment to another, analyses of variance may demonstrate whether these differences are more attributable either to characteristics of the local liturgical setting or to individual-psychological factors. The latter will be confined here to sex, age, education level, and religious commitment of the participants. Finally, when the liturgical settings appear to be a significant source of variance, we will explore in which respects the liturgical environments were different.

3.2 Subjects
The data that will be reported here are part of a larger survey into the relation between personal characteristics of church-goers, and their opinions about and evaluation of the liturgical celebration they have participated in. (In Geerts' contribution to this volume the conceptualization and operationalization of the variable symbol-experience as it has been measured in this investigation are being described). For that purpose, questionnaires have been distributed in seven parish-churches at the same weekend. Three of the parishes are situated in the city of Arnhem (one of them being a hospital chapel), the other four in suburban municipalities in the surroundings of that town. At the end of the service, the pastor asked the attenders to remain in the church for a moment. In every pew, to each second, third or fourth visitor (depending of the parish-size) a questionnaire was given. People were informed that they could fill in the questionnaire at home and that within three days, the completed questionnaire would be collected by a member of the local liturgy-workgroup. Of the 1040 distributed questionnaires, 775 were returned. For the suburban churches, the numbers of returned questionnaires were about equal (between 116 to 139). For the city-churches, there was a large discrepancy between one of them (n=145) and the other two,

among which the chapel of a hospital (n=35 each).

In the total sample, the age-group of above 50 years old is over-represented. The overall average-score for age is 53.8. In the three city-churches, subjects are older averagely than in the suburban churches. With respect to age-distribution, there were small but significant differences between the 7 groups. In one of the suburban churches the percentage of persons below 24 as well as of persons between 45 and 54 years old was greater than in the other groups. In the chapel, there are about three times as many subjects above 65 years old than in the other groups.

Of the total sample, 45.4% are men and 54.6% are women. In the separate churches, we find the same proportion, with three exceptions. In one urban and in one of the suburban churches, the proportion of women is higher (62% and 60% respectively), whereas in another suburban church the numerical relation of men and women is just the reverse in comparison with the total sample.

With respect to education level, the respondents are categorized into four subgroups: elementary school (28.9%), secondary school/lower vocational education (34.3%), high school/intermediate vocational education (20%), higher education (16.8%). Especially between the suburban churches, there are significant differences in this respect. In two of them, the proportion of respondents with only elementary education is much higher (39 to 44%), whereas in two other suburban churches the higher levels are overrepresented.

A fourth individual characteristic that may determine the degree of community-experience and of reflection, is the respondent's religious commitment. In the questionnaire, subjects have been asked about their daily prayer practises, bible reading, reading and talking with others about religious subjects, amount of time spent on self-imposed tasks for the benefit of the parish community. These items were used as indicators of religious commitment. From the answers, given to these items, a sumscore for religious commitment has been calculated for each subject, with 0.0 as minimum-value and 6.0 as maximum-value. On the basis of these sumscores, subjects can be categorized into three levels of religious commitment: low (31.2%), medium (43.5%) and high (25.2%). There are significant differences between the church-communities in this respect. In one of the urban churches as well as in the hospital chapel, higher scores for religious commitment were more frequent than in the total sample, whereas in three of the suburban churches lower scores were more frequent.

3.3 Dependent variables
Composed measures were also used for the two dependent variables

'community-feelings' and 'reflection'. To assess the degree of community-experience of the participants, the following Lickert-scale items were inserted into the questionnaire:

"The intercessions make me more committed to grief in my environment and in society."

"For me, in the intercessions all the faithfull are praying together."

"In the intercessions, I appreciate praying for the poor and the sick."

"In the intercessions, I appreciate praying for the newly baptized and married persons of the parish."

"In receiving holy communion, I feel myself bound together with the other churchgoers."

"I appreciate meeting acquaintances before and after the service."

"My co-parishioners give me a feeling of encouragement."

"For me, celebrating the Eucharist expresses my wish to be a church-community."

As a measure of each respondent's community-experience, the average of his scores to these eight items was calculated.

In order to determine how much the liturgy stimulated the participants to reflection, the following items were inserted in the questionnaire:

"In the past service, the confession of guilt brought me to think about situations of the past week, in which I did not behave properly."

"In the past service, the confession of guilt made me think about my acts and ommissions."

"In the past service, the lectures gave me a lot to think about my daily life."

"In the past service, the sermon made me linger on something, I had hardly reflected upon earlier."

"At the intercessions, I dwell for a moment on my life during the week."

"During the silence after communion, I dwelled on things that happened in the past week."

To obtain a subject's measure for reflection during the liturgy, his or her answers to these six items have been averaged.

4. Results

According to the above described design, the variance of these two dependent variables has been analysed separately in order to investigate whether differences between the seven liturgical settings have had an independent effect on it. First, the results for community consciousness will be reported. Age, education-level, and general religious commitment of the participants, also their gender probably, may cause differences in community-consciousness during the liturgical celebration. But, apart from these individual characteristics, is there also an effect from the liturgical setting as such? Table 1 shows the result of the statistical analysis of the variance in reported community consciousness. Of the output of this procedure, only the Multiple Classification Analysis is presented here. Subjects, who had not answered the items of the variable 'community consciousness (N = 148; 19%), were not inserted in this analysis. These missing observations were equally distributed over the settings.

The squared multiple R shows, that a substantial part (30%) of the total variance in the dependent variable is explained by the variables, which we assumed to be relevant predictors. Whether community consciousness is evoked by the liturgy of the Eucharist appears to depend on multiple conditions. The analysis demonstrates that the degree of religious commitment of the individual participant is the strongest determinant. The correlation (eta) between the two variables is rather high and in the expected direction: .45, which means that 20% of the variance in community consciousness is explained by religious commitment. The column 'unadjusted deviation' in table 1 shows that the average score for community consciousness of participants with low religious commitment is lower than the grand mean, whereas the average for community consciousness of highly committed participants transcends the grand mean.

Age appears to be another strong determinant. From the calculated deviations we learn that the older the respondent, the more community conscious, with the restriction that not the youngest category but the next one (25-34) has scored lowest in this respect. The correlation between age and community consciousness may be flattered, however, by the fact that the elimination of missing observations of the variable community consciousness especially thinned out the eldest categories (53% missings).

The proportion of variance that is attributable to gender, is small and not significant. The same must be concluded with respect to education. Nevertheless, the differences between the educational categories as shown in the column 'unadjusted deviations', are interesting. The highest scores for community consciousness are found with the lowest educated participants, and the lowest scores at the high school-level.

Table 1

The impact of liturgical setting, age, gender, educational level
and degree of religious commitment on community consciousness
Grand mean = 4.13

Variable + Category	N	unadjusted deviation	deviation adjusted for independants	eta	beta
Liturgical setting					
Arnhem Nicolaas	88	.11	-.01		
Arnhem Binnen	20	.62	.40		
Arnhem Chapel	16	.31	.14		
Huissen	70	-.16	-.07		
Gendt	83	-.08	-.06		
Velp	77	-.30	-.18		
Elst	94	.14	.14		
				.26	.17
Age					
15-24	29	-.54	-.38		
25-34	28	-.59	-.33		
35-44	90	-.18	-.09		
45-54	81	-.08	-.12		
55-64	123	.12	.07		
65-	97	.41	.30		
				.36	.24
Gender					
male	204	-.05	-.04		
female	244	.04	.03		
				.05	.08
Education					
elementary school	107	.22	.07		
secondary school	159	.00	.02		
high school	90	-.26	-.13		
university	92	.00	.01		
				.19	.08

Variable + Category	N	unadjusted deviation	deviation adjusted for independants	eta	beta
Religious commitment					
low	146	-.51	-.04		
medium	195	.14	.10		
high	107	.43	.36		
				.45	.35
Multiple R^2	.303				
Multiple R	.551				

This observation is all the more interesting, while in the latter category there are far less missings than in the former. However, when other factors are taken into account, the differences between educational groups largely disappear.

The analysis demonstrates that the liturgical setting also contributed significantly and independently from the other factors to the variance in community consciousness. Table 1 shows that there are large differences between the seven churches. The highest scores are found in the setting 'Arnhem Binnen', followed by the hospital chapel; the lowest scores in the suburban parish 'Velp'. It should be remarked, however, that in the two first mentioned settings, the younger age-groups are under-represented. The two-way interaction effect of liturgical setting and age on the variance of the dependent variable is significant (p = .05). However, this does not discount the independent effect of the liturgical settings. When interaction effects are taken into account, the differences between the high and low scoring liturgical settings with respect to community consciousness become smaller (see column 'adjusted deviations') but are still considerable. In the final paragraph, we will try to relate these differences to characteristics of the settings. First we must turn to the results of the analysis of the other dependent variable 'mental reflection'. Here, the number of missing observations is substantial: 283 respondents (36.5%). The analysis of variance has been calculated on the data of the remaining 492 participants.

Table 2
The impact of liturgical setting, age, gender, educational level and
degree of religious commitment on mental reflection
Grand mean = 3.09

Variable + Category	N	unadjusted deviation	deviation adjusted for independents	eta	beta
Liturgical setting					
Arnhem Nicolaas	73	.00	-.01		
Arnhem Binnen	20	-.04	-.20		
Arnhem Chapel	14	.20	.12		
Huissen	54	-.07	-.07		
Gendt	70	.03	.02		
Velp	79	.17	.14		
				.14	.10
Age					
15-24	26	-.74	-.61		
25-34	25	.11	.46		
35-44	77	-.03	.11		
45-54	63	-.12	-.22		
55-64	102	.07	.00		
65-	70	.27	.14		
				.25	.25
Gender					
male	180	.00	.05		
female	183	.00	-.05		
				.00	.05
Education					
elementary school	128	.25	.23		
secondary school	154	.04	.08		
high school	78	-.26	-.17		
university	73	-.07	-.21		
				.18	.17

Continuation table 2

Variable + Category	N	unadjusted deviation	deviation adjusted for independents	eta	beta
Religious commitment					
low	128	-.37	-.39		
medium	154	.16	.14		
high	81	.28	.35		
				.29	.31

Multiple R^2	.181
Multiple R	.426

The multiple correlation coefficient indicates that only 18% of the variance is explained by the predictors that we brought into the analysis. Again, the strongest predictor is the degree of religious commitment. The correlation (eta) is not high, but significant enough (.29). The way, in which the commitment categories deviate from the grand mean clearly demonstrates, that the less religiously committed a participant is, the smaller the chance is that the liturgical rite will make him or or her reflect. The differences between the lowly and highly committed even increase when the influence of other variables is taken into account, as the adjusted deviations show.

Age is another significant predictor of the degree in which the participants of liturgy will come to reflect. The unadjusted deviations of the age categories show that indications of reflection were hardly observed among adolescent and young adult participants (15-24 year). At first sight, persons above 65 year have most come to reflection. However, the same problem as mentioned above with respect to community consciousness is repeated here. In this age group, the majority did not answer at all the questions relating to reflection (66% missing observations against 41% in the 15-24 year-category). So it is doubtful whether the obtained score is representative. Adjustment for the other predictors has a remarkable effect on the score-pattern of the age-categories. Now, the participants in the category 25-34 year are presented as those who most came to reflection during the service. The difference with regard to the unadjusted deviations can be explained by the fact, that the majority of this age group belongs to the lowest category of religious commitment. This may have neutralized the age-effect, as the correlation between religious commitment and reflection is considerable. When the impact of religious commitment is partialled out, the high reflection-score of this age-group becomes manifest. On the other hand, with the youngest age-group, the majority of which is also lowly committed, the two effects of age and of religious commitment reinforce each other.

Whether participants come to reflection during the liturgy further depends on their level of education. The relation is weak, but remarkable regarding the fact that participants with the lowest level of education have reported more reflection during liturgy than the higher educated. Adjustment does not change the deviation, which makes clear that the high score of this education-category is not reducable to other factors. However, no less than 57% of respondents belonging to this education level has been eliminated from the analysis because of missing data for reflection, against only 33-39% from the two highest education groups. The lower score for reflection of the latter has therefore more representative value than the high score reported by the lowest educated.

Finally, table 2 proves that differences in reflection have not been caused by the liturgical setting. This factor has hardly been a source of variation in this respect (F = .71; p = .64).

5. Discussion
The results of our analysis demonstrate that the conclusion Frundt (1969) inferred from his investigation, was too general. One conclusion resulting from our analysis is that the degree in which the faithful will experience community and come to reflection during the Eucharistic ritual largely depends on ideosyncratic factors. With respect to community consciousness, religious commitment and age are strong predictors.

Is there an explanation for the remarkable fact that older churchgoers in our sample, especially those above 65 year, demonstrate more community experience than the younger? It is possible, that some of the items in our questionnaire, which were used to measure community consciousness, are more suitable to trigger the community feeling of older people. But it may also be that liturgy really fulfills its age-old community-function especially for older people in our days, while young people have many other ritual occasions outside the sacral domain of liturgy in which to experience togetherness.

Concerning reflection the analysis points out, that also in this respect the youngest age-group generally scored lowest. At first sight, older participants tend to reflect more during the liturgy than younger ones. However, when the contribution of other determinants is eliminated, the age-category of 25-34 year olds appears to have scored highest. There is a remarkable difference between the two youngest age-groups in this respect, that hardly appears to be corrected by the strong factor religious commitment. For the time being, we don't know how to account for the fact that the ritual of the Eucharist activates the 25-34 year old participants more to reflection.

Participants with a high-school level education seem to be less open to community consciousness during the Eucharist ritual than low-educated subjects. Further, the analysis made clear that these differences are partly being caused by other factors. Education does not appear to be a major factor in this respect. Remarkable however, is the inverse relation between the participants' level of education and their degree of reflection during the ritual. It is definitely not the case that the higher educated did not come to any reflection at all, but that they did so in a lesser degree than the lower educated. It might indicate, that the ritual elements that particularly stimulate reflection, are more appealing to the lower educated participants. But at the moment, there is no evidence for this assumption.

Summarizing, community consciousness and reflection - two of the effects that the ritual intends to stimulate - vary first of all with religious commitment, secondly with age and, to a lesser degree, with the level of education. The question we wanted to investigate, however, was whether fluctuations in the ritual also affect the coming about of community consciousness and reflection. With respect to community consciousness, the analysis of variance clearly demonstrated differences between the liturgical environments. In "Arnhem Binnen", participants of the ritual reported far more community consciousness than the average of the total sample. From observation we know, that the Eucharist ritual in this parish church distinguishes itself by the ceremony of the pax. This liturgical element is one of the culminating moments of the ritual, as the participants walk around then in order to exchange wishes for peace. It is very probable that this environmental characteristic caused the extreme high score for community consciousness of the respondents in "Arnhem Binnen". We can also guess why the respondents in "Velp" generally scored so low on comunity consciousness. Here, the physical environment is rather unfavourable. The church is large and the participants are sitting far from each other. This spatial formation, which the believers choose in church, seems to reflect the distance between the houses in this district.

With respect to reflection, the liturgical environment hardly contributes to the variance. This means that the liturgical environments of the seven parish churches hardly differs in this respect. This outcome of the statistical analysis corresponds with the observational data. It was evident for the observers that in each of the churches, much care had been given to the preparation of the ritual as well as of the sermon. Not any of the churches distinguished itself from the others in this respect. Consequently, differences between the participants with respect to reflection are primarily reducable to individual predispositions. The fact, that especially the higher educated believers, also the religiously committed among them, least come to reflect, should become a point of pastoral concern perhaps.

The analysis of variance has been performed with the SPSS-X ANOVA procedure. We want to express our appreciation for Ruben Konig for his assistance.

FAMILY RITUALS AS MEDIUM IN CHRISTIAN
FAITH TRANSMISSION

Adrian M. Visscher and Merle J. Stern

Religions in general, including Christian faith, have always been inextricably linked with ritual. In a variety of settings, both institutional and popular, it is ritual that expresses, celebrates and transmits the beliefs and values of a community and a culture. At the same time, religious rituals also serve as an index to the level of integration of faith in any particular group.

In our society the family provides the primary context for the daily living of beliefs and values. For this reason, the study of ritual activities of the family provides an opportunity to determine the identity and the characteristics of families as expressed in their ritual activities. We may also discover what content of faith is being transmitted through these rituals.

Two major studies underly the present project. The research of Wolin & Bennett (1984) provided us with a sophisticated framework for studying family rituals; the work of Strommen (1972) and Keeley (1976) enabled us to identify those Christian faith convictions that play a part in the intergenerational transmission of faith.

1. Background themes

Our extensive involvement with families, especially through the medium of family therapy, made us aware of the issue of Christian faith and Christian culture. The following themes served to further generate our interest in family rituals and the transmission of Christian faith values.

1.1. Christian faith or Christian culture?

Several major surveys in North America as well as in Europe surfaced fundamental questions about the extent to which contemporary Christians still believe in the major traditional tenets of Christian faith (Better Home and Gardens, 1988; Fogarty, Ryan & Lee, 1984; Gallup & O'Connel, 1986; Gallup & Poling, 1980; Harding, Philips & Fogarty, 1986; Kerkhofs, 1984; Kerkhofs & Rezsohasy, 1984; Rezsohasy & Kerkhofs, 1984). While these surveys show that the great majority of Christians professes to be believers, what they believe is less equivocal and varies according to age group and national and cultural factors. Kerkhofs (1988) suggests that the data of the European Value Systems Study Group reveal the diaspora situation of those we may call 'Christian believers' in a region where Christian culture still prevails. While Christians who practise regularly show a great variety of 'beliefs', yet most 'Christians' and a substantial majority of 'non-Christians' still expect spiritual guidance from their churches. Confessing Christians have become a minority in a culture where a large majority still proclaim their adherence to 'Christendom'. Even those who consider themselves clearly 'out', continue to bear some typically Christian relics.

These data invite us to look at the differentiation between what churches assert the faith of Christians ought to be, and the actual faith or beliefs of 'Christians'. We think that two areas of study are important in examining this question: the phenomenon of 'popular' or 'folk' religion as distinct from 'institutional' religion, and the role of the family unit in transmitting *what they feel* is important in Christian faith and beliefs. We believe that these two are related.

1.2 Popular religion

Maldonado defines popular religion as 'lived' religiosity, in contrast to 'official' or 'prescribed' religiosity (Henau, 1986:72), Meslin calls it "the quest for a more simple, more direct and more profitable relationship with the divine" (Maldonado, 1986:6). This implies that what the official Church finds important in the beliefs of Christians, is not necessarily what people feel is important.

In an earlier phase of our research (White, 1987) we found that religious activities include cognitive, affective as well as behavioral dimensions, for "the important thing is what you do, not what you think, believe or say" (Staal, 1979:4 ; Panikkar, 1977).

Popular religion expresses people's experiences as pervasively linked up with the beliefs, rituals and values of a given society, community or culture, and helps them to connect with the Holy. It is "a religion that expresses the undisguised feelings of the people themselves; they all share ... an intensity of participation and a deeply felt sense of community" (Cox, 1973:167). Pace (1987:12) suggests that popular religion is a subjective experience, autonomous from the official religious communication that is taking place in institutional worship. It takes account of subjective needs, of emotional communication, of face to face rapport as opposed to all the cold forms of functioning of the traditional religious institutions.

These characteristics of popular religion seem to play a significant role in the results of the surveys mentioned above and in their interpretation. They guided us in formulating and planning the research reported here.

1.3. The family as the 'domestic church'

The family is the arena where subjective needs are met; emotional communication is at the core of family expectations, identity and face to face rapport is a continuous event. The religious 'doing' of families is expressed in what they do together; it is this doing that will reveal what they believe and what they find important in those beliefs.

> "...(the) schooling-instructional paradigm can teach us about religion and about Christianity, but faith is expressed, transformed and made meaningful by persons sharing faith in a historical, tradition-bearing community of faith" (Westerhoff, 1976:23).

While this applies to the church as a community in its various forms, from basic group and parish communities to the universal church, it has a particular meaning for the family as the domestic church. Contemporary catechetics emphasize the indispensable cooperation of parents in religious education; family religious education complements the schooling-instructional paradigm. One may even assert the opposite: the schooling-instructional paradigm is complementary to religious education in the family. Vatican II states in 'Lumen Gentium' (Flannery, 1975:362, #11):

> "In what may be regarded as the domestic church, the parents, by word and example, are the first heralds of the faith with regard to their children."

And in 'Gravissimum Educationis' (Flannery, 1975:728, #3):

> "... (Parents) must ... be recognized as being primarily and principally responsible for (the) education (of) their children ... The role of parents in education is of such importance that it is almost impossible to provide an adequate substitute ... The family is therefore the principal school of the social virtues which are necessary to every society."

In 'Familiaris Consortio' John Paul II (1981:92) elaborates on those two themes:

> "Married couples and parents ... are called upon to communicate Christ's love to their brethren, thus becoming a saving community ... (The Christian family) stands as ... a symbol, witness and participant of the Church's motherhood."

The family communicates the faith to children in a variety of ways. However, in taking note of people's rituals, 'we discover what people consider important' (Arbuckle, 1987:10). Thus Vogeleisen (1984:26) asserts that, if we are concerned with transmitting faith to children today, we must place priority on adult formation.

What then is the function of rituals in families in regard to the transmission of Christian faith? What in Christian faith are parents intent upon transmitting to their children?

2. Family rituals

Rituals are story lines in action, they are part of everyday life, they take place over time and their meaning is embellished with the passage of time (Bausch, 1984). Stern (1987:115) writes that the point of ritual is to affect its performer and, through its regular performance, to inculcate character traits in him and inspire him with specific values.

When speaking about rituals, the matter of definition must be raised. From Van Gennep, Durkheim and Turner in an anthropological perspective, to Van der Hart and Palazoli in a therapeutic perspective, rituals and their characteristics have been defined in various and ongoing ways (Roberts, 1988). So does Worgul (1984:141) suggest that in order to be rituals, behaviors must be interpersonal, repetitive and adaptive. Steinglass, Bennett, Wolin & Reiss (1984:65) give four characteristics of family rituals: the behavior is bound in time in that it has a clear beginning and end, leaving no room for interruptions; the people involved are consciously aware that something special is happening; the behavior has primacy over any other occurring behaviors; all episodes incorporate a definite symbolic component which gives the behaviors more importance than they objectively have.

In this study we have adopted Wolin and Bennett's definition of ritual:

"A symbolic form of communication that, owing to the satisfaction that family members experience through its repetition, is acted out in a systematic fashion over time" (Wolin & Bennett, 1984:401).

Rituals reinforce the shared beliefs and common heritage of those who take part in them, and help them to make sense of their particular universe (Steinglass et al. 1987:223).

A distinction between types of rituals is also made. They fall into three categories. *Family Celebrations* are those holidays and occasions that are widely practiced throughout the culture and are special in the minds of the family; *Family Traditions* are less culture specific and more ideosyncratic for each family; the least deliberate and most covert are patterned *Family Interactions* (Wolin & Bennett, 1984:403).

3. Purpose of the present research

As the family provides the primary context for the daily acting out of beliefs and values, including religious beliefs and values, the study of

106

ritual activities of the family provides us with the opportunity to determine the identity and characteristics of families and to discover what content of faith is being transmitted through these rituals.

We will first present the methodology of this study, and secondly report some basic statistical results in reference to the characteristics of family rituals, as well as to the implications of the specific faith convictions that are linked to these rituals. A deeper analysis of the results in reference to the family as domestic church, and to the function and characteristics of popular religion as evidenced in the results, must await future publications.

4. Methodology and procedures
4.1. Family rituals
Wolin & Bennett (1984:401) explained that, depending on the commitment of families to ritual continuity (i.e. the adaptability of their ritual practices and the consistency of family ritual activities over time), families who protected their most important rituals - such as dinnertime and holidays - in spite of parental alcoholism, produced children with significantly fewer alcoholic problems in adulthood; family values and family stability remained intact. They examined such ritual characteristics as intergenerational heritage, level of novelty in ritual style, deliberateness in establishing the ritual, as well as the intent of the parents in implementing the ritual, and their experience of success. They furthermore investigated the occurrence of ritual disruption, as well as the extent of a couple's joint participation in the ritual observance.

4.1.1. Instruments and their adaption
We adapted the basic instruments used by Wolin & Bennett to our purpose of examining the religious content of rituals by replacing all references to alcoholism by those to 'faith and religion'.

4.1.1.1 Family Life Areas Questionnaire
Together with an introductory and explanatory letter, this questionnaire was sent to the participating couples before the interview. In it, each parent independently identified two family activities in the nuclear area - i.e. within the nuclear family of parents and children - and two in the non-nuclear area - i.e. activities in which extended family members and/or others participated and which, in their opinion, were specifically related to the transmission of Christian faith, its beliefs, convictions

and attitudes to their children. Thus, each couple had altogether a total of four family activities in the nuclear and four in the non-nuclear area. They were then asked to agree between them which two activities in each area would become the focus of this study.

4.1.1.2. Family History Interview and Ritual Interview

All couples participated in an interview enabling us to situate the couple's lifestyle in the perspective of the lifestyle of their families of origin. The format of this family history interview was an adapted version of Wolin & Bennett, again replacing references to alcoholism by those to faith and religion. Also, without affecting the basic information, the interview was considerably shortened by integrating the responses of husband and wife.

The Family History Interview was followed by a discussion of one nuclear and one non-nuclear family activity among the four chosen by the couples by means of the Family Life Areas Questionnaire. It followed the Standard Ritual Interview Format and prepared the couple for scoring their rituals in terms of ritual characteristics and of intended faith convictions. This Ritual Interview Format consists of five main sections: Level of Ritualization, Evidence of Developmental Changes, Comparison to Same Event in Families of Origin, Role of Faith and Religion, and finally Transmission of Faith and Religion. The whole interview lasted from one to one-and-a-half hours.

4.1.2. Scoring ritual characteristics

The observer coding system as developed by Wolin & Bennett, required extensive observer training, as well as hours of producing typewritten protocols of the interview, of scoring these protocols and of reconciling observer differences. For reasons of time economy we developed a self rating scale which the couples used to code or rate themselves.

In Wolin & Bennett's Manual for Interview Coding, various cue words indicated the identity of the ritual characteristics of family activities to be rated on a forced choice scale from 1 to 4. To convert this system into a self scoring system, we listed these cue words with their opposites on a four-point continuous scale: 1 and 2 represent Low, 3 and 4 represent High on a certain characteristic. We asked each spouse to independantly rate each family activity for the characteristic being measured. For example, question one addressed the individual's commitment to the specific family activity. Each spouse rated whether the activity was spontaneous (1) or planned (4), flexible (1) or highly structured (4) or in between. In all, the couples were required to rate ten ritual characteristics for each of the four family activities. The strength of each characteristic was rated by at least three separate scores, their average representing the overall strength of each ritual characteristic.

4.2. Christian Convictions

In an earlier stage of our research we examined the hypothesis that much of what is taught in the family with reference to Christian faith, its values and convictions, is conveyed by family rituals. We found that the adapted Wolin and Bennett instrument "enabled families to focus on family rituals which are religious in intent: (Hendrick et al., 1986; White, 1987).

In a first conclusion we realized that faith and religion are not separate from living, but find expression in daily lives, and particularly in family rituals as the participating couples pointed out to us: "All of life is religion, and there is no religion in our families outside our family life". In a second conclusion, based on a faith grid we developed on the basis of Groome's (1980) three dimensions of faith, (i.e. believing, trusting and doing), we found that, although consistent results could be obtained in the areas of 'believing' and 'doing', the results for 'trusting' were vague and left much to conjecture. We therefore decided to concentrate on the 'believing' (convictions) in the 'doing' (family rituals) of faith. This is consistent with the literature which emphasizes that effective transmission of faith takes place through experience, particularly in the family (Curran, 1987; Greinacher & Elizondo, 1984; Westerhoff, 1976).

4.2.1. Christian Convictions Instrument

Strommen et al. (1972) employed a theoretical model for understanding generational differences and similarities which held two polarities in tension, namely 'structure' (tradition) and 'newness' (spontaneity). (These polarities are also present in the work of Wolin and Bennett on family rituals.) They tested their model through a questionnaire study involving 5000 Lutherans in the United States.

Keeley (1976) in turn tested the major propositions of Strommen's model of intergenerational tensions, and his data supported the previous findings. He isolated forty three religious beliefs and values which differentiated parents from their children. In a written communication Keeley informed us that no further work had been done with this model.

We decided to use twenty eight of Keeley's convictions, leaving out those which appeared to have no relevance to family rituals such as, for example, "definite belief in morality of birth control pills for married couples". Table 1 lists these twenty eight convictions.

Table 1

List of convictions used in this study

1. Churches (Christian communities) should become involved in social problems, i.e.helping the poor and improve race relations.
2. The Bible is the source of God's truth.
3. God is our Saviour.
4. We believe in and are committed to a Supreme Being (as compared to belief in a set of morals, a Basic Principle etc.).
5. God as a Supernatural Being reveals Himself in human experiences and in history.
6. Prayer is of tremendous importance.
7. Any religion is better than none.
8. Religion deals with the supernatural rather than with this world.
9. Knowledge about religion is a high value.
10. Religious ritual and ceremony is a high value.
11. Religious experience is a high value.
12. Good works and good deeds are the behavioral dimension of religion.
13. Talking to people and seeing how they live is an important social dimension of religion.
14. Nothing on this planet is more important than human life.
15. Life is satifying.
16. Life is worth living.
17. Life has meaning and we know what it is.
18. Church doctrine is a source of conflict, bewilderment and disturbance.
19. Death should be feared.
20. Men and women are potentially good and evil depending upon their relationship to God.
21. Men and women are potentially good and evil depending upon their own efforts.
22. It is important to be a member of the Christian community (Church).
23. Our Church (Christian Community) satisfies our religious needs.
24. Our particular Christian Church denomination is a source of religious truth and values.
25. Religion is relevant to every day living.
26. Good relations with other people is important.
27. Freedom outvalues justice and law-and-order.
28. There is a continual personal existence after death.

4.2.2. Scoring the faith convictions

These twenty eight items were listed on a seven-point continuum scale, from 'very much' to 'very little'. This enabled the couples to rate for each family ritual the question "This family activity gives expression to the conviction that ... (for example) ... good relations with other people are important".

4.3. Population sampling criteria

From the North American and Canadian survey results mentioned earlier, we retained an interest in comparing the rituals and faith transmission between families that are involved and non-involved in Church affairs. We hypothesized that no differences would emerge between these two groups of families in terms of faith convictions. Hence we set out to obtain a population of involved and non-involved families. Couples for this study were selected according to their averaged combined scores on the following criteria for church involvement: church attendance, financial contribution to church, children's attendance at Sunday school or other religious instruction classes, and participation in other church social events and functions (Gallup & Poling, 1980). Couples who obtained a score of more than three out of a possible six, were considered to be involved, couples who obtained a score of less than three were considered to be non-involved couples.

As it proved difficult to obtain a sufficiently large sample of non-involved couples, the present stage of this research examines therefore a population sample of thirty-one involved families only. All these couples identified themselves as Christians, as legally married, as having an income from $ 25 000 to $ 60 000, and as having at least one schoolage child - a rather sharply defined population. We required the latter item because it appears that family rituals change significantly when the family moves into its middle years and into the children's adolescence.

4.4. Processing the data

Our present statistical computations are only basic; they refer to significant differences between nuclear and non-nuclear family activities for couples and between husbands and wives for ritual characteristics and convictions. At a later point we hope to carry out a number of analyses of variance as well as transcribe and study the massive interview data. However, we believe that the existing results are interesting and their publication warranted.

The discussion will take the following computations into account:

- Differences for Ritual Characteristics (i.e. commitment, adaptability, consistency, style, intention, success and mastery) between Nuclear and Non-Nuclear Family Activities for couples.
- Differences for Ritual Characteristics between husbands and wives across all activities as well as within Nuclear and Non-nuclear activities.
- Differences for Convictions between Nuclear and Non-Nuclear Family Activities for couples.
- Differences for Convictions between husbands and wives across all activities as well as within Nuclear and Non-nuclear activities.

5. Results and discussion
A measurement of the scoring constistency of both husbands and wives was obtained by means of a split-half randomized technique. The resulting correlation coefficients for both ritual characteristics and convictions were well within the acceptable range.

5.1. Ritual Characteristics
A first report relates to the relative strengths of ritual characteristics, or the place that family ritual activities occupy in the family.

First, no differences were found for couples between Nuclear and Non-Nuclear family activities on the ritual characteristics of Commitment, Adaptability, Consistency, Style, Intention, Succes and Mastery. Intention obtained the highest score of all characteristics (3.45 on a scale of 4).

Although we hypothesized different result for Nuclear and Non-nuclear activities, the obtained differences between those areas for husbands and wives are interesting but do not warrant this distinction. Table 2 reports therefore the results for couples and for husbands and wives across all family ritual activities. Religious rituals of the family take place both in the Nuclear and the Non-nuclear areas with consistent results with regard to their characteristics. The interpretation of the results will take this into account.

Second, when examining the differences between husbands and wives on Intention as ritual characteristic, it appears that wives score significantly higher than husbands across both Nuclear and Non-Nuclear activities; this difference is due to the significantly higher score of the wives for Intention in regard to Nuclear activities.

Intention relates to the conviction that the 'family rituals happened as they were intended'; this seemed to be more important to mothers than fathers, particularly for Nuclear family activities. Although ritual activities are uppermost in the mind of both parents, within the family

Table 2

Means for couples and for husbands and wives
for ritual characteristics

Characteristic	Couples	Husbands	Wives	Minimal difference required	Probability bility level
Commitment	(2.66)	2.68	2.65	.17	
Adaptability	(2.09)	2.13	2.06	.13	
Consistency	(2.21)	2.25	2.17	.13	
Style	(2.91)	2.84	2.98	.16	
Intention	(3.45)	3.36	3.54	.14	0.01
Success	(3.16)	3.14	3.18	.13	
Mastery	(2.42)	2.34	2.50	.20	

itself mothers feel even stronger about it than fathers, possibly reflecting a unique role of the mother in creating the family atmosphere. When asked about the extent of their joint participation in family rituals, 85% of the parents said that they did it together, whereas 13% gave the mothers a primary role and only 2% the fathers.

Third, the scores for the ritual characteristics of Commitment, Style, Intention and Success are on the high ritualization side of the four-point scale, whereas those for Adaptability and Consistency indicate low ritualization, the score for Mastery being somewhat in between. The families in this population sample are High Ritualization families (M = 3.04).

'Ritualization' constitutes the actual 'achievement' of ritual, its design and performance (Wolin & Bennett, 1984:413). They state that two dimensions determine a family's overall level of ritualization: their underlying commitment to use ritual in establishing and maintaining a family identity, (in the present research a *religious* family identity), and their ability to adapt rituals from one phase of family development to the next. This reflects the two polarities of intergenerational tension i.e. 'structure' (tradition) and 'newness' (spontaneity).

113

High-Commitment families pay close attention to the past; this historical perspective endows family life with meaning. Low-Commitment families on the other hand, downplay the importance of ritual and are oriented towards the present. They tend to allocate roles and shape power in a more egalitarian manner and generational boundaries are less precise (Wolin & Bennett, 1984: 414-415).

However, families that fare best in their use of ritual, whether high or low in the underlying commitment, also demonstrate appropriate change in ritual performance over the family life cycle. Flexibility is required of a family if its rituals are to remain relevant and effective, thus the family can accomodate their ritual life to the children's view. The ability to adapt and modify ritual observance, applies to both the type of rituals as well as their level of practice (Wolin & Bennett, 1984:416).

From the perspective of ritualization the families in the present study can be described as follows. On the one hand they are characterized by their interest and commitment to ritual activities, but on the other hand by moderation and flexibility. They are firmly in the commitment range (2.66), they believe their rituals to be purposeful, they are active and determined to continue developing their rituals (Intention = 3.45) because they know what they are doing, but these families remain flexible in the implementation and format of these rituals (Adaptability = 2.09) and Consistentency (= 2.21) in a democratic manner. This is also reflected in their fairly original and creative Style of doing rituals (= 2.91). While they rate themselves as quite Successful (= 3.16) in achieving what they set out to do in their rituals, they remain realistic about their achieved Mastery in ritual activities (= 2.42).

Fourth, parents had been asked to choose those rituals which they considered important in reference to the transmission of their Christian faith.

If one would expect that teaching the faith takes place through clearly recognizable religious rituals, our results tell us otherwise. Almost without exception, all couples chose 'dinnertime meals' as one of their religious rituals. It is around the family table that 'religious instruction' takes place. In fact, most of the 'faith transmission' rituals fall within the Family Traditions category (44%) or the Family Interaction category (36%); these categories are characterized by intense interpersonal social relationships with room for a good deal of creativity and spontaneity. The Family Celebrations category (20%) on the other hand is characterized by a strong cultural trend and standardization.

Family faith transmission appears deeply imbedded in the family experience and focussed on meaningful living and good social relationships. It is characterized by a good deal of informality within the parent-child relationships. It provides a view on the family as 'domestic church', and how this functions. This will be further discussed in the context of convictions.

Fifth, to what extent are the present rituals in this population of parents a continuation of the traditions of their respective families of origin? Forty one percent (41%) of husbands and wives said that the traditions of their respective families of origin have equally contributed to the rituals in their own family today, whereas 19% state that these rituals are essentially of their own making. It might come as a surprise that 29% considers their present family rituals to be more similar to that of the husband's family of origine, than to that of the wife (10%). In verifying these figures we found that 48% of the time husbands and wives agreed independently of one another, although it also appears that husbands tend to stress equal heritage when the wives choose their husbands' heritage as most influential. Is it a desire on the wives' part to engage their husbands in ritual activities as the earlier mentioned results on type of participation might indicate?

5.2. Convictions
Parents rated a total of twenty eight convictions in answer to the question to what extent the particular family activity under consideration expressed each conviction.

The results and discussion that follow consider primarily the five highest and the three lowest ranked convictions (See Table 3). They fall respectively within the upper quarter and the lower quarter of the actual range of means for all twenty eight convictions from 6.36 to 1.58.

5.2.1. The nature of the Christian convictions
First, parents clearly want to convey to their children that 'life is worth living', that 'good relations with other people are important', that 'religion is relevant to every day life', that 'life is satisfying', and that 'life has a meaning and we know what it is'. These convictions have a low range of variances, i.e. about half of that of other convictions. They are therefore clustered responses, and subsequently the agreement between subjects is high. Parents want to share an optimistic, meaningful and satisfying view on life in which good human relationships play an important part. Religion is not something apart from daily living. Any of these convictions could be held by non-Christian or non-religious people, or appear to be cultural values as

115

Table 3
Rank order of conviction means for couples
within the upper- and lower quarters of the scoring range

Convictions	Mean	Standard Deviation	Variance
16. Life is worth living	6.36	.89	.80
26. Good relations with others is important	6.29	1.12	1.27
25. Religion is relevant to every day life	5.93	1.38	1.93
15. Life is satisfying	5.91	1.22	1.50
17. Life has meaning and we know what it is	5.88	1.23	1.52
****************			
18. Doctrine source of conflict	2.45	1.74	3.03
8. Religion deals with supernatural	2.35	1.70	2.89
19. Death should be feared	1.58	1.03	1.07

Kerkhofs (1988) suggests. This does not invalidate these values as Gospel values, but 'doctrine' oriented convictions are conspicuous by their absence from what parents do in family religious rituals.

Second, this understanding is contextualized when those convictions are taken into account that reached the top quarter of potential scores (i.e. above 5.15):

"It is important to be a member of the Christian Community (Church)."
"Prayer is of tremendous importance."

116

"Good works and good deeds are the behavioral dimension of religion."
"Talking to people and seeing how they live is an important social dimension of religion."

"Our particular Christian Church denomination is a source of religious truth and values."
"Knowledge about our religion is a high value."
"Nothing on this planet is more important than human life."
"We believe in and are committed to a Supreme Being (as compared to belief in a set of morals, a Basic Principle etc.)."

In the religious rituals of families the emphasis is upon human and life values, rather than on specific 'Christian' or doctrine inspired beliefs. However, 'to be a member of the Christian Community', 'Prayer is of great importance', 'the Church as source of truth and values' and 'the commitment to a Supreme Being' are not absent from the parents' consciousness; they rank respectively sixth, seventh, tenth and thirteenth and function as background for what is emphasized in family religious rituals. However, convictions in this secondary category have a greater variance in scores, indicating that the agreement among subjects is less clustered and therefore weakened in its generalized meaning.

Third, faith transmission in the family by the medium of family rituals takes on an affective and experiential character. It is thus differentiated from faith values transmitted through the institutional church in other ways such as Word and Sacrament or religious instruction. They should be viewed as complimentary of each other, and in need of each other. This raises important questions. How can the Christian community assist families in profiting from this mutual complementarity? How can it encourage parents to develop a broader range of family ritual activities that links the 'domestic Church', the 'Church in miniature' with the larger Christian community? This becomes especially urgent for those families that are 'non'-involved. The nature and characteristics of 'popular religion' might provide direction in this search.

Fourth, the lowest ranked convictions also add a flavour to the faith focus of family rituals in this study. "Death should be feared" is no preoccupation at all, as it is in direct opposition to the values of meaning and satisfaction in life which parents want to convey. The low score given to "religion deals with the supernatural rather than with this world" is consistent with the vision of the parents that "religion is relevant to every day life", i.e. to the here-and-now of living. The low score assigned to "church doctrine is a source of conflict, bewilderment, and disturbance" indicates that doctrinal statements play no major role in the intention parents have for the meaning of their family religious rituals.

Yet, as Christian doctrine related convictions such as "Jesus is our Saviour", "the Bible is a source of God's truth", "there is a continual personal existence after death", and "the relationship of good and evil to God and our own efforts", remained all in the middle range of scores obtained in this study of parents' intentions with rituals, we must conclude that family religious rituals have a sharply defined 'people oriented' focus, and are less suitable to conveying 'doctrinal' truths.

Fifth, although our results indicated some significant differences between fathers and mothers on the intensity with which certain convictions are held, these did not change their overall ranking by couples and do not add much to our conclusions.

6. Summary

This study examined the relationship between subject selected family religious rituals and the intended intergenerational transmission of twenty-eight Christian convictions for thirty-one Church involved married couples. It was found that, although 'high' in ritualization, these families maintained a fair balance between 'tradition' and 'spontaneity'. In various ways it appeared that family rituals and their intended faith transmission are deeply imbedded in the family experience itself and focussed on meaningful living and good social relationships as Gospel values. 'Doctrine' related convictions form the context and the background for these rituals and need to rely upon other media of transmission either in the family or through the resources of the Christian community. These results are consistent with those of earlier studies on intergenerational transmission of values. It is suggested that 'popular religion' and the family as the 'domestic Church' offer important perspectives on faith transmission through family rituals.

FROM CHRISTIAN TO PSYCHOLOGICAL INTERPRETATION

RITUALS AND SOCIAL STRUCTURE: THE MORAL DIMENSION

K. Helmut Reich

1. Introduction

'A vision of alternative possible moral worlds brought about by the experience of ritual', that is the theme of this chapter. Let me focus the discussion right away: the world-wide spiritual communitas of the Live Aid rock marathon in London and Philadelphia on the 13th and 14th of July 1985 will be used as a central example for the thesis that such a vision is possible even in modern society. The importance of this issue is underlined by the seemingly anomic character of today's western society. Does not the very existence of the 'values clarification' movement imply a loss of common values that are accepted by all as being self-evident? In fact, whereas such issues as solidarity with the Third World or protection of the environment are being discussed (and some action is taken), a world-wide conscience-driven collective application of the 'Golden Rule' to the needy across national or continental borders, and to nature (see e.g. Kerstiens, 1987:138-40), hardly appears to be a central thrust of present-day public activity. Before discussing the Live Aid example, a theoretical framework concerning the effect of rituals on morality and symbolic rituals encountered in various social structures will be put in place.

2. Moral aspects of ritual

A ritual here is understood as a series of (formal) acts that are repeated in a more or less fixed manner. In one view (Durkheim's a.o.), rituals serve to maintain - or if need be to restore - social cohesion. Not infrequently they involve a recollection of earlier spiritual, moral or social experiences by those who have experienced them in the past, and serve simultaneously to transmit such experiences to the 'newcomers'. Recall, for instance, the pledge to the national flag in US schools: "I pledge allegiance to the flag of the United States of America and to the Republic for which it stands: One nation under God with liberty and justice for all." From this perspective rituals are an aspect of 'social engineering' by means of the emotional experience of a charismatic leader, of intense fellowship, and/or through the psychological reinforcement effect due to repetition. Seen in this way, rituals per se are morally neutral. As far as the outside world is concerned, it depends on the morality of the leaders and the content of the message whether the effect on the participants is positive or negative. For instance, the intense 'fellowship' of Ku-Klux-Klan type rituals has led to an increase in injustices of. class society. Many persons are aware of the deadly sequels of the rituals of certain football fans (Richards, 1985), not to mention the acts of concentration camp doctors or other torturers who were introduced to these atrocities by diabolic initiation rites (Vieth, 1988, ch.4: "The devil made me do it: Demonic power and human responsibility"; Sabini & Silver, 1982, ch.4: "On destroying the innocent with a clear conscience"). More positive examples are discussed below.

If that were all there is to say, how could the vision of alternative moral worlds be brought about? One obvious way would be to experience the rituals of a rather different community. Getting immersed - as a westerner - for instance, into a non-Christian, non-Cartesian culture is bound to enlarge one's moral horizon. ("Non-Christian" may mean, for instance, that the very idea of "Thou shalt love thy neighbour as thyself" (Matthew 22:39) does not exist, or that suicide is a normal, *socially approved* act - be it as an honourable issue to an otherwise unsolvable situation, or, in old age, as a means to prevent using up scarce resources. "Not-Cartesian" may involve a non-separation between subject and object and/or use of a non-Aristotelian logic, e.g. no 'exclusion of the third', no systemic thinking.) However, the thrust of this chapter goes in a different direction. The reference is to rituals which are purposely 'designed' to permit experimenting with alternative moral orientations within one's own cultural horizons.

In their *Theories of moral development* (1985), Rich & DeVitis state the following: "*Moral development* refers to growth of the individual's ability to distinguish right from wrong, to develop a system of ethical values, and to learn to act morally" (1985:7, emphasis in the original). How does such a development come about? As in other cases, the ingredients are opportunities for exercising and thence gaining experience, reflecting upon such acquired experience, perhaps encountering a person or persons serving as causa exemplaris, and, of course, having sufficient motivation to invest time and energy in such a development.

Green (1988:134) claims (controversially) that "ritual is a powerful means by which human communities convey to their members an understanding of the basis and logic of moral reasoning". Extending the work of Turner (see also Boudewijnse, *The ritual studies of Victor Turner: an anthropological approach and its psychological impact*, in this volume), Green argues that the "liminal communitas" encountered in a ritual represents "an experiential vivification of the moral point of view", provided the participants relinquish social distinctions and advantages during the ritual and "perceive the essential equality of persons that must be respected by any social order that makes an appeal to moral principles ... Ritual thus communicates the easily forgotten lesson that self-renunciation on everyone's part through moral commitment is the necessary precondition of collective flourishing" (Green, 1988:142). Implied in these and similar statements are at least two large classes of 'moral worlds': those with a 'collective conscience' feeling explicitly responsible for the common good (at least in principle), and those based on a world view where it is fully up to the individual to carve out his piece of the pie (at best according to rules aiming at a minimum level of 'orderliness' in an all-out competition).

3. Mechanisms and processes at work

As Weinreich-Haste (1986, 1990) points out, affect may play an important role in moral reasoning and engaging in a moral responsability in that it may motivate an individual going through a key experience. Living rituals are affect-laden almost by defenition, and in principle can thus act as a trigger for moral change. Furthermore, Weinreich-Haste indicates three important elements which, according to her, influence responsible moral action: (1) a creative analyzing capability, (2) the conviction that succesful moral action is possible, and (3) a personal commitment.

The first element has one dimension that is largely independent of a given individual's level of cognition, and in particular of moral judgment (Oser & Reich, 1990), viz. the sheer imagination of what an alternative moral world could look like, what could be done to make it become real, etc.. Such an imagination is not possessed abundantly by every individual. Here ritual comes in as follows: As we are discussing acts that are repeated in a more or less unchanged manner, they need not be reinvented by every single participant. In all likelihood, the most imaginative will contribute visionary aspects to the ritual. They will also be motivated to further the adhesion of other to this vision. Whereas participants to whom the alternative moral world is relatively foreign might not have been able to invent the (new) ritual, they will nevertheless at least sense what it attempts to convey, and may even dimly recognize (parts of) this message cognitively. In time they may come to understand it more or less fully, notably as a result of continued stimulation and an adequate effort.

The second element involves both the belief that this possibility exists and knowledge of how to seize it effectively. Again, in a ritual this can be made clear, at least by implication. Not only will the presence of persons with relevant experience and the sheer numbers of participants help, but the experience of togetherness, of positive feelings may also influence the judgment favourably (Schwarz, 1988).

The third element differs from person to person; not everybody is a Mahatma Ghandi or a Martin Luther King. However, in a joint enterprise there is room for many types of engagements - as in the very ritual we are discussing - thereby at least facilitating personal engagement.

4. Ritual and social structure

To be accepted - let alone to be effective - a ritual has to meet certain conditions. For Geertz the effect 'ideally' is as follows: "(when) the ritual (has) ended, (and he has) returned again to the common-sense world, a man (and presumably a woman too, K.H.R.) is ... changed. And as he (she) is changed, so also is the common-sense world, for it is now seen as but a partial form of a wider reality which corrects and completes it" (Geertz, 1973b:122). For this to happen, the moods and motivations which the symbols imbedded in the ritual induce in the participants, as well as the general conceptions of the order of existance which they formulate for the participants, must meet and reinforce one another. In other words, these symbols are at the same time models of the world, and models for acting in this world (ibid.:112). Thus they symbolize both a given world view - the picture people have of the way things are in sheer actuality, their most comprehensive ideas of order - and people's ethos - the tone, character and quality of their life, its moral and aesthetic style and mood (ibid.:89). In the optimum case (of a transmission in the traditional mode as distinct from a cognitive mode, K.H.R.), the conceptions conveyed by the symbol(s) have such an aura of factuality that the moods and motivations seem uniquely realistic (ibid.:90). This is important, because "probably the overwhelming majority of mankind are continually drawing normative conclusions from factual premises ... despite refined, in their own terms impeccable reflections by professional philosophers on the 'naturalistic fallacy'" (ibid.:141). As Geertz remarks, the need for a metaphysical grounding for values seems to vary widely from culture to culture and from person to person, but the tendency to desire some sort of factual basis for one's commitments seems practically universal (ibid.:131). Notice also, how often in everyday life factual explanations - instead of moral justifications - are given and accepted as sufficient reason to 'justify' one's 'moral' behaviour, for instance "I forgot" or "I overslept".

Particularly in times of social change the optimum case referred to above may not be within reach. Geertz (1973b:143-169) and Douglas (1973) discuss examples from the Javanese and Navajo history, respectively, which illustrate the effect of social change on world views and ritual. Douglas also hypothesizes that particular world view contents match particular social structures. For instance, if the family and neighbourhood relations are characterized by stable, close mutual

124

interdependence, she expects a rather structured 'cosmic' world view where each individual is assigned his or her position, the moral order is incorporated into that world view, and an offender is 'automatically' turned upon and in the limit excluded from the community. Every son and daughter is brought up knowing his or her position and taking pride in acting according to the moral code conveyed by the symbolic rituals. In contrast, if family and neighbourhood relations are loose, and a 'personal' stance is adopted, Douglas expects the 'factuality' (that the symbolic ritual conveys) to have to do with engagement for the (world-wide) common good and/or personal succes, because a personal justification has to start there (the 'positional' justifications being rejected on principle). Dubach (1989) reports that modern Swiss parents advocating the 'personal' world view, favour as their educational goals prosocial behaviour and critical openness over conformity.

5. Symbolic communication

Many prominent examples of symbolic behaviour from ancient and modern times can be given, think e.g. of the 'tessara hospitalis' - the little tablet which in classical times was divided and kept by the guest and host until they met again - or of the modern baptism candle which is lit for the baptised at every anniversary of the baptism, or consider, for instance, Vàclav Havel and his way of communicating (before and after he became president).

Jetter (1986) summarizes the fourfold aspect of symbolic communication as follows. *First*, communication by way of symbols is simple, simpler than with equivalent, elaborated words. Symbols can communicate something to many persons immediately, irrespective of her or his cognitive level, age, language, etc.. *Second*, such communication is potentially complex in that persons may bring into the symbol the entire world, general and personal history, birth and death, etc.. *Third*, such a communication is overarching in as much as it expresses more than can be done with words (because of taboos, of the limits of verbal expressability, or because society is not yet aware of an issue or not yet ready to thematize it). *Fourth*, symbolic communication can be directive, in so far as it invites one to cooperate in the realization of the world view expressed by the symbol. In other words, effective symbols are a bridge from this side of the river to the dimly visible embankment on the other side.

To summarize: An effective symbolic ritual immediately evokes something for many people, representing a world view of undubitable factuality, engendering moods and motivations which resonate with that world view, and carrying over such moods and motivations into everyday life. The ritual we are discussing provides opportunities for perceiving at least one different possible moral world, for manifesting and advancing in one's moral quest, for experiencing support of a non-conventional moral stance, for affirming one's values and practising their application. To be labeled 'positive' in our global village, the ritual should increase moral sensitivity, as well as a sense of world-wide communality and connectedness, of the dignity of every living being.

With all the elements in place, we can now turn to rock music festivals and to the Live Aid rock marathon of 1985 in particular.

6. The live aid rock marathon of 1985

6.1 In what ways are rock music festivals ritualistic?

A difference in behaviour at classical concerts and at rock music concerts appeared in the 1950s. It was already well developed when more than 400 000 fans listened from the 15th to the 17th of August 1969 to 32 bands and soloists at the 'Woodstock Music and Arts Fair' (which actually took place 50 miles south at Bethel). Here certain attitudes freely expressed themselves, expectations were shared and a myth was enacted, that of a world where love, not war, reigned supreme. The attitude was essentially anti-'positional'. In line with the new style, the participants were not seated in classical concert style on reserved seats, but crowded around the stage instead. As is well known, dress and general behaviour at the two types of concerts were - and still are - just as different. Thus large-scale rock music festivals already had about them an air of a "liminal communitas": there existed a strong spiritual connectedness among the participants (who behaved nevertheless as individualists) that set them apart from society at large. As one of the consequences, the rules of everyday life do not quite seem to apply under these circumstances.

While the characteristics of a communitas were maintained, certain rituals were developed in subsequent rock concerts. Foremost, these concern the kind and intensity of the communication between the performers and the participants. They have been ritualized in that participants know what to expect and how to behave. And this does not simply mean clapping hands as an expression of applause. Rather, the ritual includes raising arms (and possibly holding hands), moving them in tune with the rhythm, joining in by singing at least the refrain. (If the soloist is particularly popular, the participants may even sing the refrain on their own). When the music turns 'romantic' (ballad style) the ritual changes: As the lights dim, participants 'spontaneously' light their cigarette lighter, or whatever serves the same function, to express response and togetherness. The transmission to the newcomers and the psychological reinforcement of the rock concert experience does not only come about by the repetition of these 'formal' acts, but also by the repeated singing of the refrain(s). Most of this already having happened in London and Philadelphia, what distinguished the Live Aid rock marathon (Parry, 1985)?

6.2 What was different compared to other rock festivals?

First, the sixteen hour Live Aid rock marathon was planned primarily not for the individual enjoyment and togetherness of the immediate participants (although, of course, that was part of it), but as a demonstration of moral and material solidarity with the starving children of the Third World, particularly in Africa. A target of £10 million was set, which was surpassed five times (so that the result corresponded to about 1.5 percent of Ethiopia's annual gross domestic product).

Second, the marathon went on - partly simultaneously - in London (72 000 participants), in Philadelphia (90 000), and subsidiarily in other cities such as Moscow. It was broadcast by 14 satellites to 500 million television sets, and an estimated audience of 1.5 thousand million.

Third, some of the biggest names in pop music - The Who, David Bowie, Dire Straits, Spandau Ballet, and Elvis Costello in London, and Joan Baez, Madonna, Mick Jagger, Tina Turner and Bob Dylan in Philadelphia, not forgetting stars like Lionel Richie (USA for Africa)- participated and donated their earnings to the good cause.

Fourth, the bands and soloists were on stage not one after another as usual, but - at least for a time - together. For this occasion the microphone was handed by one soloist to the next.

Fifth, the text of the refrain of the keynote song was as follows (regrettably without the music):

> "We are the world, we are the children,
> we are the ones who make a brighter day,
> so let's start giving.
> There is a choice we're making, we're saving our own lives.
> It's true, we make a better day, just you and me."

The main distinguishing features thus being clear, let us analyze them in terms of the theories outlined above, notably those of Weinreich-Haste, Geertz, and Douglas, and of the reviews by Rich & DeVitis, and Jetter.

6.3 How does this vision of an alternative possible moral world come about?

Which alternative moral world? "There is a choice we're making" puts the issue directly in front of each participant. But there is also support, additional 'scaffolding', spelling out the moral world-view commended by the organizers: "There comes a time when we heed a certain call, when the world must come together as one"; "It's time to lend a hand so they know that someone cares". And, of course, "We are the children". This is no doubt to be understood as an identification with the hungry children world-wide, an expression of solidarity with them (just as John F. Kennedy's "Ich bin ein Berliner" expressed his solidarity with the inhabitants of Berlin). Indeed, can one not interpret the passage "we're saving our own lives" precisely as an intense identification with the dying children in the hunger-stricken areas? The official program contained a cartoon declaring that Africans are "our roots, our brothers, our sisters that are dying of starvation".

To appreciate fully the unrestricted solidarity with the needy children expressed by the lyrics, compare them, for instance, with the French national anthem "Allons enfants de la patrie, le jour de gloire est arrivé". Those are lines from a different era and occasion, of course, (and "enfants" is used metaphorically rather than literally), but do they not stand for a more or less exclusive nation-state mentality as yet so widely present in our supposedly global village? Still, those lines are not objectionable per se (the aim not being a uniform world state, but rather a political construction where allegiance to one's region, one's country, and to the world and their respective inhabitants complement each other), they simply cannot express today's wider vision. All this becomes even clearer, when compared with what is described as one of the most popular ritual chants of football fans, given here in the Aston Villa version: "We hate Nottingham Forest, we hate Albion too, we hate Birmingham City, but Villa we love you" (Richards, 1985:16) - letting alone the refrain of another football chant "You're gonna get your fucking head kicked in" (ibid.:20).

To develop a system of ethical values; to affirm them; to be convinced that moral action is possible. Whereas conceptually different, these three issues are discussed together because they are interrelated at the participants' and at the performer's level. What a magnificent causa exemplaris! Here are the idolized pop singers - some of them not known to be particularly interested in other people's difficulties, nor overly eager to help them - enthusiastically at work to further an altruistic common cause, supporting and expressing whole-heartedly values like solidarity with the needy and commitment to help them (where the governments concerned seemed unwilling or unable to do the job). And they radiate confidence that hunger can be beaten. Bob Geldof, the chief organizer, earlier on had persuaded 40 pop artists to make a recording (of which an £ 8 million profit had gone to relieve famine by the time of the Live Aid marathon). His basic organization "Band Aid" was ready to buy and distribute food. And did not the whole style of the marathon demonstrate that the organizers knew what modern technology can do: The giant screen on which the bands and soloists appeared from the local stage, from the 'other' continent, from Moscow and other cities; a performer singing and leaving by helicopter to catch a Concorde flight for crossing the Atlantic so as to appear in the USA at the same local time (the absolute time difference being five hours); the world-wide transmission of the marathon, etc.?

"To learn to act morally and to commit oneself". In the short run, any money pledge made had to be honoured, in the longer term no doubt more help was needed. How was this to be accomplished? Again, one example came from the stage. Here they were all together, the rugged, competitive individualists, used to fending for themselves, but now sharing the microphone or even singing 'with one voice' "We are the world ...". Just take this symbolic act of passing the microphone to a neighbour (who normally is a competitor). Does this not evoke sporting events - for instance the carrying of the Olympic flame from Olympia to the Games - or religious rituals like the passing of the bread and the cup?

That performers and participants (in the stadiums and to considerable extent at home in front of the TV screen) did commit themselves was evident even to a sceptical journalist (Coleman, 1985): "You have to be a bit amazed and abashed at the sheer, sweet, innocent, hopeful, impossible altruism of the whole idea, and of the thousands and thousands of people in that (Wembley) stadium. Christian missionaries are long out of fashion, but I believe some of these people have the same hope of a perfect world". The British overseas development minister, Mr. Timothy Raison stated: "I think that to have people mobilized in this way is magnificent. It shows that they really do care passionately" (Ezard, 1985).

The conceptions conveyed by the symbols have such an aura of factuality that the moods and motivations seem uniquely realistic. Even without the transmission onto the giant screen of an interview about the feeding of children at an Ethiopian refugee camp, and the singing of those children (Coleman, 1985), who could doubt that it was all sheer factuality, that "it's true, we make a better day, just you and me"? Apart from the music and the lyrics, how can it not be emotionally gripping to know that for each participant in the stadiums 10 000 people sitting in front of their TV receiver joined in and many also pledged financial support? What a world-wide community! On the other hand, notice the person-to-person touch: "... just you and me". Clearly, the underlying world view is of the personal, not the positional type.

The various aspects of symbolic communication. This symbolic ritual immediately gave something to many, many people. No doubt there were those who had primarily joined in for the music, but who nevertheless got caught up in it all even if they did not understand the lyrics. There were those who wanted to be part of the event and what it stood for, there were those who were open to the symbolism and enjoyed it, and there was mental food for those who are in the habit of reflecting on things, such as the role of music as one of a small number of activities which can bridge generations and continents, or the question of what makes a singer a moral leader. No doubt, some had memories of previous occasions, others thought of future events.

On return into the common-sense world, a participant is changed. Let me report about one witness at least. An American colleague told me that before the marathon his adolescent daughter had been involved exclusively in things like designer clothes, but afterwards became interested in the Third World and its problems. One may also note that the type of event we are discussing continues, albeit on a smaller scale. I only mention two occurences. The "Moscow Music Peace Festival" was held in the Lenin stadium on the 12th and 13th of August 1989 with the express aim of contributing to "drug prevention, nuclear disarmament, and the end of nationalism, racism and chauvinism" (Keller, 1989). A mammoth concert (by local standards) was held in the ice skating stadium of Fribourg on the 11th of May 1989. Abbé Pierre and Dom Helder Camara appealed to the several thousand participants to commit themselves to solidarity with the needy. Four hundred performers in the orchestra and the choir translated this appeal into music for all "from 7 to 77 years of age" (Stettler, 1989) with such works of art as "La joie partagée" (shared joy) and "La symphonie des deux mondes" (symphony of the two worlds). It is also noteworthy that the children of the Gardner Street primary school in Los Angeles greeted Michael Jackson by singing "We are the world ..." when he visited his old school on the 11th of October 1989 for the inauguration of the renovated auditorium (now called Michael-Jackson-Auditorium).

7. Concluding remarks

I hope to have shown, at least by way of one example, how a symbolic ritual can open the door to the vision of a possible alternative moral world. I write 'can' deliberately. Obviously there also exist other motives for participating in the type of event we have been discussing: because it is an IN-affair, because it makes you feel good to be generous to others who are worse off (and to be seen doing so), etc.. Not all seed will bring forth fruit (Matthew 13: 3-8), but that is no reason for not sowing. However, how is one to explain this diversity of responses? A particular form of reasoning seems involved.

We probably have here a case of thinking in terms of complementarity (Oser & Reich, 1987; Reich, 1989; Reich & Oser, 1990), of 'circular' complementarity to be precise. Such thinking involves the coordination of at least two descriptions of the same phenomenon that belong to different category systems, to different academic disciplines. (In contrast, in a case of 'parallel' complementarity, both 'theses' belong to the same category system, the same discipline - as, for instance, the theses of the wave-like and the particle-like behaviour of light. In such a case the mounting evidence in the end usually convinces the proponents - possibly after a paradigm change - that both theses are needed to explain the phenomenon and the subsequent work concentrates on the 'how': in what ways are the theses interrelated, how does the use of one limit the use of the other?). Here the question is: "How do rock-music and the moral atmosphere conjoin?"

In the case of circular complementarity of any two (or more) theses, this complementarity need not be evident at all, but must be justified. (This involves a circular investigative procedure in that any interrelation between the theses, any dependence of their respective explanatory weight on circumstances, etc., is brought to light by means of iterative 'boot-strapping'. Starting with some more or less well founded presuppositions, the phenomenon is examined in terms of the two theses. The findings are used to improve the presuppositions for the second round of examinations, and so on. As an example of circular complementarity, MacKay (1974:236) discusses Josephs biography (Genesis 50: 15-20) as seen by his brothers (a down-to-earth event) and by himself (part of God's plan). When this method of justification fails, a 'yoking together' of the two theses may simply be considered illogical, incompatible or even absurd by the existing culture. But even if the case is clearly one of parallel complementarity, i.e. both theses illuminate each other - at least according to some recognized experts- not everybody may agree, notably on account of a lack of motivation, because of an opposing logic or philosophical root metaphor, or because of an incomplete cognitive development. In fact, complementarity reasoning is not necessarily 'natural'. One-sided decisions, static thought, and at the limit the acceptance of a stable dynamic equilibrium are psychologically less trying behaviours (Reich, in press).

Returning to the case we are discussing, it has already been shown in what ways the rock marathon and a moral world-view were interrelated, and under which circumstances the one or the other aspect carries more weight in explaining participants' behaviour. These observations need yet to be generalized by analyzing similar events such as the Moscow Music Peace Festival, etc.. Other examples of symbolic rituals with moral objectives that come to mind (in the industrialized world) are human chains during gatherings for world peace, or a series of Sundays without motor traffic on the roads, or even fasting weeks (Müller, 1988) and world-wide non-smoking days (as organized by the World Health Organization). To be scientifically convincing, the theses put forward here should, of course, be backed by thorough, extended empirical research.

In this context one might also think of the moral dimension of the symbolic rituals led, for instance, by Mahatma Ghandi or by Martin Luther King, which were primarily aimed at *political* change. However, was it not an important part of the task of those leaders (and of others in comparable situations) to present a vision of an alternative *possible moral* world to the participants, a world of human dignity and freedom? Who can doubt that the symbolic rituals performed by thousands of people - notably in churches, on city squares and in the streets of Poland, Hungary, the Soviet Union and recently of the DDR and of Czechoslovakia - have a moral dimension? And that at least some of the mechanisms and processes we have been discussing are at work there? In fact, is it possible to imagine a more extraordinary liminal communitas than the Berliners from all over the city standing on the Berlin Wall, or a more impressive symbolic ritual than radiant people chipping away at that wall and passing the pick, the chisel or the hammer, to a neighbour? It is a matter of debate to what extent these mechanisms and processes ensure political success (as distinct from inner moral change) when facing a Stalin, Hitler or a Pol Pot; the action "sister-city" between Rumanian villages and cities and their West-European counterparts has probably contributed to the fall of Ceaucescu's regime.

A denial of cognitive value to spiritual experience is one of the tenets of our 'Age of Reason'. However, even natural scientists challenge such a view. Physicist Davies (1983:229) writes: "It is my deep conviction that only by understanding the world in all its many aspects-

reductionist and holist, mathematical and poetical, through forces, fields and particles as well as through good and evil - that we will come to understand ourselves and the meaning behind this universe, our home."

To benefit fully from the ritual, one presumably has to immerse oneself into it at three levels: the spiritual, the emotional, and the poetic. To do this in the most 'rewarding' manner may require to be adept "at seeing the same set of events from multiple perspectives or stances and at entertaining the results, so to speak, as alternative possible worlds" (Bruner, 1986:109), probably again involving complementarity reasoning.

As regards the moral dimension, is not one of the present challenges as follows? Given that responsible, active moral world-views are basically of two types - those stressing the 'good life' of the individual and those stressing the 'good life' of the community - the obvious difficulty (particularly in a non-homogenous society) is to 'combine' the two into an overarching view. This further case of complementarity reasoning involves a detailed insight into how individual good and collective good interact, limit each other, and have different weights depending on circumstances.

Even if not yet a paramount feature of western culture, complementarity reasoning will become increasingly useful in the global village. Cities with a homogenous culture and population such as Bergen (Norway), Dublin, Florence, or Kyoto will be more of a rarity, and cosmopolitan cities such as London, Montreal, New York or Singapore more the rule. How will it be possible to preserve an identity in such a pluralistic environment while remaining open to different cultures and persons at the same time? Could not symbolic rituals - far from being obsolete (Heimbrock, 1988) - play an important role for advancing in this direction? In this context remember the spirit behind St. John's cathedral at La Valetta (Malta) with its chapels expressing particularities of the regions 'Provence', 'Auvergne', '(Isle de) France' and 'Bavaria' inside a common framework (De Liederkerke, 1989).

To sum up: It seems not unreasonable to claim that living symbolic rituals can provide an otherwise rather rare experience in the industrialized western world. Such rituals can open new vistas, allow one to be part of a genuine communitas which serves as a causa exemplaris of a society built on truly universal moral principles. Such rituals can provide an opportunity - as well as give emotional support- for one's moral development towards increased moral sensitivity, even if it differs from that of the majority (who do not yet participate in the ritual). Occasionally there may even arise a cognitive challenge within such rituals, which may stimulate the development of moral judgment. A few specific examples seem to support such claims; more systematic research beyond these pointers would be needed for a full confirmation. Speculatively, an important role is ascribed to (implicit) complementarity reasoning for achieving optimum results.

Acknowledgments: I wish to thank Wolfgang Althof for helpful comments on an earlier draft of this chapter, and F.B. Singleton, librarian, for providing the articles from The Guardian.

WOMEN'S RITUALS:
REFLECTIONS ON DEVELOPMENTAL THEORY

Eva Ouwehand

1. Introduction

Religious development is an important theme in the psychology of religion. Inspired by Piaget, people like Oser & Gmünder and Fowler are engaged in the research of the development of religious thinking in the life of children and adults. Erikson has emphasized the importance of ritualization in identity-development. In this article, I will look critically at the above-mentioned theories from the perspective of women's experiences in ritual praxis and ask some questions with respect to their starting-points and conclusions.

In the first part, the aim of female ritual praxis will be at stake: what exactly do women want to achieve or enjoy in the rituals they celebrate? I will sketch in outline the context of their origin: a tendency in the women's liberation movement to recognize the necessity for change, not only politically, but also of the symbolic order, which has a profound influence on the attitudes of human beings. The creation of new religious symbols and rituals is an indication of female protest against a society and religion which are dominated by men, and is at the same time the expression of the search of women for their own identity. Secondly, I'll try to clarify on which points the above-mentioned search of women for inner and outer change challenge the cognitive structural theories of Oser & Gmünder and Fowler. To this end I will make use of the descriptions of rituals such as women have given them to me in interviews, and describe some rituals in which I have participated myself. As an illustration of a subjective ritual theory I will cite one woman (a member of the Women's Spirituality Movement) in particular. As my research on women's rituals is still in an explorative phase, it is not my intention to present a new theoretical framework to interpret rituals, but to point out in which direction psychological development theory might move.

2. Women's rituals

2.1 Two examples

Rituals performed within feminist groups usually do not have a fixed form, although certain elements return in every ritual (formation of a circle, invocation of the power of the four elements, etc.). In Dutch spirituality groups the rituals are usually prepared in advance, each time by (one or two) different women, who look for a form that suits the time of the year and the situation of the group.

Situated in a Dutch training centre where several different courses are being given, during a week devoted to women's spirituality a few lesbian women prepare a ritual which is to be performed with the participating group. The ritual takes place around a fire and commences with a greeting ceremony. Everybody says: "I welcome the Goddess in the shape of my friend ...." and then every woman in her turn says her name. The whole group repeats this name the same way the woman presented herself. One can feel the power of this ceremony, as if every woman is worthy to bear the name of the divine. Then, all are asked to take a branch and to throw it, one by one, into the fire while expressing what one wants to say about lesbian women or expressing something else which occupies one's mind at that moment. It has to be something one wants to be transformed by the fire. The atmosphere is open and women come forward with things that really touch them. Some speak about prejudices against lesbian women, others about their pain and fear, caused by the invisibility of their existence. Some women speak with pride about their 'coming out' as a lesbian. The victims of discrimination against lesbians are commemorated.

A second example is taken from the Dutch weekly magazine *Hervormd Nederland*. During the "Women-Church" conference (in a centre of the Grail-movement in december 1987), the following story was presented. A woman told her group about the years she had had an incestuous relationship with her father. While she was a child, she could only avoid this by hiding herself under a big forsythia-bush. The women in her group then performed a ritual for her and with her. They stood around her in a protective way, each holding a forsythia-branch in the hand. Now the bush had become a hiding-place consisting of the living bodies of her sisters. During the difficult time that followed whilst reliving her past experience, this celebration was printed in her mind as a luminous and powerful moment (Hervormd Nederland 44, July 1988: 20).

2.2 The feminist context of women's rituals
From the seventies onwards women in several European countries and the United States have come together regularly in meeting groups, workshops and courses to create and perform rituals. Although not strictly organized, one can speak in this respect of the *Women's Spirituality Movement* and the *Movement for Feminism and Theology*.

In feminist spirituality women connect spirituality with a feminist view. The designation 'Women's Spirituality Movement' is used for certain specific forms of women's spirituality: the *Goddess-movement, feminist witchcraft,* and a growing interest in rituals, female art, natural symbols, the endeavour to come into contact with deeper layers of the personality and the search for a female or androgynic origin, often based on insights from Jungian psychology. In these forms of feminist spirituality, inner growth - by methods derived from humanist psychology, eastern spirituality and western occultism - is being emphasized. Especially female and natural symbols play an important role in the rituals and expressions of art of these women. Women of the Women's Spirituality Movement find identification-figures in goddesses and heroines of ancient non-Christian cultures, which are reinterpreted and thus form a source of inspiration for the Women's Spirituality Movement. Often, at least in the literature, the Women's Spirituality Movement explicitly rejects the Christian tradition as an essentially sexistic religion (cf. Spretnak, 1982).

The movement of Feminism and Theology, represented by women like Redford Ruether and Schüssler Fiorenza, is more closely connected to the Christian tradition and lays its emphasis more on social justice than on inner growth, although even in feminist theology these two can't be seen as totally opposite. Feminist theology observes the Women's Spirituality Movement from a critical distance.

The rituals that are being performed in these movements can only properly be apprehended against the background of certain tendencies in the women's liberation movement and in the feminist criticism of what they call 'patriarchy'. Women want to liberate themselves from images, values and norms that allow them only a restricted role in society and that limit their possibilities to develop themselves freely. During the initial stages of the second feminist movement, the emphasis was mainly put on the analysis of social structures leading to the inferior position of women, and on political action to change this situation. Today, spirituality has become part of women's strategies to change unjust male/female relationships (King, 1989). In addition to the continuous struggle for economic equality, better child-care, better educational chances for women, and other feminist issues, women try to reshape the *symbolic* order. In feminist spirituality the positive value of earth and nature, corporality and sexuality, the commonness of religious experience and emotionality, and the inseparability of political and personal transformation is being stressed and given form in new ritual and symbolic forms. In this way feminists call into question the dualistic mode of thought which in their eyes has dominated western society and Christianity for centuries.

This cultural protest of women must be seen in the context of a broader field of changes in the religious domain, which has become especially clear since the counter cultural revolution of the sixties. In the seventies the *New Age Movement, holism* and the *Women's Spirituality Movement* emerged from it. In the brief outline of this article it is impossible to present a historical overview of these developments (cf. Hummel, 1980; Chowdhury, 1986; Schorsch, 1988).

2.3 The aim of feminist rituals

What exactly do women have in mind when performing their rituals? From the scarce literature on the subject and the interviews I had with women from the Women's Spirituality Movement, a few often returning subjects can be identified. In feminist rituals women are searching for their own *identity* as a woman or a human being in a society dominated by men and 'masculine' values. The recovery and confirmation of 'female' *power* is an important element in feminist rituals. For centuries women have been denied access to power. Now that they do find access the very meaning of the concept is being changed. In feminist rituals power is not seen as power of people *over* each other, but as a lifegiving force, an empowering presence *for* each other. The feminist slogan that the personal is political can also be applied to feminist spirituality. Women want to accomplish a profound *transformation* of society and of the existing religious traditions being part of it, but this can only be achieved by a profound *change of consciousness* as the ultimate ground and matrix of women's experiences. As internalized misogynist images from the Christian tradition form a hindrance to personal growth, transformation of religious institutions will be difficult. Feminists acknowledge the necessity of *female bonding* in a community, not only in order to be able to continue the political struggle for equality, but also to help each other face the fear and uncertainty which inevitably arise when deeply rooted value-systems begin to change (see also Christ, 1979; Redford Ruether, 1985; Schüssler Fiorenza, 1983, 1984; K. Turner, 1982).

As has been said before, women have discovered the necessity to change the symbolic order as well as the social order. The images and symbols with which they were brought up, today can no longer express their experiences as women adequately; they are even felt as impediments to their spiritual quest. This has resulted in an explosion of experiments with symbols and rituals which can express the changing relationship between men and women and can, at the same time, give direction to the whole process of change. In my opinion, research on goddesses, heroines, matriarchies, women in the scripture and the

138

history of Christianity, in many cases is not as much an attempt to reconstruct history, as an indication of the search of women to find their own identity as women and to construct new models of a society based on justice. The meaning of the concepts 'masculinity' and 'femininity' is shifting; the feminist movement has shown the impossibility of linking these concepts to a 'natural' order. In this connection the concepts of *corporality* and *sexuality* are being revalued in feminist spirituality, not only by considering their meaning, but also by actually experiencing body and sexuality in rituals.

2.4 Women's rituals: protest and quest

On the one hand, feminist rituals have to be interpreted as a sign of protest, as has been said before. The two examples mentioned both contain a critical element towards the usual images of women in our society. These examples, like others, such as menstruation rituals that are being performed in the Women's Spirituality Movement, can only properly be understood against the background of feminist criticism of pornography and sexual violence, of the distortion of sexuality into a commercial product, of the taboo against menstruation and of the hetero-sexual norm which is dominant in western society and particularly in western religion. Celebrating with the whole body and expressing one's feelings corporally instead of just sitting quietly on a bench while listening to what the preacher has to say - as is usual in most white middle- and upperclass churches in the West - can be seen as a sign of protest against the body/mind dualism which has prevailed in the main currents within Christian tradition.

On the other hand, in the above-mentioned rituals women *celebrate* their female bodily existence, their sensuality and erotism. They recover the power and energy their bodies contain. They try to heal their wounded sexuality and transform the negative images they have internalized during their personal development into positive ones. In short: in feminist rituals the reliving of past negative experiences of being a woman is at stake in order to develop a positive self-image as a woman, of which one's own body forms a substantial part.

The question is: how can we relate the above-mentioned experiences of women to the cognitive structural theories of Oser & Gmünder (1984) and Fowler (1981, 1988) or to the psychoanalytic identity-development theory of Erikson. Each of these theories illuminates quite different aspects of religious development. Oser & Gmünder, following Kohlberg's track, try to discern different cognitive structural stages of the development of religious judgements on the basis of interviews about certain dilemmas. In their theory, religious judgement refers to the ultimate meaning of life.

Although Fowler is greatly indebted to cognitive psychology, he attempts to integrate the psychoanalytic insights of Erikson into his theory by taking the concept of 'trust' as the basis for his understanding of human faith. In Fowler's theory, faith as 'meaning making' is not just a cognitive process; it implies trust in other people, mutual relationships in a community which are deepened and formed by a common loyalty to what Fowler calls 'centers of supraordinate values'. In the course of the development of his theory, Fowler broadens his perspective in an attempt to avoid the one-sidedness of theorizing by means of the logic of rational certainty of the natural sciences. In his opinion the mind has different modes of constitutive-knowing, one of which is connected with the right hemisphere of the brain and is expressed in art and faith. The development of these more affective, imaginative, and holistic modes of knowing follow another logic, the logic of conviction, which, in Fowler's view, is complementary to the logic of rational certainty.

Erikson regards religious development from again a different angle. In *Toys and Reasons* (1977) he connects the individual life-cycle and social institutions with the concept of 'ritualization'. In each stage of human development, play and ritual take different forms in order for human beings to grasp reality, to feel at home in an otherwise immense and chaotic world and to come to terms with the ground-conflict which accompanies each specific stage. In daily rituals the child is also being initiated into the world-view and social institutions of the community. The different forms of adult ritualization - like for example trial in court, sports, theater and war - all originate in different stages of ritualization in the life-cycle.

The question arises: can we interpret women's rituals in the light of these theories? Should we for example interpret these, to a great extent spontaneously arising rituals of protest - which at the same time express women's search for a new identity - as an expression of the "role confusion" that characterizes adolescence in Erikson's view? Erikson speaks in this respect about the inclination of adolescents towards improvised anti-rituals in order to get a grasp on the tension between the search for one's own identity and the confirmation of existing models offered by the community (Erikson, 1977). Also, should we regard a "herbal charm" which is performed in the Women's Spirituality Movement as a ritual of magic (Starhawk, 1979), or as an indication that the performers are in the "do-ut-des" stage such as described by Oser & Gmünder? In my view this way of dealing with women's experiences doesn't lead to a proper understanding of female ritual praxis. Even within those theories, when looking at aspects of the religious development of women other than ritual, women would appear to be more mature than I presented in the above-mentioned examples. Although the theories of Oser & Gmünder, Fowler and Erikson each emphasize different aspects of development, they agree with each other in one respect: they describe stages of development without taking into account the self-understanding of the people researched. My main criticism of these theories is, that the meaning *women* attach to religious concepts like ritual or religious development or quest, is not related to the definitions given by the researcher. In the next paragraph I will give a more detailed explanation of my criticism.

3. Cognitive structural theories on religious development: some questions
In the field of research on religious development an extensive body of literature has come into being during the past few years. There are three issues concerning the theories of Oser & Gmünder and Fowler which I would like to mention here.

First of all, the relationship between religious judgement and religious action will be questioned. My focus will be on ritual action and in this respect the subject corporality - which often returns in literature about feminist spirituality and in interviews with women of the Women's Spirituality Movement - will be discussed. The question is in what way corporality influences mental processes and how the relationship between mind and body must be seen.

Secondly the question is put forward whether the separation which is made within cognitive structural theories of development between structure and content, is a valid one. If it isn't, their claim of universal validity is untenable.

The third question asked is which relationship exists between individual religious images and the social context in which they arise. This subject is closely linked to the structure/content problem. Following current developments in the comparative study of religion and cultural anthropology, in which the biased look of western researchers is being criticized and the universal validity of theories that explain religious phenomena is being seriously challenged, one must come to the conclusion that a universal theory is an impossibility, because the concepts used are part of a specific western context and can't be applied without implicitly being normative.

3.1 Is religious development exclusively a cognitive matter?
Although both Oser and Fowler probably wouldn't deny the importance of religious action, they don't take it into consideration in their theories on religious development. In Oser's view the relationship of a

person to the Ultimate is of central importance to religious development. He clearly differentiates between social relationships and the relationship of an individual to the Ultimate, which, in his opinion, transcends the social. One's relationship with the Ultimate manifests itself particularly in the following basic activities: when a person tries to come to terms with situations of contingence; in the meaning one gives to his of her own life; in the interpretation of religious messages; in prayer and other forms of inner, meditative dialogue (Oser, 1988:48). This leaves little room for a more immanent interpretation of the ultimate, as is current in the New Age movement and the Women's Spirituality Movement, in which the ultimate is situated, among other things, in the intrinsic connection one has as a human being with other people and creatures, and in which human beings, whenever they stand in a free and just relationship to each other, are considered to be holy. In this mode of thought it is impossible to make a strict division between the social and the ultimate or between religious judgement and religious action (in the sense of doing justice). Oser doesn't take religious action into account because it is of secondary importance to him, but the problem is that in doing so, he implicitly attributes a normative meaning to his concept of religious judgement.

In Fowler's theory faith is seen as a human activity taking place in relationships of which trust and loyalty are the basic aspects. But here also the connection between religious knowing and religious action remains in the dark (Parks, 1988). Bukow doubts whether the ability to make religious judgements really is an intrinsic part of daily religiousness at all (Bukow, 1989). Dijkstra proposes, as an alternative to Fowler's definition of faith, a more action-oriented one. He suggests that faith is "appropriate and intentional participation in the redemptive activity to God" (1986:55). But here the same problems with regard to the determination of what is appropriate and intentional participation, emerge.

Heimbrock has another emphasis. He is interested in *ritual* action in particular and discloses the insufficient explanation of cognitive structural interpretation on this point. In principle, the performance of ritual acts can be taken into consideration within Fowler's "symbolic function", although Fowler doesn't show much interest in the subject. In the theory of Oser & Gmünder however, rituals are interpreted one-sidedly as magical - a passing phenomenon in the "do-ut-des" stage. According to Oser & Gmünder children (and 'immature' adults) perform rituals in order to fulfil certain wishes: when being good to God, He certainly will pay rewards. In the third stage children transcend such an argumentation because they start to recognize their own responsibility and the limits of God's influence. In the view of Oser &

Gmünder, a rejection of religious practices such as rituals is the result.

Looking at the interviews, it can be concluded that the women concerned neither interpret symbols and rituals in the "fundamentalistic" way which Fowler describes as typical for the third stage of development, nor in the "demythologizing" way of stage four (1981:163). These women reflect on the meaning of rituals and symbols and describe how they undergo the power of a ritual while performing it. They are able to discern the adequacy or inadequacy of symbols to express what is going on in a particular situation, without considering these symbols as superfluous because they can verbally express their meaning. In Fowler's outline these women could possibly be situated in stage five with regard to the symbolic function.

3.1.1 Subjective ritual theory: an example

To illustrate my argument I will now present part of an interview with a forty-year-old teacher who is a member of a women's group in the Dutch Women's Spirituality Movement. I chose this example because it clearly expresses several issues in women's criticism of the Christian tradition that could be expanded to cognitive structural theories of religious development as well.

Tineke reinterprets the traditional 'pax-christi' symbol in a specific way. In her view the X (chi) stands for the connection between the four elements (earth, air, water and fire) and the P (rho) for the connection between heaven and earth:

> "I think it is a pity that this is completely lost in Christianity, whilst I think that is in fact what the symbol means. Christianity has become so much a mental exercise with its concentration on the divine. The humanity, one's bodily existence as a human being, one's connection as a human being with creation, with the earth, with other people, with animals and plants and with the cosmos, it is this I miss in the Christian tradition."

As I indicated before, I have now tacitly made the transition from a remark about women's *modes* of speaking about symbols to the *content* of their views, because exactly this content contains a critique to both Oser & Gmünder's and Fowler's approach of religious development. According to Tineke mental development must be seen in its connection to other aspects of development, including corporality. This becomes clear in her vision on the essential elements of a ritual:

"For me there are a few things that are a 'must' in a ritual. They have simply to do with the four elements: earth, air, water and fire. Earth for me is, roughly speaking, first of all the body, body-consciousness, the acknowledgement: this I am as a body. Furthermore it means: everything one possesses, one's family and living conditions, God knows what, everything connected with the earth anyhow. In a proper ritual, this is one of the points of concentration. If you leave this out, you are not grounded. One needs some kind of body-work, whether it is dancing or, for my part, exchange of energy or massage or anything else, as long as it is something expressive with the body."

As a second element Tineke mentions air. Air has to do with mental power, ideas, fantasies, intellect etc. In a ritual a mental point of concentration is also necessary. Then, as a third element, there is water, which is connected with feeling, with emotions and desires. It also has to do with the unconsciousness, with dreams:

"and the driving force that is behind all this. One doesn't come out of nowhere. We are the result of trillions of years of development, not just like that, bang! No, we are the result of a long evolution. From the beginning we were there, as mind and matter. This is in short the emotional aspect on which one has to concentrate. I found out it often works out best when one starts from emotionality, because the emotions usually are the clearest expression of what is going on. Finally it is feeling which is nearest to being a human being."

According to Tineke the fourth element, fire, has to do with energy, with the power of action. In a ritual, the action must be suited to the word. Tineke also associates this element with blood, because the course of one's blood is the transmitter of energy throughout the body.

Tineke compares these four aspects, which are essential for a ritual, to the four legs of a chair. They are the poles of humanity which have to be brought in balance with each other. In addition to this, a fifth aspect is important. Human beings take part in a cosmic evolutionary process. One can increasingly get in tune with this process. Tineke calls this aspect: power of light, the cosmos, omnipotence or primeval power. To come into contact with this power is essential in a ritual and this can only happen when the four elements are in balance with each other. For Tineke, performing ritual means purification:

"Get rid of old lumber, trying to clarify one's insights. If one completes something, one can start something new and let the ballast fall down ... For me life is in fact evolution, nothing else. Life is

144

development, permanent change ... In seven months time not one of the cells in my body is still the same, they are all, exept for the brain, replaced! This is something unbelievable, there is so much power in it. Such an unconceivable hope, I must say. Hope for the possibility to change things, to change the world".

I have cited Tineke extensively, because it is evident that she understands human development - and for her this is religious development - as a process in which all aspects of humanity are involved. Spiritual growth even has a relationship to corporal development.

3.1.2 The body/mind relationship

The unity of human beings, incorporating bodily and mental aspects, is an often returning theme in feminist spirituality. One of the feminist authors theorizing about the relationship between mind and body from a psychological angle is Goldenberg. According to her, feminist theory should abandon the division of mind and body into two totally separate entities and should research the influence of the body on mental processes. In Goldenbergs conception we must learn to "think through the body":

> "Let us not cling to disembodied ways of thinking which lead us to disparage women in particular and physical life in general. We need to show how the much-disparaged bodies of both women and men give rise to all so called higher intellectual activity. We need to inspire thought that supports physical life by understanding in detail how physical life gives birth to thought" (Goldenberg, 1985:64).

In Goldenberg's opinion psychoanalysis can help us investigate the "corporal ground of our intelligence" (1985:65). Freud connects mind and body by using the concept of the instincts ('Triebe'):

> "We assume that the forces which drive the mental apparatus into activity are produced in the bodily organs as an expression of major somatic needs" (Freud according to Goldenberg, 1985:67).

These instincts can't express themselves in any other way than in ideas. This means that, in Freud's vision, all our images, fantasies and ideas find their origin in the body.

According to Goldenberg it is Winnicott who formulates the clearest definition of the concept of 'psyche': "the imaginative elaboration of somatic parts, feelings and functions" (Winnicott according to Goldenberg, 1985:69). Our soul makes it possible for us to see reality in

145

a symbolic or metaphorical way, and therefore it can simply be said that images and symbols are "bodily feelings perceived pictorially ... Psyche or soul is body visualized" (ibid.). Art, for example, is understood by Goldenberg as a creative expression of male and female bodily experience, of the physical sensations and desires people have. Winnicott assumes that the mind in fact is not an entity at all, but something which develops differently in each individual as a special function of the body/mind unity. The development of the mind originates as a reaction to the failure of the child's environment to satisfy its needs:

> "Through cognitive understanding and mental control, the infant transforms the imperfect environment into the perfect one. Mind thus has its origins in the attempt to gain control of the environment" (Goldenberg, 1985:70).

The more unreliable the environment, the greater the distance which is experienced by the individual between mind and body. According to Winnicott this distance is expressed (among other things) in the notion that the mind would be situated in the head. Goldenberg extends this line of thought to Jung's theory of the archetypes and to Jewish and Christian representations of God, in which she perceives a continuing dissociation of the body/mind unity.

As regards the relationship between mental development and corporality, Piaget has done an interesting observation of a girl of sixteen months old. When a box which was slightly opened was put in front of her, she looked at it attentively and then opened and closed her mouth several times. Piaget's interpretation of this event is that out of the desire to open the box, the girl used physical action, the opening and closing of her mouth, signifying through her body her wish to open the box (Piaget, 1936).

In the light of the above-mentioned discussion, fundamental questions must be asked with regard to theories concerning the development of mental processes. What is the relationship between motorial action and cognitive processes in early childhood? In the example of Piaget, movement seems to precede the act of imagination. A next question would be if this "thinking through the body" is only a passing stage in human development, which according to Piaget would proceed towards an increasing capacity to think objectively and abstractly. If one agrees to this point, the danger exists that the development of presentative symbolism (Langer, 1974 (1942)) with its sensory basis, and the development of body language - both authentic expressive abilities of

146

humanity - are highly neglected. Much as they are based on the piagetean perspective, with regard to cognitive structural theories of religious development the question arises whether they are not in fact describing the development of *discursive* symbolism (Langer, 1974 (1942)) and if they aren't, because of that, reflecting more the rationalization of the modern worldview (Bukow, 1989) than that they are offering an insight in the specifics of *religious* development.

In the investigation of religious development the processes in which the development of presentative symbolism and body language are embedded, should be of central concern. Winnicott, Lorenzer and Pruyser have offered useful insights with regard to the relationship between religion and human imaginative processes.

Lowen's bio-energetical approach and Perl's Gestalt-therapy have given rise to interpretation-models for body-language in a therapeutical setting, which might be useful for the research of religious action generally and of rituals in particular. Inevitably this leads to further theoretical questions concerning the relationship between body-experience and the reflection on it, or concerning the relationship between corporal and verbal expression (Wimmer, 1982). These questions however can't be answered within the scope of this article.

3.2 Structure and content of the developmental stages

The basis of cognitive structural theory of religious development, the devision between structure and content, is questioned by several authors (a.o. Schweitzer, 1987; Parks, 1988). Their main criticism applies to stage six, which both in Oser & Gmünder's and in Fowler's work appears to be defined in terms derived from the Christian tradition (Parks, 1986, 1988; Schweitzer, 1987; Broughton, 1988; Zwergel, 1989), in spite of their claim of universal validity. Apart from Ghandi, Fowler only mentions people from a Jewish-Christian background as examples of stage six, and among them only one woman can be found. In analogy to Gilligan's critique of Kohlberg's theory, which reveals its implicit normativity by unconsciously excluding women's way of coming to moral judgements, one could ask if a more gender specific analysis of Fowler's interview-material would lead to a different description of the six stages.

The problem at stake however, is that structure and content can't be divided in such a strict way as cognitive structural theories of religious development do.

"Religiöse Vorstellungen sind jedoch, wie die Religionsgeschichte lehrt, hochkomplexe, sehr variable, nicht eindeutig relationierbare, sondern vielmehr lebensweltlich gebundene und hingenommene Bestandteile des

147

Alltagslebens. Es gibt keinen Grund, ausgerechnet bei der Aneignung einer so komplexen Materie wie der Religion - jedenfalls in Bezug auf deren wesentliche Aspekte - von Stadien auszugehen, die altersbezogen und sequentiell-linear, irreversibel, hierarchisch aufeinander aufbauend sowie von soziokulturellen Einflussen wie Machtinteressen frei konzipiert werden, die also letztendlich über konkrete Lebenssituationen erhaben sind" (Bukow, 1989:67).

Bukow points to the influence of the socio-cultural environment and religious socialization on the ability to make religious judgements. His criticism is, and it is shared by others (e.g. Heimbrock, 1986), that there is an implicit normativity in cognitive structural theories of development, which illegitimately presents *one* model of religious development as the only possible one and thus distorts the multi-interpretable reality of human development. The problem with theories which try to reduce human experience to its 'essential' structures by universalizing this experience, is that they lead to a simplification of historical and cultural varieties. In short: the conceptual framework of the theories discussed is not sufficient to apprehend adequately the possible varieties in development in different cultural contexts.

In my opinion it is impossible to answer the question if humanity is, psychologically speaking, one, and thus develops the same way everywhere. In order to be able to do so, one should compare the concepts of development of different religious and secular contexts with each other. Because of the cultural embeddedness of the concept of development in modern western society (Hull, 1988), the enterprise to expand development theories in such a way that their claim of universal validity is justified seems too pretentious to me. There might possibly exist religions in which our conception of development doesn't play a decisive role at all and others in which even much more differentiated stages of development are being formulated.

2.3 Psychological research within cultural contexts
Within cultural anthropology and the comparative study of religion a discussion has been going on for several decades about methods of understanding different cultures and the different religions being part of them. The evolutionistic approach of anthropologists like Tylor and Frazer, which characterizes the beginning of this century and interprets 'primitive' religions as restricted ways of knowing the world that precede our western science, is considered to be biased.

In the more recent discussion about the interpretation of magic, western ethnocentrism is profoundly criticized and anthropologists have

148

now become much more cautious in their application of western models of interpretation to understand cultural phenomena that initially appear to be 'strange' to them (Wilson, 1970 (1979)); Kippenberg & Luchesi, 1978). It is a pity that this whole field of discussion is scarcely being mentioned in the psychology of religion, although the same theoretical questions are at stake.

In the comparative study of religion several authors judge religion to be of such a complexity, that all religious phenomena can't possibly be catched within one definition of religion. These authors try to understand religious concepts in the context of their praxis rather than to place them in a previously given theoretical framework (Lauwers, 1974; Kippenberg, 1983; Cohen, 1985). Although an investigator inevitably enters his or her field of research with a specific frame of reference, in this approach the point of issue is the clarification of sense-giving of the 'objects' of research themselves; their way of giving sense to their own lives. In the second instance, this "local knowledge" (Geertz, 1983) can be connected with existing definitions and theories of the phenomena at stake. Geertz speaks in this respect of

> "a continuous dialectical tacking between the most local of local detail and the most global of global structure in such a way as to bring them into simultanious view" (1983:69).

The point is, that in this hermeneutical circle, which according to Geertz also takes place in sciences other than anthropology, "experience-near" and "experience-distant" concepts have to be set in a dialectical relationship to each other:

In my opinion, this incorporation of the personal and social composition of meaning into one theory, forms a real challenge to the psychology of religion. While anthropologists are mainly interested in the social context of religious concepts, this doesn't mean that one has to restrict oneself to this aspect of the investigation of symbols and rituals:

> "Symbols are often defined as things 'standing for' other things. But they do not represent these 'other things' unambigiously: indeed, as argued above, if they did so they would be superfluous and redundant. Rather, they 'express' other things in ways which allow their common form to be retained and share among members of a group, whilst not imposing upon these people the constraints of uniform meaning. Because symbols are malleable in this way, they can thus be made to 'fit' the circumstances of the individual" (Cohen, 1985:18).

Why does one woman judge the lesbian fire-ritual to be perfectly suiting to the occasion while another woman experiences it as a coercive confession of 'sins' against lesbians? Both have attended the same ritual, but what has taken place in each of their minds (and bodies) and why, is a psychological issue.

My conclusion would be that, seen from the aforementioned mode of thought in cultural anthropology, psychological theories of universal validity are not only an impossibility, but in fact distort the multi-varied reality of human experience by forcing it into a biased, implicitly normative frame of interpretation. Because pan-psychological investigation is too pretentious, psychological research should always explicitly be situated within a cultural context and should relate its frame of reference to the meaning-making of human individuals.

PSYCHOTHERAPEUTIC AND RELIGIOUS RITUALS: THE ISSUE OF SECULARIZATION

Patrick Vandermeersch

1. Introduction

The question whether psychotherapy has to a certain degree replaced religion and the questions concerning the current relationship between both fields have, apparently, still not been solved. Time and again- sometimes in a rather simplistic manner, sometimes more nuanced- some people defend the position that the psychiatrist is a substitute for the pastor. Yet within the same range from subtle distinctions to brazen militantism, others insist that it must be understood once and for all that psychotherapy and the pastoral field have nothing in common. The vehemence with which the debate flares up again at the least provocation, as recently occurred in The Netherlands, proves that western man is still struggling with the issue of secularization.

In this context moreover, we wonder whether we can truly speak of "the" secularization and its significance for "the" western person. In the field of mental health care, more than in any other domain, one can observe the different roles which secularization has played in various western countries. These differences result not only from the fact that the mental health services are not structured in the same manner and thus fit differently into the system of social services. Nor do they solely result from local differences regarding socially accepted theoretical options and psychotherapeutic theories. The differences between the Christian churches among themselves and the numerous religious sensitivities spread throughout the West, especially influenced the way in which mental health care and pastoral work oppose, cooperate with, cross-fertilize or ignore each other.

Within the scope of this article, we cannot adequately discuss the whole issue of the relationship between psychotherapy and pastoral work. Following a brief description of the historical setting of the conflict concerning competence, we will approach the problem from one well-defined angle: the observation that psychotherapists devise and apply rituals which closely resemble religious rituals. Usually, a pastor would react uncomfortably to this practice. He is accustomed to having the therapist reproach him for not limiting himself to the pastoral field and for improperly infringing upon the psychotherapeutic field. Now the opposite seems to be taking place. The therapist appears to be moving into the pastor's field. Should the pastor in turn voice his protest? Or should he be pleased that the previous unity between religion, or at least its philosophical disposition, and psychotherapy is being restored?

2. Psychotherapy versus pastoral work

Anyone who is somewhat familiar with the origins of psychotherapy will not be surprised to learn that psychotherapy and pastoral work can come into conflict with each other. Contrary to what is sometimes heard, psychiatry did not become a medical specialization due to the conviction that a psychic disturbance could be traced back to a physical cause. The account which is found in quite a number of psychiatric handbooks, and which appears to be a more informed rendering of the historical setting, is equally more legend than reality. Here, it is claimed that Philippe Pinel (1745-1826) liberated the insane, who until then had been locked away in the most inhumane conditions, and that he considered them, not as being criminals but as being "sick people".

This ideological tale, however, which perpetuates the pre-eminently humanitarian image of the physician, overlooks the most essential element (Postel, 1981). While not excluding his immediate British predecessors, one can indeed posit that to a certain degree psychiatry emerged during the French Revolution thanks to Pinel. Indeed, he did attempt to heal the insane by means of a specific treatment. This treatment, however, was anything but medical according to our understanding of the word. Pinel himself, for that matter, called it a "moral treatment". Currently, we would more than likely label it anachronistically as a "systematic psychological manipulation". In any case, the main object of the treatment was "to in a way overpower and tame the alienated, by bringing him into a close relationship with someone who, by his mere physical and moral qualities, inescapably holds him in his grip" (Pinel, 1801:50).

The application of this moral treatment immediately led to a heated conflict with regard to competence. Did one have to be a physician in order to employ the "moral treatment" or were philosophers, lawyers or pastors allowed to apply this treatment as well? The dispute was settled at that time, not on theoretical grounds but solely due to the historical events which were taking place. In revolutionary France, the physicians easily won the debate. They had set themselves up as moral leaders in almost every aspect of social life within modern society. Shortly thereafter, when the Napoleonic armies overran Europe, the French model which entrusted the treatment of insanity to physicians, was adopted everywhere. Thus, long before taking a biological turn, psychiatry emanated from the militant slogan: "not in the name of religion or philosophy but in the name of medicine, may one psychologically manipulate people". During the second half of the 19th century, the success of anatomic research affirmed the medical character of the psychiatric field which had been appropriated by the medical profession over the past half century. It was only at this point that psychiatry became truly "medical" in the current sense of the word. This exclusive state, however, was soon to be challenged, though not by pastors nor by philosophers. In most countries, these had suffered a considerable loss of authority. Rather, the psychiatrist found himself confronted with new rivals, namely, the psychotherapists. Ever since the beginning of the present century, psychotherapy has contested the medical status of the psychiatric field which, in the course of the past two centuries, has undergone both expansions and shifts and whose inner cohesion is still not very clear (Vandermeersch, 1984).

The source of conflict between philosophers and pastors, on the one hand, and physicians, on the other hand, can be rather easily described in the beginning stages of psychiatry. What was at stake was the authority, or rather, the qualifications needed in order to obtain the right to exercise influence on someone's inner life. In the meantime, psychoanalytic experience discovered the deep psychological layers upon which a person's acceptance of authority is based. Keeping in mind the complex construction process of the ideal of the ego as well as the even more archaic fantasms inhabiting the human unconscious, the question regarding the references needed in order to be qualified as a psychotherapist, becomes even more complicated.

The fact that psychoanalysts, from the start, were very interested in primitive cultures, rituals and religion, was probably not coincidental. But perhaps they themselves were initially unaware of what motivated their interest in this direction. At first, they primarily investigated the possible contribution of the study of these phenomena to the individual psychology of the person. Gradually, a second question was raised. How did these rituals succeed in integrating the instinctual individual into the broader context of society?

Propelled by the inner logic of the research, one had to gradually abandon the originally adopted stance of faith in a superior evolution. While religious rituals were initially considered to be primitive forms of psychotherapy, one now wondered whether psychotherapy was not a specific ritual answering a specific need within the crisis-ridden western society. Victor Turner gives this question a new impetus. In his anthropological studies, he further develops the fact that the core of traditional rituals, as they are encountered in most cultures, consists of bringing the individual into a "liminal state". This connotes a condition of depersonalization, the fading of the otherwise very important social distinctions such as gender, class, possessions, and authority. It also implies a condition of deep humbleness and subordination. Turner, however, indicates that this "liminal state" should not be solely interpreted as a deconstruction of the distinctions which normally constitute the fundamental structure of social life. What is at stake is not merely a regression to the nadir, after which an integration into social structures can be attempted a second time. Rather, this liminal state possesses its own, positive characteristics. It restores a state of "communitas", the most fundamental feeling of meaningful communal humanity which at the same time offers the experience of establishing contact with the fundaments of existence (Turner, 1977a (1969)). According to Turner, this is also an experience of the sacred. Consequently, he points out that Christianity contains many characteristics of the "communitas" experience. He claims that even in more highly developed religions, one can to a certain degree encounter organized, ritual forms of "communitas". These rituals offer a counterbalance (an "anti-structure") to the structure imposed by society upon its members. One wonders whether western psychotherapy, insofar as it leads a patient back to original relational experiences, is not fulfilling the role of the traditional rituals and even of the more developed religions, though in a modern context (Moore, 1983).

This, once again, raises the question concerning the scope of secularization. Yet, this question is now being posed in a far more complex manner than it was at the time of the conflict concerning the moral treatment, which was settled by the mere historical circumstances. The question apparently has rather alarming implications, which could explain why one so easily returns to the much simpler theme of authority, when one wishes to affirm the necessary distinction between psychotherapy and religion. But what is this confusion which inspires such fear that one attempts to avoid the complexity of the problem by reverting to the outdated discussion held at the time of the moral treatment, when authority and power seemed to be simple matters?

3. Psychotherapeutic rituals
At first sight, the psychotherapeutic practice appears rather confusing. Therapists who devise rituals might ask a patient suffering from continuing grief over the death of someone for example, to write a letter to the deceased, reproaching him for all the negative aspects of his personality and later to write a second letter, thanking him

elaborately for all the good things which they shared. Afterwards, both letters would be burned in the presence of the therapist. In other instances, children's clothes might be buried or pictures of deceased loved ones might be burned. Sometimes, a funeral is re-enacted and, to this purpose, a procession is held with a table symbolizing the coffin. A therapist might take a group of drug addicts to an isolated place, fast with them, let them take off their old clothes and burn them, take a ritual bath with them in the nude and afterwards, help them put on the clothes of the "new person" (van der Hart, 1978 and 1981).

Are these religious rituals? At first sight, one would be inclined to say no. The therapist definitely does not intend to evoke the sacred or the transcendent. He has another reason for often making his rituals appear similar to traditional rituals which usually originate in a context of sacredness. On the one hand, the therapist designs his ritual with a very specific and individual problem in mind. He designs a particular ritual for a particular client. On the other hand, he is convinced that the efficiency of a ritual flows from the fact that rituals belong to the archaic layers of a culture and of the human psyche. Therapeutic rituals are therefore somewhat different than the common rituals of a surrounding culture. Yet at the same time, they do correspond to the traditional rituals sufficiently enough to help an individual cope with a crisis by means of the familiar power of symbolic deeds.

It is therefore understandable that one would want the therapeutic rituals, as illustrated above, to be similar to known and customary rituals. Psychotherapeutic rituals cannot be too eccentric for then they would run the danger of no longer being effective as rituals. Therapists who devise rituals aim at a technique other than that of the psycho-drama developed by Jacob Moreno (1892-1974). The object of Moreno's psychotherapeutic technique was to symbolically enact, within a structured therapeutic group, one's inner conflicts. In the case of the patient who was unable to cope with his father's death and for whom the funeral was re-enacted in the corridors of the hospital, one might wonder whether this is not an example of psycho-drama rather than a specific example of a therapeutic ritual. When therapists create their rituals, they intend to go beyond the technique of psycho-drama. They do not only seek to symbolize. They also aim at evoking the structuring power which symbols, within the framework of traditional rituals, have always been able to wield in someone's inner life. For this reason, one often makes use of fasting, baptizing and burying. These are indeed ritual gestures which are anchored in our culture. So by burning an object, for example, one is appealing to a primordial symbol. This is the reason why therapists strive for a certain resemblance between the traditional and therapeutic rituals. Therapists like to point to the human phenomenon of the transforming power of ritual gestures not only because they don't wish to appear too unfamiliar but also because they claim the right to gain from insights based on past experiences. Rituals belong to a culture's heritage. Since time immemorial, they appear to have been powerful instruments in manipulating emotions. Why then should the therapist not be allowed to employ these instruments which have been passed down to him by his culture?

4. The model of the rite de passage

The model which the therapist has in mind clearly is the *rite de passage* (Van Gennep, 1969 (1909)). In a schematic form, the ritual can be described as follows. By means of symbolic actions, an individual is integrated into the social order. These rituals are related to birth, maturing, marriage and death. For generation after generation, these gestures have been repeated in a recognizable manner and according to a fixed pattern.

Why does a society employ such rituals? What became most conspicuous to therapists was the fact that these rituals affected people's emotions. For instance, at the time of the rite de passage, the individual is undergoing a transitional stage or a crisis. The ritual aims at bringing him to a new integration. In order to achieve this, rituals allow for the expression of emotions, sometimes even intensifying them. Yet they also channel emotions and weaken them. In the case of death for example, rituals help people to cope with the grieving process by letting them express their regret, their fear, as well as their aggression. This last emotion is often even provoked. The example which is frequently quoted to illustrate this is the obligation to tear one's clothes. Yet simultaneously, the ritual curtails the expression of emotions. The emotional discharge has to occur at a certain moment, in a well-defined context and in the presence of specific people. All of this is performed in the same manner as it has been in the past by others who had experienced similar crisis situations. The ritual thus exercises both a stabilizing and comforting function when it allows for the venting of emotions. In a certain way, therefore, a ritual depersonalizes. One who participates in a ritual assumes a clearly defined role.

At this point, we need to make a clear distinction between the person who undergoes the ritual and the one who administers it. I am aware of the fact that this distinction is often disputed. It is indeed true that the person who undergoes the ritual performs certain gestures as well. Nevertheless, on closer inspection, two clearly different positions are always present. On the one hand, there is the person who is transformed by the ritual and who is submitting himself to this process. On the other hand, there is the person who, as it were, represents society, or maybe we can also say the "order" (the French Lacanians would call it the "symbolic order"), which supports the rituals. Alongside the depersonalization, this distinction between two positions explains the fact why one often changes clothes when performing a ritual. The person administering the ritual does not do so in his own name. He is representing someone else. The person undergoing the ritual however, is much more personally involved. He is acting as himself but he is experiencing this "himself" within a process of changing persons. He is living through a critical moment which should somehow transform him into someone different. The ritual demands that both positions are made present in their distinction so that the person undergoing the ritual may feel assured of his culture's support the moment he submits himself to the process of transforming his person.

Besides these rites de passage, there are other rituals whose object is not so much the individual going through a crisis period, but rather the safety and meaningfulness of time and space as well as the identity of the community. These rituals are based on myths, which can also play a role in the rites de passage. Such myths or edifying symbolic stories are important for our argumentation for two reasons. First, one should question whether therapeutic rituals, which are constructed here and now and not on the basis of a mythical story, can be so easily compared to traditional rituals. Here perhaps we touch upon the fundamental reason why therapeutic rituals aim at resembling traditional rituals in one way or another, or at presenting some sort of theory as their own edifying myth. When discussing myths, however, we touch upon a second problem. Traditionally, it is stated that philosophical thought emerged in the West when the mythical world view was ruptured. As a consequence, western philosophers have experienced rituals as something very problematic. Early Christianity adopted this suspicion and added another motif, namely, the specific Christian experience of the divine as "transcendent". Although Christianity held on to some ritual elements, it constantly attempted to make the divine presence felt in ways other than the mythical opposition between the sacred and the profane world. This presents yet another potential difficulty for the therapist who, rooted in a western world characterized by two thousand years of Christianity, wants to draw inspiration from the rites of other cultures.

5. A psychotherapeutic ritual: a ritual without a myth?
The rituals which serve as the therapist's model are usually rituals which took place within the framework of a culture characterized by myths. Now, however, they are being performed in an entirely different setting. Does this create any problems?

In answering this question, one can refer to data from various experiences. One can draw attention to the fact that the emotional power of rituals does not necessarily disappear when they are extracted from their traditional context. Theatrical experiments can sometimes be more impressive than certain rituals which have become all too familiar and which begin to appear timeworn. Further, should not the fact that special efforts are regularly needed to breathe new life into traditional religious practices teach us a lesson? To take a more recent example, in Catholic circles some twenty years ago, one took great pains to make the liturgical experience "more authentic". "Authentic" in this context meant that one would consciously make certain gestures by which the experience of the participants would become tangible. This implied no special garments, no separate space and no fixed texts. One was supposed to express one's personal, religious feelings to the participants who were actually present.

This example teaches us that, when extracting a ritual from a too classical and worn-out context, one can acquire an intensified emotional experience. The same example, however, immediately shows the impasse to which such a process can lead. A liturgy constructed in this way quickly became very annoying. One had passed over the context essential to the ritual in order for the individual to be able to surrender to his emotions. Because the ritual had been made so personal and so tangibly emotional, it no longer effected the symbolic integration of the individual into a tradition. It was no longer the mysterious, supporting basis of existence which was concretely made present, but rather the personal-affective relationship between the minister of the ritual and the people actually present. The experience of freedom was no longer there, neither in the administration nor in the undergoing of the ritual.

In the example of a specific psychotherapeutic ritual, one can clearly observe that the participants are aware of this danger and attempt to correct it (van der Hart, 1978:191). The case involves a child who was taking too much medication and who had clearly developed the impression that he was ill. Therefore, the child felt it was no longer in any way responsible for its actions. The therapist devised a ritual in order to break through this deadlock. The object of the ritual was to make clear to the child that he was not sick but just angry and misbehaved. Accordingly, the whole family went in procession to the toilet. "Ritually", one box of medicine after the other was thrown into the toilet and flushed down. Every time this was done the father repeated: "The doctors said that you are nothing but a naughty child."

We should pay particular attention to the formula pronounced by the father. He does not say: "*I* tell you, you're nothing but a naughty child". He says: "The *doctors* said that you are nothing but a naughty child". In fact, the father effaces himself as a concrete father and, within the ritual, he becomes a sort of actor, a performer of deeds in the name of someone else. I believe this is essential. If the father was not to do this, then there would have been a normal, direct interaction between a concrete father and a concrete son and the mobilization of emotions by means of this impressive gesture would have had the character of applying violent power.

Within the framework of a ritual, to say "*I* tell you" or "*I* am doing this to you" is only possible when the cultural context is made present to a strong degree and when the performer of the ritual has become the representative of the order to such an extent that he is, at that time, no longer approachable as an individual. Catholics for instance can recall the emotional atmosphere aroused by the words "ego te absolvo" (*I* absolve you from your sins) from the penance ritual or the words of consecration "hoc est enim corpus meum" (for this is *my* body). It was essential to the sacrament of penance that one confess to this unknown priest who was no longer approached as an individual. Likewise, the priest seemed to be someone else when he pronounced the words of consecration.

But perhaps these examples from present liturgical practices fall short since we in fact live in a secularized world in which religion no longer has the emotional impact that initially emanated from the primitive sacred world. Perhaps we ought to turn to theater, preferable to those forms which portray the most archaic aspects of humanity, as for example a performance of Japanese Buto theater. We could also turn to those forms of drama which employ more narrative material and thus more myth, such as Kafka's *The Penal Colony* as performed by Pip Simons' London-based theater company. It is possible that one becomes emotionally affected and that one would be inclined to speak of a therapeutic ritual in those cases. But imagine, as in the case of Simons' production, that one had witnessed the most gruesome tortures until it became truly unbearable and that one was then chased out of the hall for apparently remaining willing to act as a voyeur and an accomplice: "Who were you to think that you could stay settled in the comfortable role of 'public'?" Indeed, one can witness the most affecting situations taking place on the stage because one knows that spectators are

159

spectators and actors are actors. One knows there will be an end to the performance, that there really is a cloakroom where one can get one's coat and that the actors will return to their normal lives after the show.

These examples probably shed some light on the difference between traditional rituals and the intentionally constructed psychotherapeutic rituals. The latter are no longer concerned with making certain gestures in the same way as it has been done by previous generations or by others in similar situations. Yet even when there is room for unusual behavior whose content is not established beforehand, such as in theater performances or at the yearly carnival festivities, such behavior still occurs at well-defined places and times. Moreover, the claim that "in any case this is traditional" acts as a justification. However, when rituals are detached from their traditional context in order to be used by the therapist, this form of legitimation disappears. That is why I find the discussion very confusing if it isn't clearly posited that a psychotherapeutic ritual is something other than a traditional ritual. Precisely because it is not rooted in culture as is the traditional ritual, the psychotherapeutic ritual has the potential danger of permitting a more radical exercising of personal authority. The guarantees, which were assured by tradition, are lacking in the case of a psychotherapeutic ritual.

Psychoanalytic theory itself has become more and more attentive to the importance of the meaning-giving context in which a ritual takes place. The attention given to the interpretation of possible eccentric gestures which are made, as far as content is concerned, has shifted to the background. In this regard, it is worthwhile to recall Freud's first article concerning religion entitled *Obsessive Actions and Religious Practices*. From this text, in which Freud elaborated upon the difference between religious rites and obsessional rites, one often remembers only the notorious statement: "In view of these similarities and analogies one might venture to regard obsessional neurosis as a pathological counterpart of the formation of a religion, and to describe that neurosis as an individual religiosity and religion as a universal obsessional neurosis." (Freud, 1953 (1907):126-7). Though there are many issues in this article which have become outdated, it still contains an element which deserves further attention, i.e. the fact that obsessional rituals always take place in secrecy. The patient is afraid to be caught performing them. The same stress on secrecy is also encountered in another type of pathology, perversion. While perversion has nothing to do with neurosis, the ritual aspect in both cases often occupies a

160

central position, though in completely different modes. In perversion, the ritual is not experienced as a strange, meaningless act which the patient feels himself forced to undertake against his will. Rather, the act is experienced as being lustful. It offers a unique "kick". Although this pathology falls outside of the context of neurosis, once again, the secret character of the ritual, which is essential in perversion, draws our attention (Clavreul, 1987).

With these reflections, we have arrived at the question of how rituals can be understood as specific forms of intrapsychic experiences of reality. Psychoanalysis has barely touched upon this question and it is too early to even formulate an hypothesis. What is conspicuous is that the fact, that both the rituals of obsessional neurosis and of perversion are characterized by secrecy, points in the same direction as the analysis of the ritual's social function. In order for the ritual not to deviate, it needs to be framed by the social order. Does this imply that psychotherapeutic rituals should not be allowed? That would be a rash conclusion. However, it does imply that one should be especially cautious, since the fact that psychotherapeutic rituals appear externally similar to traditional rituals might cause the need for a safety mechanism to be mistakenly overlooked.

Devising psychotherapeutic rituals which resemble traditional rituals can therefore be very misleading. The exterior similarities in gestures and symbols hide the fundamental distinction between the cultural context, which clothes the traditional ritual with meaning, and the completely different context in which the therapeutic ritual occurs. The latter involves a concrete therapist who prescribes a ritual for a concrete patient. This ritual however, in spite of its similarities with the traditional ritual, is anything but common in the patient's experience. The danger of being absorbed by an all too direct relationship in which the ritual no longer protects the individual, is not too farfetched.

Once again, does this imply that psychotherapeutic rituals should not be permitted? We don't think so. Perhaps it is possible to use the emotional powers which rituals are able to arouse in therapy. It would therefore be valuable to conduct further research into the intrapsychic dynamics of the ritual. Thus, from what has been said, it can only be concluded that a reference to extant traditional rituals does not suffice to justify the use of rituals by the therapist. He should provide his own specific context or, to put it more traditionally, construct his own "mythology" to which he could later refer.

6. Traditional and psychotherapeutic rituals: different objectives

Here, we touch upon another, yet equally essential question. Since antiquity, the West has developed a very unique relationship with ritual practices. Both philosophy and Christianity have influenced this development. Moreover, during the past several centuries, the West has become characterized by the unique process of secularization. This process is unknown to most of the cultures from which the therapist derives traditional rituals and to which he refers. Pastors who employ rituals within a religious or explicitly philosophical context, have a completely different objective in mind than those who apply a ritual which originated in a primitive culture. Therefore, it is not be surprising that the therapist working with rituals such as they appear in a traditional culture but nevertheless retaining their outward resemblance with the religious rituals of modern western culture (at least as far as exterior elements are concerned) creates a confusion which eventually has to lead to conflict. One could of course dispose of the problem by stating the following. In traditional rituals, there usually is a cohesion between the ritual, on the one hand, and religion (or, more broadly, philosophy), on the other hand. This cohesion is lacking in psychotherapeutic rituals. These rituals have originated in a clearly secularized climate. Is this difference relevant? So many aspects of life have become secularized in the meantime. So why should rituals not become secularized as well?

How far one can pursue this argumentation depends on a number of things, not in the least on one's concept of religion and philosophy. Whatever these views may be, we should realize that the question of whether something is religious or not, is a new question. Those who look into other cultures or past times in order to gain insight into how rituals function, will always encounter them within the framework of a religious culture. Our own culture, however, is one of the few cultures which underwent the process of secularization. When attempting to answer the question of how rituals operate within a secularized culture, we cannot look for the answer in cultures where this process has not yet occurred. The same is true for religious rituals. Unless one can view religion as nothing else than a remnant from a bygone era, as did 19th century scientism, one has to accept the fact that a religion belonging to a culture which underwent the process of secularization, also changed because of that process. For that matter, the interaction of the western religious world with rituals has a long history. Greek philosophy which has profoundly influenced western thinking, experienced rituals as problematic from the very beginning. The replacement of the meaning-giving context of myths by a personal quest for truth did not remain without consequences as far as rituals were concerned (Bousquet, 1981). Christianity for the most part integrated this Greek way of thinking. Moreover, it contributed its own religious motive in order to discredit the traditional rituals which portrayed the distinction between the profane and sacred worlds as a distinction between two radically different domains. In Christian thinking, the spatial and temporal metaphors contained within this distinction incorrectly expressed God's transcendence, as if the relationship of mankind with God was a relationship of two "others". The interiorization of the cult and especially of the notion of sacrifice as a "sacrifice of the spirit", is very characteristic of this change in thinking (Yon, 1981).

The correct interpretation of God's transcendence as opposed to his immanence has, even until now, been the subject of much discussion within Christianity. The Jewish concept of ritual was also a special topic of discussion. This concept had demystified nature and had exclusively combined God's intervention with the commemoration of historical events in light of the concept of the covenant. Should not the process of universalization, which Christianity hoped to achieve by linking Jewish and Hellenistic elements, lead to a new type of cult? Obviously, we do not intend to present here all the theological problems and possible options. It is important to note, however, that the notion of ritual within the context of Christianity became the bearer of a new meaning in which both the contact between an individual believer and God and the submission of one's life to regulation by a personally acknowledged ultimate truth were attributed an important significance. This certainly differs from the objectives of the traditional ritual. The emotional aspect in particular was regarded very critically for religious reasons. This becomes clear in the continued uneasy reception of the charismatic movements within Christianity.

Secularization sharpened this problematic relationship between the West and rituals. The question of the pastor's significance is concerned with the way in which he is able to transmit faith in the absolute as well as the specific dynamic of the western religious tradition. He cannot deny the existence of secularization as a historical fact. Yet he cannot help but wonder whether secularization results from the logical development of this religious tradition. And when he does make those old, familiar gestures, he makes them very cautiously because he realizes that his religious world no longer contains the evident and all-embracing function which the sacred enjoyed in traditional cultures.

When employing a ritual, the therapist's concern is whether that ritual is efficient or not. This is precisely *not* the concern of the pastor. His interest is whether the particular ritual, besides its didactic or clarifying functions, serves the quest for "the Truth". I leave this expression vague since the Christian tradition has produced pastors of all kinds. No matter how this "Truth" is further defined, whether by a humanistic, Protestant or Catholic tradition, all pastors have much in common which they should defend. It is good that the different accents are not immediately placed in the foreground. It is crucial that philosophies are not reduced to something merely "useful" but that they remain linked to the free quest for truth. For this reason, a religious ritual is always a "broken" ritual. The therapeutic ritual intends to transform a person by means of the ritual into someone who, in the eyes of one's own ego, is felt to be more satisfactory. The religious ritual expresses respect and trust in a reality which goes beyond us, which grounds our freedom and which asks to be more profoundly known. This is indeed something quite different and, for that matter, not always "useful".

CHRISTIAN PILGRIMAGE
Motivational Structures and Ritual Functions

Marinus H.F. van Uden & Joseph Z.T. Pieper

1. Introduction

In this article we'll first concentrate on the results of a research project on the motivational structure of pilgrims to Lourdes. We relate these results to the motives of pilgrims going to two other places of pilgrimage: Wittem and Banneux. Second, attention is given to the effects of pilgrimage on personal wellbeing. Finally we'll deal with the question as to how these effects can be explained. In this context we consider pilgrimage as a ritual of transformation.

Some years ago we presented the results of a first exploratory study on the motivational structure of pilgrims to Wittem, a small village in the south of the Netherlands and the effects of this pilgrimage on well-being (Oosterwijk, Van Uden, Hensgens, 1986). Since then we have done comparable exploratory work in Lourdes and in Banneux, a place of pilgrimage in the Ardennes in Belgium. At this moment we are conducting a large scale investigation among 600 pilgrims to Lourdes in addition to the completed pilot-studies. Control groups are planned as well. In the last years an increasing scientific interest in the phenomenon of pilgrimage can be observed (Bax, 1984; Scharfe, Schmolze, Schubert, 1985; Guth, 1986; Van Uden, Post, 1988). Also the number of pilgrims to different places seems to be increasing and on television and radio the issue is rather frequently paid attention to. Especially a new place of pilgrimage in Jugoslavia, Medjugorje, has received quite some attention. Explanations for this increase of attraction of modern pilgrimage are scarce. As to why the individual pilgrim goes on pilgrimage and what it does to him, few answers are available. In general a lack of empirical knowledge is noticed about the motives of pilgrims (see Guth, 1986).

In this paper we'll report some results of the pilot study in Lourdes. We'll also refer to some results of the Wittem and Banneux-study. Lourdes, with about 5 million visitors each year, is still the most important center of pilgrimage in Europe. We'll deal with two aspects of this pilgrimage: the motives of the pilgrim and, secondly, the effects of the pilgrimage on his psychological well-being. In the discussion we relate these effects to Victor Turner's thinking on myths and rituals. The results of the Lourdes pilot-study are especially interesting because a particular group of respondents could be distinguished with a motivational structure fundamentally different from the motivational structures found in the Wittem and Banneux research. This makes it possible to raise the question whether pilgrims with different motivational structures also differ in the effects the pilgrimage has and how these matters can be explained from a theoretical point of view.

2. Research design and response

One of the purposes of our study was to determine possible effects of pilgrimage on personal well-being. We investigated this effect by administering a questionnaire before (the pre-test) as well as after the pilgrimage (the post-test). In the pre-test 78 questionnaires were distributed randomly among pilgrims travelling by train from the Netherlands to Lourdes in October 1985. This pilgrimage was in fact a combination of three pilgrimages: 1. The 132th National Pilgrimage, 2. The Third Pilgrimage for Young People, 3. The Limburger Pilgrimage. Of the 78 questionnaires 71 were returned (response 91%). 51 pilgrims disclosed their names and received post-test questionaires, of which 50 were returned. This means that from 50 (= 64%) of the 78 persons contacted we received both a pre-test and a post-test. This is a high response which is probably due to the personal contacts we had with the pilgrims.

The age of our respondents varied between 15 and 78 years. Of them 70% was female. In sum 36 of our respondents were younger than 35 years of age; we refer to them as the younger pilgrims (mean age 22 years). 35 were older than 35; we call them the older pilgrims (mean age 58 years).

Due to the fact that so many young people participated in our pilgrimage this division was feasible. In this way we especially gained some insight into the motives of the younger pilgrims, a group which, according to some authors (e.g. Guth, 1986), is rather different from the traditional, older pilgrims.

3. Analysis of the motives

In our research the pilgrims on their train journey to Lourdes received a list of 34 possible motives. By means of a 5-point Likert-scale the pilgrim could indicate to what extent a particular motive was applicable.

In the data-processing for this report the reactions to the motives were treated as binary responses. This means they were put in two categories: applicable ("very applicable" and "applicable") and not applicable ("completely unapplicable", "not applicable" and "don't know").

166

3.1 The motives of the younger and older pilgrim

The pattern of the motives of all the pilgrims is difficult to interpret. However, when we look at the younger and older pilgrims separately, clear lines emerge. In the next part we deal with the motives of the younger pilgrim first and subsequently with the motives of the older ones. The motives are ranked according to their percentage 'applicable'.

Let us first have a look at the motivational top-ten of the younger pilgrim (n = 36). (See Table 1).

Table 1

Motives of the younger pilgrim

"This time I go to Lourdes..."

		In %
1	to meet others	89
2	to divert myself	80
3	out of curiosity	69
4	because the atmosphere appeals to me	66
5	to gain new strength	64
6	because I like to experience my faith together with many others	56
7	to strengthen my faith	56
8	to pray for a better world	53
9	because of the opportunity for reflection	53
10	to pray for the healing of others	50

Remarkable is the fact that the most important motives of the younger pilgrim deal with diversion/recreation, meeting others and curiosity. In our original list of 34 motives there were several explicit non-religious items. They occupy the first three places of this top-ten.

Let us now have a look at the motivational top-ten of the older pilgrims (n = 35). (See Table 2).

Table 2
Motives of the older pilgrim

"This time I go to Lourdes..."

		In %
1	because of Mary	80
2	to gain new strength	74
3	to pray for the need and misery in the world	71
4	to give thanks	69
5	to strengthen my faith	68
6	to pray for the healing of others	65
7	to pray for a better world	65
8	to beseech help and assistance	63
9	to beseech God's blessing	63
10	to give thanks for acquired favours	61

Looking at the older pilgrim to Lourdes all the important items are religious. Explicit non-religious motives do not belong to their top-ten of motives. If we would present the motivational top-ten of the Wittem study (Oosterwijk, Van Uden, Hensgens, 1986) and the Banneux one (Pieper, Van Uden, 1988), studies in which hardly any younger pilgrims were involved, exactly the same ten items constitute the top-ten (except for Gerard, who takes Mary's first place in Wittem). One could say all these respondents belong to the same population of elder pilgrims.

If we compare the motives of the older and younger pilgrims the following can be noticed. Only four motives are found in both top-tens: "to gain new strength", "to pray for the healing of others", "to pray for a better world" and "to strengthen my faith". The three non-religious motives, that were most important for the younger pilgrim ("to meet others", "to divert myself" and "out of curiosity") only reach place 21, 13 and 34(!) in the motivational hierarchy of the older pilgrim. The most important item for the older pilgrim, "because of Mary", ranks 17 for the younger pilgrim. In other words, the motivational structures of the younger and older pilgrim look fundamentally different.

Regarding the question as to whom their faith is directed we can conclude that for the older pilgrims Mother Mary is most important. For them, God is important too. The item "to beseech God's blessing" ranks 9 for the older, 29 for the younger pilgrim. With the younger pilgrim, on the other hand, Jesus is more popular. Within the triad Mary, God and Jesus, Jesus scores highest. The item "because Jesus from Nazareth appeals to me" is at place 11 for the younger, and only at place 27 for the older pilgrim. So, in their preferences for God, Jesus and Mary, the older and younger pilgrims clearly differ as well.

3.2 Results of a factor analysis

To gain more insight into the interdependencies and meaning of the various motivational descriptions we will now deal with the results of the factor analysis. The principal components factor analysis with varimax rotation (for more details: see Oosterwijk, Hoenkamp-Bisschops, Pieper & Van Uden, 1987) we conducted, led to three factors (see table 3). The motives within each factor are ranked according to their factor loading. Also the percentages which each motive scores for the younger as well as the older pilgrim are given. To each factor a name is given that represents our interpretation of this factor as a whole.

Let us now have a closer look at the various factors.

Factor 1 deals with what we call "deepening of faith". To this factor belong the items "to learn to pray", "because they preach so well there", "to strengthen my faith", "to experience the Universal Church" and "to be converted". Items referring to God and Jesus are explicitly present in this factor. Further analysis shows a significant correlation between a high score on factor 1 and an affirmative reaction to the item "my personal faith is primarily focused on God". This underlines the relation between this factor and God. The items forming this factor are applicable to 33% of the younger and 30% of the older pilgrims.

Factor 2 we called "beseeching help and cure". Apart from the item "to beseech help and assistance", we find in this factor the item "to be cured" with a high factor loading. Furthermore the items "because I made a promise" and "because my partner (or someone else) asked me to" belong to this factor. We also find here an item referring to God's blessing and an item that relates this factor to Mary. The item "out of curiosity" loads negative, which means that pilgrims who score high on the other items of factor 2, usually don't agree to the motive "out of curiosity". More detailed analysis showed that pilgrims affirming to the item "my personal faith is primarily focused on Mary" score high on factor 2. The items forming this factor are applicable to 20% of the younger and 53% of the older pilgrims.

Table 3

The three factors

motive	description	loading	% applicable	
			old	young
Factor 1: Deepening of faith				
20	to learn to pray	.71	24	23
28	because they preach so well there	.71	12	17
6	to honour God	.58	44	39
26	to strengthen my faith	.57	68	56
16	because Jesus from Nazareth appeals to me	.56	27	50
15	to experience the Universal Church	.41	26	36
4	to be converted	.33	9	11
			30%	33%
Factor 2: Beseeching help and cure				
2	to beseech help and assistance	.75	63	25
27	to beseech God's blessing	.69	63	17
1	because of Mary	.66	80	42
17	to be cured	.66	36	6
5	because I made a promise	.42	21	9
22	because my partner (or someone else) asked me to	.34	16	11
13	out of curiosity (inverted)	-.61	94	31
			53%	20%
Factor 3: Looking for peace and quietness				
10	because Lourdes is situated in such a beautiful environment	.71	30	50
32	because of the opportunity for reflection	.68	44	53
3	to look for silence	.55	37	31
30	to divert myself	.52	47	80
7	to meet others	.50	38	89
			39%	61%

Factor 3 concerns "looking for peace and quietness". This factor includes motives that express a certain atmosphere, a particular situation: the beautiful environment, diversion and the meeting with other people. We find these motives together with items like "because of the opportunity for reflection" and "to look for quietness". This suggests that the first motives cannot be strictly interpreted as recreational motivations, but must be seen as motives that create positive conditions for quietness and reflection. Notice that in this factor there is no item referring to God, Jesus or Mary. Further analysis showed that pilgrims scoring high on factor 3 usually disagree with the item "my personal faith is primarily focused on Mary". The items forming this factor are applicable to 61% of the younger and 39% of the older pilgrims.

When we look at the applicable percentage of the items forming the various factors, we notice that the younger as well as the older pilgrim scores relatively low on factor 1 ("Deepening of faith"). Furthermore we see that older pilgrims score highest on factor 2 ("Beseeching help and cure") and younger pilgrims on factor 3 ("Looking for peace and quietness"). The older pilgrims score lowest on factor 1 while the younger pilgrims score lowest on factor 2. The older pilgrim can be characterized by his looking to Mary for help; the younger by his desire to look for peace and quietness together with others.

All in all, the factor analysis supports the conclusion that there is a fundamental distinction between the motivational structure of the younger and the older pilgrims.

4. The effects on psychological well-being

In a contribution entitled *The effect of pilgrimage on anxiety, depression and religious attitude*, Morris (1982) put forward that, although much has been written about the physical condition of pilgrims before and after a visit to Lourdes, hardly any investigation into their emotional state has been undertaken. Therefore Morris, in his own investigation, tries to discover what benefit pilgrims with physical complaints gain on an emotional level. Two rating scales were used to assess the level of anxiety and depression of people planning to visit Lourdes. In the month following their return these two rating scales were completed again. A significant drop in anxiety and depression could be observed. 10 months later the same procedure was undertaken. It appeared that the reduction of anxiety and depressive feelings was still present.

We decided to replicate Morris' investigation to see whether our group of pilgrims showed similar signs of improvement. At the same time we could determine possible differences between younger pilgrims and older ones regarding these psychological effects. We used two different rating scales: the ZBV and the Zung-D.

The ZBV is a rating scale, used to measure the level of anxiety. It is the Dutch equivalent of the STAI, Spielbergers State-Trait Anxiety Inventory (Van der Ploeg, Defares, Spielberger, 1980). The STAI was used by Morris in his investigation. The ZBV consists of two separate scales, measuring State anxiety (i.e. how subjects feel at a particular moment in time) and Trait anxiety (i.e. how they have generally felt over a period of time). Because we were especially interested in long-term effects, we only used the Trait Anxiety Scale. This scale consists of 20 items, like "I feel pleasant" and "There are some thoughts I can hardly get out of my mind". The respondent can choose from four possible answers: "hardly ever", "sometimes", "often" and "nearly always". The total score ranges from 20 to 80 points. The lower the score, the less the level of anxiety. Before visiting Lourdes the average score of the pilgrims (n = 42) was 40.0 (s.d. = 10.1), after their visit it was 36.0 (s.d. = 13.5). This drop of four points is statistically significant at a 0.01 level. The younger pilgrims (n = 26) showed a decrease in anxiety from 39.8 (s.d. = 10.9) to 36.1 (s.d. = 14.4) points, significant at a 0.05 level. The scores of the older pilgrims (n = 16) dropped from 40.6 (s.d. = 8.6) to 35.8 (s.d. = 11.8) points, significant, too, at a 0.05 level.

The Zung-D is a rating scale, used to measure the level of depression (Zung, 1965). Here too we used a Dutch version. The Zung-D consists of 21 items, like "In this period I didn't sleep very well" or "In this period I felt nervous and couldn't sit still". Respondents could choose from the same four answers as with the ZBV. Here the total score of the scale can vary from 0 to 63 points. The lower the score, the less the degree of depression. The average score of the pilgrims (n = 43) dropped from 19.1 (s.d. = 11.4) before to 13.6 (s.d. = 9.4) after. This decrease in depressive feelings was statistically significant (0.01 level). After the pilgrimage the respondents felt less depressed. This was especially true for the older ones (n = 16). Their scores dropped from 21.9 (s.d. = 12.8) to 13.2 (s.d. = 10.8), significant at a 0.01 level. But the younger ones (n = 27) showed similar effects. Their scores dropped from 17.4 (s.d. = 10.3) to 13.8 (s.d. = 8.8), significant at a 0.05 level.

Taking these results together, the overall conclusion is that pilgrims, three weeks after their pilgrimage, feel less anxious and depressed. In the Wittem-study (mainly older pilgrims) a comparable significant drop in depression (from 17.7 to 12.8) and in anxiety (from 36.5 to 34.5) was observed. The results of Morris are therefore confirmed. This improvement, as the Lourdes-study suggests, applies to the older as well as to the younger respondents. In other words, two groups with quite different motivational structures for their visit to Lourdes, show the same positive effects regarding psychological well-being. Whether these effects are due to the pilgrimage itself can only be discovered by further research, in which an adequate control group is included.

5. Discussion

Recently some other authors have also pointed to differences between younger pilgrims and older ones as to how they experience their pilgrimage. Bank (1982) investigated the motives of about 1600 Dutch pilgrims to Lourdes. He determined three basic motivational structures. The most important is a cluster of motives of a religious nature, relating to praying for salvation, favours, comfort and strength. Next are religious motives that point in the direction of a "deepening of faith", such as "to strengthen my faith", "to meet Christ" or "to join the Universal Church". Thirdly and lastly are the non-religious motives, such as "out of curiosity" and "for diversion". These non-religious motives, as in our study, especially apply to the younger pilgrims.

In 1984 Robbrecht (1986) questioned a 1000 pilgrims to the Flemish place of pilgrimage called Scherpenheuvel. He discerned three main categories of motives. Devotional motives, such as "I come for a good prayer" and "I come because the month of May is devoted to Mary" are most often mentioned: 49%. Then motives follow which are related to actual needs, such as "to get a favour for myself", "to get a favour for someone else" or "to have my car blessed". This group of motives applies to 28% of those investigated. Finally the non-religious motives follow, such as "I come as a tourist" or "just to see what's happening". On the average 22% of the respondents agree to this kind of motives. But here too, respondents younger than 35 agree more frequently.

In these two studies there is a strict division between 'religious' and 'non-religious'. Our investigation showed that younger pilgrims often agree to motives, which at first sight seem to be related to recreation and social contacts, but which are also related to motives of a more existential nature, like "looking for silence" and "finding an opportunity for reflection". Our description of the younger pilgrim is much in accordance with the results of an investigation of the sociological center E.S.T.A. in Paris, held in 1977. On the basis of interviews with 40 French pilgrims to Lourdes four types of pilgrims were distinguished. The description of one of these types (the aspirant pilgrim, the new generation) shows many parallels with our description of the younger pilgrim. In this description the new generation is characterized as follows. They know little about the apparitions at Lourdes and are hardly interested in the rites taking place. Mary is not an important point of reference. Instead they are moved by silence and prayer and the social contacts in the group are especially important and stimulating.

In our view, a strict division between religious and non-religious motives (at least for the younger pilgrims) is less adequate. We suggest that the most interesting domain for future research on pilgrimage is this twilight zone between strictly religious and strictly non-religious motives. Here the feeling of "communitas" belongs: feeling close to one another through shared experiences. Brückner (1984) relates this searching for "communitas" to the discomfort of the younger pilgrim with our consumer society. He supposes that the younger pilgrims react to this consumer society by searching for real fellowship. One expression of this search is the revival of the "foot-pilgrimage": walking with a group of fellow pilgrims to the place of pilgrimage.

Motives, such as "because of the silence and the peaceful environment", "to contemplate" and "to meditate and reflect" also belong to this "in between zone". Further research (with additional in depth research methods, like interviews) has to be carried out in order to discover to what degree this reflection refers to religious (Christian) or non-religious meanings or, to speak with Turner and Turner (1978), to what degree the shared human experiences are identified with religious or non-religious paradigms. What we do know is that for many youngsters the Christian interpretation of the meaning of Lourdes is no longer popular.

Another matter concerns the effects of the pilgrimage. Younger as well as older pilgrims report positive changes on the level of emotional well-being. They are less anxious and depressed. We must however point at two limitations with respect to the interpretation of the observed changes. In our research we have not yet investigated whether these effects are long lasting. Secondly, because of the lack of a control group, it is difficult to point at a causal factor. Is it the pilgrimage, is it the effect of the pre-test itself ("testing" as a source of invalidity) or are there still other factors involved?

Supposing that at least some part of the effects observed is due to the pilgrimage, we wonder in what way the pilgrimage leads to beneficial changes. Searching for answers we studied Victor Turner, who regards pilgrimage as ritual. In his book *Image and pilgrimage in Christian culture* (1978), which he wrote together with his wife Edith, several characteristics of pilgrimage are given. Pilgrimage is described as a liminoid phenomenon:

174

"Pilgrimage has some of the liminal phase attributes in passage rites: release from mundane structure; homogenization of status; simplicity of dress and behavior; communitas, both on the journey, and as a characteristic of the goal, which is itself a source of communitas, healing, and renewal; ordeal; reflection on the meaning of religious and cultural core-values; ritualized reenactment of correspondences between a religious paradigm and shared human experiences; movement from a mundane center to a sacred periphery which suddenly, transiently, becomes central for the individual, an axis mundi of his faith; movement in general (as against stasis), symbolizing the uncapturability and temporal transience of communitas; individuality posed against the institutionalized milieu; and so forth. But since it is voluntary, not an obligatory social mechanism to mark the transition from one stage to another within the mundane sphere, pilgrimage is liminoid rather than liminal" (Turner and Turner, 1978:253-4).

Although one may wonder what the precise implications of the distinction between liminal and liminoid are, the Turners here present an anthropological look at the phenomenon of pilgrimage. From the point of view of the psychologist of religion the most interesting part of the description is: "...ritualized reenactment of correspondences between a religious paradigm and shared human experiences." Here is a starting point for explaining the transforming power of rituals (cf. Van Uden, 1987). Van der Hart (1981) also dealt with these matters. He claimed that in fact there is always one complex of myth - in which, in Turners words, a religious paradigm is expressed - and ritual. Myths can be seen as stories, which in the society in which they are being told, are regarded as true reports of what used to be. Myths, as Turner (1968a:576) put it, are "sacred narratives". Myths relate how one state of affairs became another; how chaos became cosmos. In a complex of myth and ritual the negative experiences of an individual can be expressed within the context of the myth. The myth becomes the medium through which human experiences can be symbolically shaped and altered. By participating in the ritual, changes, as presented in the myth, are followed by changes at a subjective level.

This explanation seems especially applicable to the older pilgrims, for whom a religious paradigm, in which Mary and God play a crucial role, is clearly available. Their motives point in a vertical, transcendent direction. The motives of the younger pilgrims, on the other hand, seem to have a more horizontal, immanent character. Here the religious frame of reference is less clear. Still, it may be possible that the open mind for nature, for the environment and the fellow pilgrim, creates an open attitude for the transcendental as well. Maybe the younger pilgrim meets God in the others and in nature, while the older pilgrim - mediated by Mary - searches for the Other: God. Yet we think that for the younger a less circumscribed myth for structuring their experiences can be distinguished.

This leads to some questions. Is it true that the experience of the younger pilgrim disappears sooner? And is this explained by the fact that after coming home the "myth of the group" quickly fades into an illusion? Sooner than he or she expected and hoped, despite reunions, the group desintegrates and the remembrance of a crucial confrontation with existential questions vanishes. The younger pilgrim reenters the consumer society to which we referred earlier. For the older pilgrim this is different. For him continuity is realized through weekly churchgoing, by which the myth, in which Mary is so prominently present, is actualized. But even apart from this churchgoing, the devotion to and identification with Mary remains possible in a process of role-playing and role-taking (Sundén, 1966b). For the older pilgrims the group of people with whom the pilgrimage was undertaken plays a minor role. Their "communitas" is of a different nature than that of the younger pilgrims. One could suppose that the myth of the younger pilgrims is created by the random group of pilgrimating, physically present others. The myth of the older pilgrim is constituted by a community that transcends this concrete situation, a community rooted in a tradition. But how will pilgrimage survive when the older generation disappears and their religious myth dies with them?

Thus, many questions still remain. Our future research in this field hopefully leads to as many answers.

BIBLIOGRAPHY

Arbuckle, G.A.
1987 Communicating through symbols. In: *Human development*, 8(1), pp. 7-12.

Augustinus, A.
1872-73 *Oeuvres Complètes*. Librairie de Louis Vivès, Paris.

Austin, D.J.
1981 Born again ... and again and again: Communitas and Social Change among Jamaican Pentecostalists. In: *Journal of Anthropological Research*, 37(3), pp. 226-46.

Bank, F.J.
1982 Waarom gaat men nú naar Lourdes? In: *Ons Geestelijk Leven*, 59, pp. 256-264.

Barbour, I.G.
1984 *Myth, Model and Paradigms. The Nature of the Scientific and Religious Language*. London.

Batson, C.W. & Ventis, W.L.
1982 *The Religious Experience. A Social-Psychological Perspective*. Oxford University Press, New York.

Bausch, W.J.
1984 *Storytelling: Imagination and Faith*. Twenty Third Publications, Mystic, Conn..

Bax, M.
1984 *"Officieel geloof" en "Volksgeloof" in Noord-Brabant: veranderingen in opvattingen en gedragingen als uitdrukking van rivaliserende clericale regimes*. In: Sociologisch Tijdschrift, 10, pp. 621-647.

Berger, P. & Luckmann, T.
1966 *The Social Construction of Reality. A Treatise in the Sociology of Knowledge*. Anchor Books/Doubleday, Garden City, N.Y.; English ed., 1967, Penguin Books, Harmondsworth.

Better Home and Gardens
1988 Religion, Spirituality and American Families; Attitudes and opinions of 80.000 respondents. In: *Better Home and Gardens Magazine*, Meredith Corporation.

Bock, P.K.
1980 *Continuities in Psychological Anthropology*. Freeman and Co., San Francisco.

Bousquet, F.
1981 Et la chair se fit logos. Essai sur la réaction philosophique au rite. In: F. Bousquet et al., *Le Rite* (Philosphie 6), Beauchesne, Paris.
Broughton, J.M.
1986 The Political Psychology of Faith Development Theory. In: C. Dykstra & S. Parks (eds.), *Faith Development and Fowler,* pp. 90-115, Religious Education Press, Birmingham, Alabama.
Brückner, W.
1984 Fusswallfahrt heute. Frömmigkeitsformen im sozialen Wandel der letzten hundert Jahre. In: L. Kriss-Rettenbeck & G. Möhler (eds.), *Wallfahrt kennt keine Grenzen.* Themen zu einer Ausstellung des Bayerischen Nationalmuseums und des Adalbert Stifter Vereins München, pp. 101-113, Schnell und Steiner, München.
Bruner, J.
1986 *Actual minds, possible worlds.* Cambridge, Mass./London, Harvard University Press.
Bukow, W.D.
1989 Religiöse Sozialisation und Entwicklung des religiösen Urteils: Einige kritische Bemerkungen zur Theorie der religiösen Urteilentwicklung aus der Perspektive der religiösen Sozialisation.
In: A. Bucher & K. Reich (eds.), *Entwicklung von Religiosität: Grundlagen, Theorieprobleme und praktische Anwendung,* pp. 65-76. Universitätsverlag, Freiburg.
Canda, E.R.
1988 Therapeutic Transformation in Ritual, Therapy and Human Development. In: *Journal of Religion and Health,* 27(3), pp. 205-20.
Canter, D.V. & Craik, K.H.
1981 Environmental Psychology. In: *Journal of Environmental Psychology,* 1, pp. 1-11.
Capps, D.
1982 The psychology of petitionary prayer. In: *Theology Today,* 39, pp. 130-141.
Carminati, G.
1988 Una Teoria semiologica del Lingguaggio Liturgico una verifica sull' "ordo missae". In: *Ephemerides Liturgicae,* 102, pp. 184-233.
Chowdhury, T. & et al.
1986 *Holisme en New Age-bewustzijn.* Theologische Faculteit Tilburg. Elka, Tilburg.

Christ, C.
1979 Why Women need the Goddess: Phenomenological, Psychological and Political Reflections. In: C. Christ & J. Plaskow (eds.), *Woman Spirit Rising*, Harper & Row Publishers, San Francisco.

Clavreul, J.
1987 *Le désir et la loi. Approches psychoanalytiques*, Denoël, Paris.

Cohen, A.P.
1985 *The symbolic construction of community*. Ellis Horwood, Chichester/Tavistock Publications, London.

Coleman, T.
1985 Missionary zeal in a world of famine. In: *The Guardian*, 15th July. Manchester/London.

Coppolillo, H.P.
1976 The transitional phenomenon revisited. In: *International Journal of the American Academy of Child Psychiatry*, 15, pp. 36-48.

Cox, H.
1973 *The Seduction of the Spirit; the Use and Misuse of People's Religion*. Simon and Schuster, New York.

Curran, D.
1978 *In the Beginning there were the Parents*. Winston Press, Minneapolis.

Daiber, K. & et al.
1980 *Predigen & Hören. Ergebnisse einer Gottesdienstbefragung*. Chr. Kaiser Verlag, München.

Davies, P.
1983 *God and the new physics*. Dent, London.

Doorn, P. & Bommeljé, Y.
1983 *Maar men moet toch iets wezen. Nieuwe gegevens over ontkerkelijking in Nederland*. Humanistisch Verbond, Utrecht.
1987 *Ontkerkelijking en verzuiling*. Humanistisch Verbond, Utrecht.

Douglas, M.
1973 *Natural Symbols: Explorations in Cosmology*. Barrie & Jenkins, London.

Dubach, A.
1989 Weg von Akzeptanz - hin zu Selbstentfaltungswerten. In: *Katechetische Blätter*, 114, Heft 10, pp. 744-749.

Durkheim, E.
1912 *Les Formes Elementaires de la Vie Religieuse. Le système totémique an Australie*, Bibliothèque de philosophie contemporaine, Paris.
1971 *The Elementary Forms of Religious Life*. Allen & Unwin, London.

Dykstra, C.
1986 What is Faith? An Experiment in the Hypothetical Mode. In: *C. Dystra and S. Parks (eds.), Faith Development and Fowler*, Religious Education Press, Birmingham, Alabama.

Eliade, M.
1988 *Symbolism, the Sacred & the Arts*. Crossroad, New York.

Erikson, E.H.
1966 Ontogeny of Ritualization in Man. In: R.M. Loewenstein et al. (eds.), *Psychoanalysis - A General Psychology. Essays in honour of Heinz Hartmann*, International University Press, New York.

1958 *Young Man Luther: A study in psychoanalysis and history*. W.W. Norton, New York.

1977 *Toys and Reasons. Stages in the Ritualization of Experience*. W.W. Norton, New York.

Evenshaugh, O. & Hallen, D.
1989 Readiness for religion - revisited. An educational perspective. In: *Proceedings of the fourth symposium on the psychology of religion in Europe*, Nijmegen.

Ezard, J.
1985 Band Aid gears up for action after the 'ultimate day'. In: *The Guardian*, 16th July, Manchester/London.

Faber, H.
1976 *Psychology of Religion*. London/Philadelphia.

1988 De Betekenis van de huidige Psychoanalyse voor het Inzicht in Religie. In: J.A. van Belzen & J.M. van der Lans (eds.), *Rond Godsdienst en Psychoanalyse, pp.9-22*, Kok, Kampen.

Felling, A., Peters, J. & Schreuder, O.
1982 Gebroken identiteit: Een studie over christelijk en onchristelijk Nederland. In: *Jaarboek Katholiek Documentatie Centrum*, no. 11-1981, pp. 25-81, Nijmegen.

Finney, J.R. & Malony, H.N.
1985 Empirical studies of Christian prayer: a review of the literature. In: *Journal of Psychology and Theology*, 13, pp. 104-115.

Flannery, A.P.
1975/1985 *Documents of Vatican II*. Eerdmans Publ., Grand Rapids.

Fogarty, M., Ryan, L. & Lee, J.
1984 *Irish Values and Attitudes; The Irish Report of the European Value Systems Study*. Dominican Publications, Dublin.

Fowler, J.W.
1974 Toward a developmental perspective on faith. In: *Religious Education*, LXIX, 2, pp. 202-19.

1981   *Stages of Faith. The Psychology of Human Development and the Quest for Meaning.* Harper & Row, San Francisco.

1986   Faith and the Structuring of Meaning. In: C. Dykstra & S. Parks (eds.), *Faith Development and Fowler,* pp. 15-45, Religious Education Press, Birmingham (Al.).

1988   Die Berufung der Theorie der Glaubensentwicklung: Richtingen und Modifikationen seit 1981. In: K.E. Nipkow, F. Scheitzer & J.W. Fowler (eds.), *Glaubensentwicklung und Erziehung,* pp. 29-48. Gerd Mohn, Gütersloh.

Freud, S.

1972   Zwangshandlungen und Religionsübungen. (Orig. 1907). In: S. Freud, *Gesammelte Werke,* Bd. VII, pp. 129-139, S. Fischer Verlag, Frankfurt.

1973   Totem und Tabu. (Orig. 1912/13). In: S. Freud, *Gesammelte Werke,* Bd. IX, Fischer Verlag, Frankfurt.

1953-74 Obsessive Actions and Religious Practices.
In: *The Standard Edition of the Complete Psychological Works of Sigmund Freud,* IX, pp. 115-127, Hogarth Press, London.

1982   Das Unbehagen in der Kultur. (Orig. 1930).
In: S. Freud, *Studienausgabe,* Bd.IX, pp. 191-270, Fischer Verlag, Frankfurt am Main.

Fröbe-Kapteyn, O. (ed.)

1951   Mensch und Ritus. In: *Eranos Jahrbuch* (1950), Bd.XIX, Rhein-Verlag, Zürich.

Frundt, H.J.

1969   Rite involvement and community formation. In: *Sociological Analysis,* 30, pp. 91-107.

Fuchs, W.

1985   Konfessionelle Milieus und Religiosität. In: A. Fischer, W. Fuchs & J. Zinnecker, *Jugendliche und Erwachsene '85: Generationen im Vergleich.* Leske & Budrich, Leverkusen.

Gallup, G. jr. & O'Connell, G.

1986   *Who do Americans say that I am?* Westminster Press, Philadelphia.

Gallup, G. jr. & Poling, D.G.

1980   *The search for America's Faith.* Abingdon Press, Nashville.

Gay, V.P.

1983   Ritual and Self-Esteem in Victor Turner and Heinz Kohut.
In: *Zygon, Journal of Religion and Science,* 18(3), pp. 271-282.

Geertz, C.

1966   Religion as a cultural system. In: M. Banton (ed.), *Anthropological Approaches to the Study of Religion,* pp. 1-46, Tavistock Publications, London.

1973a Religion as a cultural system. (Orig. 1966). In: C. Geertz, *The Interpretation of Cultures*, pp. 87-125, Basic Books, New York.
1973b *The Interpretation of cultures*. Basic Books, New York.
1983 *Local Knowledge. Further essays in interpretive anthropology*. Basic Books, New York.

Gehlen, A.
1964 *Urmensch und Spätkultur*. (Orig. 1956). Athenäum Verlag, Frankfurt am Main.

Gennep, A. van
1909 *Les rites de passage. Etude systématique des rites*. Emile Nourry, Paris.
1960 *The Rites of Passage*. Routledge and Kegan Paul, London.
1969 *Les rites de passage. Etude systématique des rites*. Johnson, New York.

Gergen, K.J.
1985 The social constructionist movement in modern psychology. In: *American Psychologist* 40(3), pp. 266-275.

Gill, S.D.
1987 Prayer. In: M. Eliade (Ed.), *The Encyclopedia of Religion*, Vol. 11, pp. 489-494, MacMillan and Free Press, New York.

Gilligan, C.
1982 *In a Different Voice. Psychological Theory and Woman's Development*. Harvard University Press, Cambridge, Mass..

God in Nederland
1967 Van Ditmar, Amsterdam.

Goddijn, W., Smets, H. & Tillo, G. van
1979 Opnieuw: God in Nederland. In: *De Tijd*, Amsterdam.

Goffman, E.
1967 *Interaction Ritual*. Doubleday Anchor Books, New York.

Goldenberg, N.
1985 Archetypal Theory and the Separation of Mind and Body. In: *Journal of Feminist Studies of Religion*, 1.

Gordon, A.J.
1967 *The Nature of Conversion*. Boston

Greeley, A.M.
1971 Godsdienstige symboliek, liturgie en gemeenschap. In: *Concilium*, 7(2), pp. 58-68.
1979 *Crisis in the Church*. The Thomas More Press, Chicago.

Green, R.M.
1988 *Religion and moral reason. A new method for comparative study*. Oxford University Press.

Greinacher, N. & Elizondo, V. (eds.)
1984 Handing on the faith to the next generation. In: *Concilium*, 174, IX-X.

Grimes, R.L.
1985 *Research in Ritual Studies: A programmatic essay and bibliography*. The Scarecrow Press, London.
1987 Ritual. In: M. Eliade (Ed.), *The Encyclopedia of Religion*, Vol.11, pp. 405-425. MacMillan and Free Press, New York.

Groome, T.
1980 *Christian Religious Education*. Harper & Row, San Francisco.

Grünewald, F.
1982 Das Gebet als spezifisches Übergangsobjekt. In: *Wege zum Menschen*, 34, pp. 221-228.

Guth, K.
1986 Die Wallfahrt. Ausdruck Religiöser Kultur. In: *Liturgisches Jahrbuch*, 36, pp. 180-201.

Harding, S., Philips, D. & Fogarty, M.
1986 *Contrasting Values in Western Europe: Unity, Diversity and Change*. MacMillan, London.

Hart, J. de
1989a Secularization or the return of the sacred? Reflecting on meaning and new religious movements among Dutch high school students. In: *Proceedings of the fourth symposium on the psychology of religion in Europe*, Nijmegen.
1989b *Levensbeschouwelijke en politieke praktijken van Nederlandse middelbare scholieren*. Dissertation. Kok, Kampen.

Hart, O. van der
1978 *Overgang en bestendiging: Over het ontwerpen en voorschrijven van rituelen in psychotherapie*. Van Loghum Slaterus, Deventer.
1984 *Rituelen in Psychotherapie: Overgang en Bestendiging*. Van Loghum Slaterus, Deventer.

Hart, Onno van der & et al.
1981 *Afscheidsrituelen in Psychotherapie*. Ambo, Baarn.

Haste, H.
1990 Moral responsibility and moral commitment: The integration of affect and cognition. In: T. Wren (ed.), *The Moral Domain*, pp. 315-359, Massachusetts Inst. of Technology Press, Cambridge (MA).

Heidegger, M.
1972 *Sein und Zeit*. (Orig. 1927). Max Niemeyer, Tübingen.

Heiler, F.
1921 *Das Gebet, eine Religionsgeschichtliche und Religionspsychologische Untersuchung*. Verlag von Ernst Reinhardt, München.
1958 *Prayer*. Galaxy Books, New York/Oxford University Press.

1961 Erscheinungsformen und Wesen der Religion. In: Ch. Schröder (Ed.), *Die Religionen der Menschheit*, W. Kohlhammer Verlag, Vol.1, Stuttgart.

Heimbrock, H.G.

1977 *Phantasie und christlicher Glaube*. Christian Kaiser Verlag, München/Mainz.

1986 The Development of symbols as key to developmental psychology of religion. In: J.A. van Belzen & J.M. van der Lans (eds.), *Current issues in the psychology of religion. Proceedings of the third symposium on the psychology of religion in Europe*, pp. 38-43, Rodopi, Amsterdam.

1988 Religiöse Entwicklung und die rituelle Dimension. In: K.E. Nipkow, F. Schweitzer & J.W. Fowler (Eds.), *Glaubensentwicklung und Erziehung*, pp. 193-207. Gerd Mohn, Gütersloh.

Helve, H.

1989 The formation of the world views of young people. A longitudinal study of young Finns. In: *Proceedings of the fourth symposium on the psychology of religion in Europe*, Nijmegen.

Henau, E.

1986 Popular religiosity and Christian faith. In: *Concilium*, 186, pp. 71 - 81.

Hendrick, R., Morrissey, T. & Nielsen, P.

1986 *The Contribution of Family religious Practices (Rituals) in the Transmission of Christian Faith: an Adaption of the Wolin and Bennett Method for the Study of Family Rituals.* (Unpublished Research Memoir). Saint Paul University, Ottawa.

Holloman, R.E.

1974 Ritual Opening and Individual Transformation: Rites of passage at Esalen. In: *American Anthropologist*, 26, pp. 265-280.

Holmes, U.T.

1973 Liminality and Liturgy. In: *Worship*, 47(7), pp. 386-97.

Hood Jr, R. W.

1978 Anticipatory Set and Setting: Stress incongruities as elicitors of mystical experience in solitary nature situations. In: *Journal for the Scientific Study of Religion*, 17(3), pp. 279-287.

Hood Jr., R.W. & Morris, R.J.

1981 Sensory Isolation and the Differential Elicitation of Religious Imagery in Intrinsic and Extrinsic Persons. In: *Journal for the Scientific Study of Religion*, 20(3), pp. 261-273.

Hull, J.
1988 Menschliche Entwicklung in der modernen kapitalistischen Gesellschaft. In: K.E. Nipkow, F. Schweitzer & J.W. Fowler (Eds.), *Glaubensentwicklung und Erziehung*, Gerd Mohn, Gütersloh.

Hummel, R.
1980 *Indische Mission und neue Frommigkeit im Westen*. Kohlhammer Taschenbuch, Stuttgart.

Hutsebaut, D. & Verhoeven, D.
1989 The adolescents' representation of God from age 12 till age 15. In: *Proceedings of the fourth symposium on the psychology of religion in Europe*, Nijmegen.

Huxley, Sir Julian & et al. (eds)
1966 A Discussion on Ritualization of Behavior in Animals and Man. In: *Philosophical Transactions of the Royal Society of London*, Series B, 251, pp. 247-526.

James, W.
1902 *The Varieties of Religious Experience*. Longmans, New York
1982 *The Varieties of Religious Experience*. Penguin Books Ltd, Harmondsworth.

Janssen, J., Bego, H. & Berg, G. van den
1987 *TekstTabel*. Nijmegen, Internal publication Psychological Laboratory.

Jetter, W.
1986 *Symbol und Ritual. Anthropologische Elemente im Gottesdienst*. Vandenhoeck & Ruprecht, Göttingen.

John-Paul II
1981 *Familiaris Consortio*. Canadian Conference of Catholic Bishops, Ottawa.

Johnson, P.E.
1945 *Psychology of Religion*. Abingdon Press, New York.

Jung, C.G.
1940 *Psychologie und Religion*. Rascher, Zürich.
1952 Symbole der Wandlung. In: C.G. Jung, *Gesammelte Werke*, Bd. 5, Walter Verlag, Olten.

Keeley, B.
1976 Generations in tension: intergenerational differences and continuities in religion and religion-related behavior. In: *Review of Religious Research*, 17 (3), pp. 221-231.

Keller, B.
1989 Heavy Metal is music to Moscovites' ears. In: *International Herald Tribune*, 14th August, Zürich.

Kerkhofs, J.
1984 Young people and values in Western Europe. Pro Mundi Vita Dossiers, 4.
1988 Between Christendom and Christianity. In: *Journal of Empirical Theology*, 1(2), pp. 88-101.
Kerkhofs, J. & Rezsohazy, R.
1984 *De stille Ommekeer*. Lannoo, Tielt.
Kerstiens, L.
1987 *Das Gewissen wecken. Gewissen und Gewissensbildung im Ausgang des 20. Jahrhunderts*. Julius Klinkhardt, Bad Heilbrunn/ Obb. (FRG).
King, U.
1989 *Women and Spirituality. Voices of Protest and Promise*. Mac-Millan Education LTD, London.
Kippenberg, H.G.
1983 Diskursive Religionswissenschaft. In: B. Gladigow & H.G. Kippenberg (eds.), *Neue Ansätze in der Religionswissenschaft*, Kösel, München.
1986 Religionssoziologie ohne Säkularisierungsthese: E. Durkheim und M. Weber aus der Sicht der Symboltheorie. In: H.G. Hubbeling & H.G. Kippenberg (eds.), *On Symbolic Representation of Religion. Groninger Contributions to Theories of Symbols*, pp. 102-118, Walter de Gruyter, Berlin/New York.
Kippenberg, H.G. & Luchesi, I. (eds.)
1978 *Magie. Die sozialwissenschaftliche Kontroverse über das Verstehen fremden Denkens*. Suhrkamp, Frankfurt.
Kohut, H.
1977 *The Restoration of the Self*. New York.
Langer, S.
1974 *Philosophy in a New Key*: a study in symbolism of reason, rite and art. (Orig. 1942). Harvard Univ. Press, Cambridge, (MA).
Lans, J.M. van der
1980 *Religieuze ervaring en meditatie. Een godsdienstpsychologische studie*. Van Loghum Slaterus, Deventer.
1984 De functie van het symbool in de liturgie. In: J.M. van der Lans (ed.), *Spiritualiteit; sociaalwetenschappelijke en theologische beschouwingen*, pp. 42-56, Ambo, Baarn.
1988 Geloven: Een kwestie van fantasie. In: A.G. Weiler (ed.), *Een nieuw christelijk mensbeeld*, pp. 69-83, Ambo, Baarn.
Lauwers, J.
1974 *Secularisatietheoriën. Een studie over de toekomstkansen van de godsdienstsociologie*. Universitaire Pers, Leuven.

Leach, E.
1968 Ritual. In: D.L. Shils (ed.), *International Encyclopedia of the Social Sciences*, XIII, pp. 521-526. MacMillan & Free Press, New York.

Leege, D.C., Welch, M.R. & Trozzolo, T.
1986 Religiosity, church social teaching, and socio-political attitudes: A research note on homogamy as social context for U.S. Catholics. In: *Review of Religious Research*, 28, (3), pp. 118-128.

Lévi-Strauss, C.
1973 *Structural Anthropology*, vol.2. Penguin Books, Harmondsworth.

Liederkerke, A. de
1989 Malte, l'île forteresse, va retrouver ses chevaliers. Sous l'emblème de l'ordre de Saint-Jean, ils étaient six cents rassemblés dans le fief de l'ordre. In: *Figaro-Magazine*, 28th October, Paris.

Loofland, J.
1977 *Doomsday cult: A Study of Conversion, Proselytization, and Maintenance of Faith*. Irvington, New York.

MacKay, D.M.
1974 Complementarity in scientific and theological thinking. In: *Zygon, Journal of Religion and Science*, 9, pp. 225-224.

Maldonado, L.
1986 Popular religion: Its dimensions, levels and types. In: *Concilium*, 186, pp. 3-11.

Malinowski, S.
1948 *'Magic, Science and Religion' and other Essays*. Selected by R. Redfield. Trade ed. Beacon Press, Boston, Mass.; Text ed. The Free Press, Glencoe, Illinois.

Meadow, W. & Kahoe, R.
1984 *Psychology of Religion*. Harper & Row, New York.

Meissner, M.M.
1984 *Psychoanalysis and Religious Experience*. Yale University Press, New Haven/London.
1987 *Life and Faith. Psychological Perpective on Religious Experience*. Georgetown University Press, Washington.

Moore, R.L.
1983 Contemporary Psychotherapy as Ritual Process: An initial Reconnaissance. In: *Zygon, Journal of Religion and Science*, 18(3), pp. 283-294.
1984a Space and Transformation in Human Experience. In: R.L. Moore & F. Reynolds (eds.), *Anthropology and the Study of Religion*, pp. 126-143, University of Chicago Press, Chicago.

187

1984b Ministry, Sacred Space, and Theological Education: The legacy of Victor Turner. In: *Theological Education*, autumn 1984, pp. 87-100.

Moore, R.L. & Reynolds, F.E. (eds.)
1984 *Anthropology and the Study of Religion*. University of Chicago Press, Chicago.

Moore, S.F. & Meyerhoff, B.G. (eds.)
1977 *Secular Ritual*. Van Gorcum, Assen/Amsterdam.

Morris, B.
1987 *Anthropological Studies of Religion; an introductory text*. Cambridge University Press, Cambridge.

Morris, P.A.
1982 The effect of pilgrimage on anxiety, depression and religious attitude. In: *Psychological Medicine*, 12, pp. 291-294.

Müller, P.
1988 Fasten - Heilmittel oder Modeerscheinung? (Erfahrungsbericht über die jährliche Rottweiler Fastenwoche). In: *Katechetische Blätter* 113, pp. 58-64.

Müller-Pozzi, H.
1975 *Psychologie des Glaubens. Versuch einer Verhältnisbestimmung von Theologie und Psychoanalyse*. Ibris, München.

Neumann, E.
1978 Zur psychologischen Bedeutung des Ritus. (Orig. 1978). In: E. Neumann, *Kulturentwicklung und Religion*, pp. 9-50, Fischer Taschenbuch Verlag, Frankfurt.

Nieuwenhuis, J.
1978a *Volgend jaar misschien*. Ambo, Baarn.
1978b *Tussen twaalf en zestien*. Ambo, Baarn.

Ogden, Th.H.
1985 On Potential Space. In: *Int. Journal of Psycho-Analysis*, 66, pp. 129-141.

Oosterwijk, J.W., Uden, M.H.F. van & Hensgens, L.
1986 Pilgrimage: motivation and effects. In: J.A. van Belzen & J.M. van der Lans (eds.), *Current Issues in the Psychology of Religion. Proceedings of the third symposium on the psychology of religion in Europe*, pp. 173-182. Rodopi, Amsterdam.

Oosterwijk, J.W., Hoenkamp-Bisschops, A.M., Pieper, J.Z.T. & Uden, M.H.F. van
1987 *Steun en ontmoeting. Een onderzoek onder bedevaartgangers naar Lourdes*. UTP, Heerlen.

Oser, F.
1980 Stages of religious judgement. In: C. Brusselmans & J.A. Donahoe (eds.), *Toward moral and religious maturity*, pp. 277-315, Morristown, New Jersey.
1988 Genese und Logik der Entwicklung des religiösen Bewusstseins: Eine Entgegnung auf Kritiken. In: K.E. Nipkow, F. Schweitzer & J.W. Fowler (eds.), *Glaubensentwicklung und Erziehung*, pp. 48-91, Gerd Mohn, Gütersloh.
1989 Stufen religiöser Entwicklung: Fakten oder Fiktionen? Ein Gespräch mit Fritz Oser. In: A. Bucher & K. Reich (eds.), *Entwicklung von Religiosität*, pp. 239-255, Universitätsverlag, Freiburg.

Oser, F.K. & Gmünder, P.
1984 *Der Mensch. Stufen seiner Religiösen Entwicklung*. Benzinger Verlag, Zürich.

Oser, F.K. & Reich, K.H.
1987 The challenge of competing explanations. The development of thinking in terms of complementarity of 'theories'. In: *Human Development*, 30, pp. 178-186.
1990 Moral judgement, religious judgement, world view and logical thought: A review of their relationship. In: *British Journal of Religious Education*, 12(2), pp. 94-101, (3), pp. 172-181.

Otto, R.
1917 *Das Heilige. Ueber das Irrationale in der Idee des Göttlichen und sein Verhältnis zum Rationalen*. Stuttgart.

Ouwerkerk, C. van.
1984 Het gebed: enkele godsdienst-psychologische aantekeningen. In: *Leer ons bidden*, pp. 21-32, Utrecht.

Pace, E.
1987 The paradigms of popular religion. In: *Archives de Sciences sociales des Religions*, 64(1), pp. 7-14.

Panikkar, R.
1977 Man as a ritual being. In: *Chicago Studies*, 16(1), pp. 5-28.

Pargament, K.I. & Silverman, W.H.
1983 Exploring some correlates of sermon impact on catholic parishioners. In: *Review of religious research*, 24(1), pp. 31-39.

Parks, S.
1986 Imagination and Spirit in Faith Development: A Way Past the Structure-Content Dichotomy. In: C. Dykstra & S. Parks (eds.), *Faith Development and Fowler*, pp. 137-157. Religious Education Press, Birmingham, Alabama.
1988 James Fowlers Theorie der Glaubensentwicklung in der nordamerikanischen Situation. In: K.E. Nipkow, F. Schweitzer & J.W.

Fowler (eds.), *Glaubensentwicklung und Erziehung*, pp. 91-108, Gerd Mohn, Gütersloh.

Parry, G.
1985 Live Aid records £ 50 million. In: *The Guardian*, 15th July, Manchester/London.

Peirce, C.S.
1935 *Collected Papers*. Eds. C. Hartshorne and P. Weiss. Cambridge, 1931-1935.

Piaget, J.
1926 *La représentation du monde chez l'enfant*. Presses Universitaires de France, Paris.

Pieper, J.Z.T. & van Uden, M.H.F. van
1988 *Bidden in Banneux. Een onderzoek onder bedevaartgangers naar Banneux*. UTP, Heerlen.

Pinel, Ph.
1801 *Traité médico-philosophique sur l'aliénation mentale ou la manie*. Richard, Caille & Ravier, year IX, pp. 58, Paris.

Ploeg, H.M. van der, Defares, P.B., & Spielberger, C.D.
1980 *Handleiding bij de Zelf-Beoordelingsvragenlijst*. Swets & Zeitlinger, Lisse.

Postel, J.
1981 *Genèse de la psychiatrie. Les premiers écrits de Philippe Pinel*. Le Sycomore, pp. 39-46, Paris.

Pratt, J.B.
1910/11 An empirical study of prayer. In: *American Journal of Religious Psychology and Education*, 4, pp. 48-67.

Proshansky, H.M. & Altmann, I.
1979 Overview of the field. In: W.S. White (ed.), *Resources in environment and behavior*, American Psychological Association, Washington, D.C.

Pruyser, P.W.
1973 Sigmund Freud and his Legacy: Psychoanalytic Psychology of Religion. In: C.Y. Glock & P.E. Hammond, *Beyond the Classics. Essays in the scientific study of religion*. Harper & Row, New York.

1982 *Between Belief and Unbelief*. Sheldon Press, London.

1983 *The Play of the Imagination*. International University Press, New York.

Randall Nichols, J.
1985 Worship as anti-structure: the contribution of Victor Turner. In: *Theology Today*, 41(4), pp. 401-409.

Redford Ruether, R.

1985 *Woman-Church. Theology and Practice of Feminist Liturgical Communities.* Harper & Row Publishers, San Fransisco.

Reich, K.H.

1989 Between religion and science: Complementarity in the religious thinking of young people. In: *British Journal of Religious Education,* 11, pp. 62-69.

1990 The Chalcedonian Definition, an example of the difficulties and the usefulness of thinking in terms of complementarity? In: *Journal of Psychology and Theology.*

Reich, K.H. & Oser, F.

1990 *Konkret-operatorisches, formal-operatorisches und komplementäres Denken, Begriffs- und Theorieentwicklung: Welche Beziehungen?* In: F. Oser & K.H. Reich (eds.), *Bericht über die Arbeitsgruppe "Entwicklung von Denkprozessen und Argumentationsfiguren" auf der 9. Tagung "Entwicklungspsychologie" vom 18-21 September 1989 in München,* pp. 41-66, Pädagogisches Institut, Fribourg.

Reik, Th.

1919 *Probleme der Religionspsychologie* (Bd.1, *Das Ritual*). Int. Psychoanalytischer Verlag, Vienna.

1964 *Pagan Rituals in Judaism.* New York.

Religion in America: 50 years: 1935-1985

1985 Princeton: The Gallup Organization.

Rezsohazy, R. & Kerkhofs, J.

1984 *L'Univers des Belges.* Ed. CIACO, Louvain-la-Neuve.

Rich, J.M. & DeVitis, J.L.

1985 *Theories of moral development.* Charles C. Thomas, Springfield, Illinois.

Richards, J.

1985 The hooligan culture: Violence and the undermass. In: *Encounter* LXV, No. 4, pp. 15-23.

Rieff, Ph.

1973 *The Triumph of the Therapeutic. Uses of Faith after Freud.* (Orig. 1966). Penguin, Harmondsworth.

Rizzuto, A.M.

1979 *The Birth of living God. A Psychoanalytic Study.* University of Chicago Press, Chicago.

Robbrecht, I.P.

1986 *Mariaverering te Scherpenheuvel. Proeve van een hedendaagse pastoraal in een mariaal bedevaartsoord.* Eindverhandeling Licentiaat. Leuven.

191

Roberts, J.
1988 Setting of the frame: definition, functions, and typology of rituals. In: E. Imber-Black, J. Roberts & R. Whiting (eds.), *Rituals in Families and Family Therapy*, Norton, New York.

Ross, M.E. & Ross, Ch.L.
1983 Mothers, Infants and the Psychoanalytic Study of Ritual. In: *Signs: Journal of Women in Culture and Society*, 9(1), pp. 26-39.

Sabini, J. & Silver, M.
1982 *Moralities of everyday life*. Oxford University Press, Oxford.

Sallnow, M.J.
1981 Communitas Reconsidered: The sociology of Andean Pilgrimage. In: *Man (N.S.)*, vol. 16, pp. 163-182.

Scharfe, M., Schmolze, M. & Schubert, G.
1985 *Wallfahrt. Tradition und Mode. Empirische Untersuchungen zur Aktualität von Volksfrömmigkeit*. Tübinger Vereinigung für Volkskunde, Tübingen.

Scheer, A.H.M.
1985 De beleving van liturgische riten en symbolen. In: J.A. Van der Ven (ed.), *Pastoraal tussen ideaal en werkelijkheid*, pp. 105-120. Kampen.

Schleiermacher, F.
1955 *On Religion. Speeches to its Cultured Despisers*. (Orig. 1799). New York.

Schorsch, C.
1988 *Die New Age Bewegung*. Utopie und Mythos der Neuen Zeit. Gerd Mohn, Gütersloh.

Schreuder, O. & Peters J.
1987 *Katholiek en Protestant. Een Historisch en Contemporain Onderzoek naar Confessionele Culturen*. Instituut Toegepaste Sociale Wetenschappen, Nijmegen.

Schüssler Fiorenza, E.
1983 *In Memory of Her*. SCM Press, London.
1985 *Bread not Stone*. Beacon Press, Boston (MA).

Schwarz, N.
1988 Stimmung als Information. Zum Einfluss von Stimmungen und Emotionen auf evaluative Urteile. In: *Psychologische Rundschau*, 39, pp. 148-159.

Schweitzer, F.
1987 *Lebensgeschichte und Religion. Religiöse Entwicklung und Erziehung im Kindes- und Jungendalter*. Breklumer Druckerei, München.

Sidenap, K.
1989 *Spring inverted. A tope analysis*. Belinge Press.

Smith, W.C.
1978 *The Meaning and End of Religion. A revolutionary Approach to the great religious Traditions*. New York.
Sölle, D.
1965 Gebed. In: H.J. Schultz (Ed.), *Theologie voor Niet-Theologen. Een Abc van het Protestantse Denken*, pp. 126-133, Ambo, Utrecht.
Spretnak, C. (ed.)
1982 *The Politics of Woman's Spirituality*. Essays on the rise of spiritual power within the feminist movement. Anchor Books, Garden City, N.Y..
Spilka, B., Hood, R.W. & Gorsuch, R.L.
1985 *The psychology of religion. An empirical approach*. Prentice Hall, Englewood Cliffs.
Staal, F.
1979 The meaninglessness of ritual. In: *Numen*, 26, pp. 2-22.
Starhawk
1979 *The Spiral Dance*. Harper & Row Publishers, New York.
Steinglass, P., Bennett, L.A., Wolin, S.J. & Reiss, D.
1987 *The Alcoholic Family*. Basic Books, New York.
Stern, J.
1987 Reference modes in Judaic rituals. In: *Religious Studies*, 23(1), pp. 109-128.
Stettler, W.
1989 Mammutkonzert in der Eishalle. Teamwork von Kirchenarbeit und Tonkunst. In: *Freiburger Nachrichten*, 12th June, Fribourg.
Strommen, M.P., Brekke, M.L., Underwager, R.C. & Johnson, A.L.
1972 *A study of Generations*. Augsburger, Minneapolis.
Sundén, H.
1966a *Religionen och rollerna. Ett psykologiskt studium av fromheten*. Verbum, Stockholm.
1966b *Die Religion und die Rollen. Eine psychologische Untersuchung der Frömmigkeit*. Töpelmann, Berlin.
Terrien, S.
1978 *The Elusive Presence*. San Francisco.
Tillich, P.
1926 *Die religiöse Lage der Gegenwart*. Berlin.
Turner, K.
1982 Contempory Feminist Rituals. In: *The Politics of Women's Spirituality*. pp. 219-234, Anchor Books, Garden City, NY.
Turner, V.W.
1957 *Schism and Continuity in an African Society; a study of Ndembu village life*. Manchester University Press, Manchester.

1967 *The Forest of Symbols; aspects of Ndembu ritual.* Cornell University Press, Ithaca, NY.

1968a Myth and Symbol. In: *International Encyclopedia of the Social Sciences,* 10, pp. 567-582.

1968b *The Drums of Affliction; a study of religious processes among the Ndembu of Zambia.* Clarendon Press, Oxford.

1974a *Dramas, Fields and Metaphors: Symbolic action in human society.* Cornell University Press, Ithaca, NY.

1974b *Liminal to Liminoid, in Play, Flow, and Ritual; an essay in comparative symbology.* In: *Rice University Studies,* 60, pp. 53-92.

1974c Symbols and social experience in religious ritual. Worship and ritual in Christianity and other religions. In: *Studia Missionalia XXIII,* pp. 1-22.

1974d Pilgrimage and Communitas. In: *Studia Missionalia,* pp. 305-327.

1977a *The Ritual Process: Structure and Anti-structure.* (Orig. 1969). Cornell University Press, Ithaca, NY.

1977b Variations on a theme of liminality. In: S.F. Moore & B.G. Meyerhoff (eds.), *Secular Ritual,* pp. 36-52, van Gorcum, Assen/Amsterdam.

1978 Encounter with Freud: The Making of a Comparative Symbologist. In: G.D. Spindler (ed.), *The Making of Psychological Anthropology,* pp. 558-583, Univ. of California Press, Berkely.

1982 *From Ritual to Theatre.* Performing Arts J. Publications, New York.

1983 Body, Brain and Culture. In: *Zygon, Journal of Religion and Science,* 18(3), pp. 221-245.

1984 Liminality and the Performance Genres. In: J. Macaloon (ed.), *Rite, Drama, Festival, Spectacle,* pp. 19-41. ISHI, Philadelphia.

1986 Dewey, Dilthey, and Drama: an essay in the anthropology of experience. In: V.W. Turner & E.M. Bruner (eds.), *The Anthropology of Experience,* pp. 33-44, University of Illinois Press, Urbana/Chicago.

Turner, V.W. & Turner, E.

1978 *Image and Pilgrimage in Christian Culture: anthropological perspectives.* Basil Blackwell, Oxford.

Tylor, E.

1958 *Religion in Primitive Culture.* (orig. 1871). Harper & Brothers Publishers, New York.

Uden, M.H.F. van

1987 Gejaagd door de wind. Over de werking van rituelen in psychotherapie. In: *Tijdschrift voor Psychotherapie,* 5, pp. 274-282.

Uden, M.H.F. van & Post, P.G.J.
1988 *Christelijke Bedevaarten. Op weg naar heil en heling.* Dekker & van de Vegt, Nijmegen.

Vandermeersch, P. (ed.)
1984 *Psychiatrie, godsdienst en gezag. De ontstaansgeschiedenis van de psychiatrie in België als paradigma,* Acco, Leuven.

Vieth, R.F.
1988 *Holy power, human pain.* Meyer-Stone, Bloomington, Indiana.

Vogeleisen, G.
1984 Catechesis: Handing on the faith today. In: *Concilium,* 174, pp. 63-70.

Volkan, V. & Corney, R.T.
1968 Some Considerations of Satellite States and Satellite Dreams. In: *British Journal of Medical Psychology,* 41, pp. 283-290.

Walker Bynum, C.
1984 Women's Stories, Women's Symbols: A critique of Victor Turner's Theory of Liminality. In: R.L. Moore & F.E. Reynolds (eds.), *Anthropology and the Study of Religion,* pp. 105-125, CSSR, Chicago, Illinois.

Weinreich-Haste, H.
1986 Moralisches Engagement. Die Funktion der Gefühle im Urteilen und Handeln. In: W. Edelstein & G. Nunner-Winkler (Eds.), *Zur Bestimmung der Moral. Philosophische und sozialwissenschaftliche Beiträge zur Moralforschung,* pp. 337-406. Suhrkamp, Frankfurt am Main.

Westerhoff, J.
1976 *Will our Children have Faith?* Seabury Press, New York.

White, H.
1987 *The Contribution of Family Practices (Rituals) in the Transmission of Christian Faith.* (Unpublished Research Memoir). Saint Paul University, Ottawa.

Wikström, O.
1987 Religion, Roles and Attributions. In: *Journal for the Scientific Study of Religion,* 3, pp. 390-400.

Wilson, B.R. (ed.)
1979 *Rationality.* (Orig. 1970). Basil Blackwell, Guildford.

Wilson, E.O.
1978 *On Human Nature.* Harvard University Press, Cambridge.

Wimmer, M.
1982 Der gesprochene Körper. Zur Authentizität von Körpererfahrungen in Körpertherapien. In: D. Kamper & C. Wulf, *Die Wiederkehr des Körpers,* pp. 82-97. Suhrkamp, Frankfurt am Main.

Winnicott, D.W.
1958 The Capacity to be Alone. In: Int. Journal of Psycho-Analysis, 39.
1978 Mind and its Relation to the Psyche-soma. In: *Winnicott, Through Paediatrics to Psycho-analysis*. Hogarth Press, London.
1986a Transitional Objects and Transitional Phenomena. (Orig. 1951). In: D.W. Winnicott, *Playing and Reality*, pp. 1-30, Penguin Books, London.
1986b The Use of an Object and Relating through Identifications. (Orig. 1969). In: D.W. Winnicott, *Playing and Reality*, pp. 101-111, Penguin Books, Harmondsworth.

Wolde, E.J. van
1989 *A Semiotic Analysis of Genesis 2-3; A semiotic theory and method of analysis applied to the story of the Garden of Eden*. Assen.

Wolin, S.J. & Bennett, L.A.
1984 Family rituals. In: *Family Process*, 23(3), pp. 401-420.

Worgul, G.S. Jr.
1984 Ritual as the interpreter of tradition. In: *Louvain Studies*, 10, pp. 141-150.

Yon, E.D.
1981 Deux figures du rite dans le christianisme. Leur notion de transcendance et de médiation. In: F. Bousquet et al., *Le Rite* (Philosphie 6), pp. 205-246. Beauchesne, Paris.

Zadra, D.
1984 Victor Turner's Theory of Religion: Towards an Analysis of Symbolic Time. In: R.L. Moore & F.E. Reynolds (eds.), *Anthropology and the Study of Religion*, pp. 77-103, CSSR, Chicago, Illinois.

Zoest, A. van
1978 *Semiotiek. Over tekens, hoe ze werken en wat we ermee doen*. Ambo, Baarn.

Zung, W.K.
1965 A Self-Rating Depression Scale. In: *Archives of General Psychiatry*, 12, pp. 63-70.

Zwergel, H.A.
1989 Höchste Stufen religiöser Entwicklung: Kritische Rückfragen. In: A. Bucher & K. Reich (eds.), *Entwicklung von Religiosität*, pp. 51-63, Universitätsverlag, Freiburg.

TABLE OF CONTRIBUTORS

H.B. Boudewijnse, Groningen, The Netherlands
C. den Draak, Nijmegen, The Netherlands
H. Faber, Maarn, The Netherlands
H. Geerts, Nijmegen, The Netherlands
J. de Hart, Nijmegen, The Netherlands
H.G. Heimbrock, Groningen, The Netherlands/Frankfurt am Main, FRG
J.A.P.J. Janssen, Nijmegen, The Netherlands
J.M. van der Lans, Nijmegen, The Netherlands
E. Ouwehand, Groningen, The Netherlands
J.Z.T. Pieper, Heerlen, The Netherlands
K.H. Reich, Fribourg, Switzerland
M.J. Stern, Ottawa, Canada
M.H.F. van Uden, Heerlen, The Netherlands
P. Vandermeersch, Leuven, Belgium
A. Visscher, Ottawa, Canada
O. Wikström, Uppsala, Sweden